THE HORIZONTAL SOCIETY

EMUNOT: JEWISH PHILOSOPHY AND KABBALAH

ACADEMIC
STUDIES
PRESS

The Horizontal Society

Understanding the Covenant and Alphabetic Judaism

José Faur

2

Boston
2008

Library of Congress Cataloging-in-Publication Data

Faur, Jose.
The horizontal society : understanding the covenant and alphabetic Judaism / Jose Faur.
p. cm.
Includes bibliographical references.
ISBN 978-1-934843-18-5
1. Rabbinical literature—History and criticism. 2. Bible. O.T.—Criticism, interpretation, etc. 3. Tradition (Judaism) 4. Philosophy, Jewish. I. Title.

BM496.6.F385 2008
296.3—dc22
2008020009

Book design by Yuri Alexandrov
On the jacket: Elaine Langerman. Liver Series #6: «Through His Creations»

Published by Academic Studies Press in 2008
145 Lake Shore Road
Brighton, MA 02135, USA
press@academicstudiespress.com
www.academicstudiespress.com

In Memoriam

With the Publication of this Important Work
We Honor the Memories of our Dear Father
Sam E. (Sonny) Haddad
And Grandparents
Sophie and Eli Haddad
Victoria and Aslan Safdeye
ת.נ.צ. ב.ה.
May their steadfast dedication to the principles
and values of our Holy Tora
Continue to inspire Generations to Come...
Eli and Lillian Haddad

Hebrew Transliteration Table

א	’	ל	l
ב	b	מ, ם	m
ג	g	נ, ן	n
ד	d	ס	s
ה	h	ע	‘
ו	v, w	פ, ף	f, p, ph
ז	z	צ, ץ	ṣ
ח	ḥ	ק	q
ט	ṭ	ר	r
י	y	ש	sh, s
כ, ך	k, kh	ת	t

Abbreviations

Ac	*Acts*	*IShG*	*Iggeret Sherira Gaon*
AdRN	*Abot de-Ribbi Natan*	*Jer*	*Jeremiah*
Am	*Amos*	*Jn*	*John*
Ar.	Arabic	*Lk*	*Luke*
Ch	*Chronicles*	*Mac*	*Maccabees*
Col	*Colossians*	*Mal*	*Malachi*
Cor	*Corinthians*	*Matt*	*Matthew*
Dan	*Daniel*	*MT*	*Mishne Tora*
Dt	*Deuteronomy*	*Mk*	*Mark*
Ec	*Ecclesiastes*	n.d.	no date
Eph	*Ephesians*	n.p.	no place; no pagination
Est	*Esther*		
Ex	*Exodus*	*Neh*	*Nehemiah*
Ez	*Ezekiel*	*Nu*	*Numbers*
Gal	*Galatians*	*Pet*	*Peter*
Gn	*Genesis*	*Sam*	*Samuel*
Hab	*Habakkuk*	*Song*	*Songs of Songs*
Heb.	Hebrew	*Thess*	*Thesssalonians*
Hos	*Hoshea*	*Tim*	*Timothy*
Is	*Isaiah*	*Zeph*	*Zephaniah*

Contents

APPENDICES

1. Vocalization of the Scroll of the Tora

A Scroll of the Tora that has been vocalized is 'ritually invalid' (פסול), even if one were to erase the vowels. The authority for disallowing a vocalized *Sefer Tora* is a work attributed to R. Judah al-Bargeloni, ed. Elkan Adler, *An Eleventh Century Introduction to the Hebrew Bible* (Heb.) (Oxford: Private Circulation, 1897), p. 38:

> It is forbidden to vocalize a Scroll of the Tora; a vocalized Scroll is ritually invalid. As we were instructed concerning Scrolls: 'One cannot read from a vocalized [Scroll]. Even if he were to erase the vowels [still] it [the Scroll] cannot be used [for liturgical] reading.' R. Yehudai Gaon (8th century) of blessed memory said: 'One may not put a colon [used in Hebrew as a period] at the end of the verse; if one puts it, then he should erase it. R. Hayye Gaon sent the following *responsum* to R. Nissim's Academy (of blessed memory), in Arabic: Concerning a Scroll of the Tora that had been vocalized... we have written on this matter in [our work] *Rules for Scribes*: "A vocalized Scroll of the Tora may not be read in public, even if the vowels had been erased. If it was taken out (to be read in public) it must be returned and another Scroll must be taken out in its place. It should not be kept, since with this blemish it had forfeited the status of Scroll of the Tora."

Before proceeding further we must call attention to the expression 'heads of the [Scriptural] verses' ('ראשי פסוקים'), found in rabbinic literature. It is generally understood to refer to the 'beginning' of the verse, as in *Midrash Zuṭa, Ruth* (Buber) II, 8; in which case this would be an ellipsis for ראשי *תיבות של*פסוקים 'the first letters [or words] of the verses," cf. *Midrash Tanḥuma* ([Warsaw] Lublin, 1913), *Ha'azinu* V, 5, p. 213; and cf. *Tosafot Yoma* 37b, s.v. *be-sirrugin*. (A similar ellipsis is found in *Shabbat* 12b: "ראשי פרשיות" for ראשי *תיבות של* פרשיות). In my view this expression is not always an ellipsis. In the case of "ראשי פסוקים" it stands for "the superlinear punctuation at the head of the verses"—a reference to the punctuation in vogue in Babel and Israel. See *Bereshit Rabba*, Ms. Vatican Ebr. 30, Facsimile (Jerusalem: Makor, 5731/1971) XXXV, 41b: אלו ראשי פסוקים; *Bereshit Rabba*, eds. Theodor-Albeck, 3 vols. (Jerusalem: Wahrman Books, 1965), p. 342. In *Yerushalmi Megilla* IV, 1, 74d, the rabbis associated

"ראשי פסוקים" with the verse "and they understood the Scripture" (*Neh* 8:8). Support for this interpretation is to be found in the parallel version, *Megilla* 3a, as quoted by R. Baḥyye b. Asher, *Perush*, vol. 1, p. 169, which reads: "and they understood—this is ניקוד," i.e., 'vocalization.' Accordingly, the rule in *Massekhet Soferim* III, 7, ed. Dr. Michael Higger (New York: Debe Rabbanan, 1937), pp. 125–126 disallowing a Scroll "שעקרו ראשי פסוקים" refers to a Scroll that had been vocalized after which "the superlinear vocalization was erased," which then remains ritually invalid, and "one should not read from it." (For parallel sources and bibliography, see ed. note *ad loc.*). This rule was recorded in *Maḥzor Viṭry* #524 and thereof in *Haggahot Maymoniyot* on *MT Sefer Tora* 10:1 (b); see *Bet Yosef* and *Shulḥan 'Arukh Yore De'a* CCLXXIV, 7.

The above rule in *Massekhet Soferim* coincides with the Geonic decision cited above in two fundamental points. First, the Scroll is ritually void (פסול). Second, it retains the status of ritually void (פסול) even if the vowels were to be erased. It is generally assumed that vocalization renders the Scroll void because the Tora should bear no 'marks.' This explanation cannot be accepted for the following two reasons. First, according to scribal tradition some consonants of the Tora are occasionally marked with a point on top; see, for example, *Berakhot* 4a, *Nazir* 23a, *Horayot* 10b, etc; *AdRN*, A, XXXIV, p. 100. Furthermore, a Scroll with errors may be amended. Accordingly, why should a vocalized Scroll retain the status of ritually void (פסול) after the vowels have been erased? As we shall see, the theory for disallowing such a Scroll pertains to the Hebrew concept of 'lettering' and 'reading.'

The Hebrew 'letter' (אות) stands for a 'distinctive' mark or sign. God is referred to "as 'letter'" (אות)—in the sense of being 'absolutely distinctive and unique'—even "among myriads (of heavenly angels)"; see *Midrash Tanḥuma* (Buber), vol. 2, p. 39 and *Golden Doves*, p. 83. A 'letter' is not only 'different' from all other signs of the alphabet, but it must be inscribed within a blank, *writable* space, from all its sides. The blank-space is not merely to ensure that one letter does not touch another: it pertains to the very *action* of writing. In Hebrew, 'to write' is an intransitive verb. Therefore, you don't write *a* book but you write *in* a book or *on* a parchment (see below Appendix 2). However, once a letter has been inscribed in a suitable blank-space it retains its 'written' status even when there is no longer any space around it. Consider the following rule: if a letter was written around a punctured parchment, so that the perforation is contained within the letter or between two letters, the Scroll is void (פסול), although the perforation does not affect any letter. However, if the perforation within a letter, or between two letters, or between two words, occurred *afterwards*, the Scroll is valid, providing that the perforation had not expunged a letter. Borges, too, included blank spaces in his definition of writing; see *Golden Doves*, p. 116.

Hebrew reading warrants *successive synthesis*; see *Golden Doves*, pp. 30–35. A vocalized Tora is void because, in effect, vocalization links the letters and words *semantically* to one another, canceling, thereby, the blank space between the letters. A vocalized text allows only for *simultaneous synthesis*; the reader plays a passive role, 'picking up the sound from the page.' In this case, someone would be 'reciting from memory,' rather than 'reading.' Moreover, vocalization would limit the countless interpretations comprehended in the consonantal text of the Tora; see *Golden Doves*, pp. 136–137, and would exclude the possibility of successive 'reading'; see *Golden Doves*, pp. 118–123. According to this theory, even Maimonides, who in extreme circumstances permits the use of a void Scroll (ספר פסול) for liturgical services, would disallow the use of a vocalized Scroll, since in such a circumstance, the text would be 'recited' rather than 'read'; cf. *Homo Mysticus*, pp. 186–187. It should be noted, in passing, that apophasis and the entire realm of negative theology pertain to *successive synthesis*. A Hebrew letter it *is* not. Rather, by synthesizing it successively to the next, the reader creates something fundamentally different than each letter in isolation; see *Homo Mysticus*, part I. (This coincides with the syntagmatic character of the Hebrew Alphabet: a 'letter' (אות) signifies in that it is *different* than all other letters; see *Golden Doves*, pp. xxiv–xxv). Finally, vocalized writing would function as an 'idol' standing between God and his creatures; like with hieroglyphics a vocalized text would border on idolatry, by making openness to God and a reciprocal relationship impossible.

Halakhic scholars debated whether it would be permissible to vocalize a bill of divorce. The standard practice among Sephardic scribes is to use diacritic marks (as an apostrophe or a dot) to transliterate a foreign *consonant* into Hebrew; see R. Moses b. Ḥabib, *'Azarat Nashim* (Leipzig, 5619/1859), 101b–103a, but not to vocalize the text; see R. Ovadiah Yosef, *Yabbia' Omer*, vol. 7 (Jerusalem, 5753/1993), *Eben ha-'Ezer*, #22, p. 380.

2. Hebrew 'Writing' and 'Reading'

Jewish law interprets 'to write' (כתב) as an intransitive verb, as if it were a 'complete' action needing no direct object. The expression "he shall write a *sefer*" (*Dt* 24:1) in reference to the bill of divorce does not contain a preposition indicating the object of the verb. Accordingly, it is taken to mean to 'write in a precise wording or formula' specifying the divorce (in which case *sefer* is an adverb of "write") not a 'parchment' or a 'scroll'!—see *Giṭṭin* 21b; cf. *Soṭa* 16a and R. Abraham ha-Levi, *Ginnat Veradim*, vol. 2 (Constantinople, 5476/1716), *Eben ha-'Ezer* I, #5, 3d–4d. Thus, 'writing' may take on an existence of its own, independent of the parchment or material on which it was written. (This may explain the rationale for permitting, in extreme cases, to write the Tora on a parchment which was not prepared adequately; see Saul Lieberman, *Shkiin* [Jerusalem: Bamberg & Wahrman, 1939], p. 25). Consider the following rule. One who executes a work on the Sabbath with the intention of damaging an object is exempted. And yet if one were to write on a parchment with the intention of damaging the parchment, he stands guilty since in writing the "infraction is not because of the place on which the writing took place [= the parchment], but because of the writing (itself)" (*MT Shabbat* 11:9). Therefore, on witnessing a scroll of the Tora burning, one must rend his garment twice, once because of the destruction of the parchment and once because the destruction of the writing; see *Mo'ed Qaṭan* 26a. Similarly, R. Ḥanaya ben Teradyon (2nd century), while burning at the stake together with the Scroll of the Tora, "saw [only] the parchment burning, while the letters flew away"; see *'Aboda Zara* 18a. Cf. Roland Barthes, "To Write: An Intransitive Verb?" in eds. Richard Macksey and Eugenio Donato, *The Structuralist Controversy* (Baltimore: Johns Hopkins University Press, 1972), pp. 134–155.

The preposition 'on' (על-, ב) can be used to render 'to write' as a transitive verb, as the rule stipulating that the king "shall write (כתב) for himself a summary of this Tora *on* a scroll (על-ספר)… and he shall read *in it* (קרא בו)…" (*Dt* 17:18–19; cf. Section III, n. 129). As noted by the commentators, the masculine preposition *in it* (קרא בו) clearly indicates that the object of the verb is the actual Scroll, which is masculine, rather than the 'Tora' which is feminine; cf. Rashi on *Dt* 29:20. That is why the Talmud interprets the clause "Someone reading (קורא) from (ב-) the Tora" (Mishna *Berakhot* 2:1) as an ellipsis for the clause "Someone that was reading from *the Scroll* of the Tora"; therefore, concluding that the reference is to "Someone reading from [*the Scroll* of the Tora] for the purpose of proof-reading (בקורא להגיה) it; see *Berakhot* 13a and Section I, n. 2. For the meaning of the expression "summary of this Tora," see *Golden Doves*, pp. 53–54.

'Book' is a Jewish invention (see above Chapter 7). This will help us understand why Arabic speaking Jews used the term *kuttab*, root KTB 'writing'—having to do with the *ketab* system discussed in Section I—to designate 'elementary-school.' There was a good reason for this choice. The classical designation of the Hebrew-primary school (*Talmud Tora* and *Bet ha-Sefer*) has to do with 'book.' However, when Jews began to settle in the

Arabian Peninsula (particularly from the 2nd century on to escape Roman persecution, see Chapter 40), 'writing' was unknown in the region. Before the advent of Islam (7th century), native pagans were referred to as *jahiliya* 'analphabets.' The root KTB 'writing' was unknown in Arabic—and it is one of the many key-terms from Hebrew and Aramaic introduced by Jews to the Arabic lexicon; cf. A. S. Yahuda, *'Eber ve-'Arab* (New York: Ha-Histadrut ha-'Ibrit be-Ameriqa, 1946), p. 138, n. 6; and p. 152 n. 2. [For a penetrating analysis of this early period, see Charles Cutler Torrey, *The Jewish Foundation of Islam* (New York: Jewish Institute of Religion Press, 1933). On the impact of rabbinic thought and terminology on the formative period of Islam, see Abraham I Katsh, *Judaism in Islam* (Heb.) (Jerusalem: Kiryat Sepher, 1957); and A. S. Yahuda, *Al-Hidaja* (Leiden: E. J. Brill, 1912), pp. 82–91. Cf. Appendix 27]. Instead of KTB, the Arabic root ZBR (sing. *zabar*; pl. *zubur*), 'engraving,' 'embellishment'—has to do with the Greek *grámma* used for 'letter,' but actually meaning 'lines of drawing,' and 'picture'; and the Greek *graphes* used for 'writing,' but actually meaning 'drawing,' 'delineation,' and 'picture (= Heb. *roshem*). This root—rather than *ketab* (see Section I, n. 5)—was used in Arabic to designate 'writings' and 'books' in general (more specifically the *Psalms*; see *Koran* 26:195). Briefly, if one is to understand 'book' in its Hebrew connotation—that is, *writing* made of *letters* (rather than 'drawings' made of 'pictures'), composed for *reading*, then the Arabic language *does not* have a term for 'book.' (Arabic-speaking Jews use *sifr*, from the Hebrew *sefer* to designate the Scroll of the Tora; and Arabic *maṣḥaf* from *ṣaḥifa* 'page' of a 'notebook,' to designate a 'volume.' This term indicates the outer form of a codex; that is, 'pages written on the recto and verso, bound into a single volume'—not its content). Arabic *kitab* (pl. *kutub*) stands for *writing*, not for *book*; that is the term used by Muhammed to describe the Tora (see *Koran* 2:41, 50, 79, 81, 83, etc.). Again, the word *Qur'an* used to designate the Muslim Holy Scripture is an Arabization of the Hebrew *miqra* (root QR'), which Jews introduced to the Arabic language; it has to do with 'reading'—not with 'book.'

In such an environment, a 'book' is nothing more than a paranormal object, which one may want to possess for esthetic or religious purposes, like an amulet; as with Kien, in Canetti's *Auto da Fé*; see *Golden Doves*, pp. 4–7, 9; and cf. Section I, n. 65. Accordingly, the purpose of Jewish elementary education was *kuttab*, instruction in the *ketab* system, so that the children would grasp the concept of 'book.' Thus Jews identified themselves as *Ahlu-l-Kitabu*, usually translated as 'people of the book,' but actually meaning 'people of the writing.' The term *kuttab* in modern Arabic came from the Jews. Another term having to do with education, *madrasa* 'religious school' and the corresponding verb *daras* 'to study,' were introduced by Jews; they are Arabizations coined, respectively, from the Hebrew *midrash* and *darash*. For the Arabic source, see Abraham Shalom Yahuda, "A Contribution to Qur'an and Hadith Interpretation," in *Ignace Goldziher Memorial Volume,* part I, p. 290.

3. Alphabetization and *Masora*

Hebrew writing warrants an alphabetic script, rather than hieroglyphics; or else, writing would border on idolatry; cf. José Faur, "God as a Writer: Omnipresence and the Art of Dissimulation," *Bible and the Intellectual Life* 6 (1989), p. 32; and above Appendix 1. Eventually, Egyptian scribes learned to write in alphabetic script, but it was not used systematically; see Cyrus H. Gordon, *The Ancient Near East* (New York: W. W. Norton, 1965), pp. 54–55. For some insights on the Hebrew Alphabet, see idem, *Before Columbus* (New York: Crown Publishers, 1971), pp. 99–100.

An index of Jewish alphabetization is the *Masora* appended to the Hebrew Scripture—unique in textual history—where even minute orthographic irregularities, odd letters, as well as unusual morphological and phonological phenomena, including vowels and accents, are minutely accounted for and catalogued. For an excellent overview of this highly complex subject, see A. Dothan, "Massorah," *EJ* vol. 16, cols. 1402–1482. This apparatus is a fundamental condition for registering the text of Scripture; see *Golden Doves*, p. 108. Of course, to the analphabetic and monoliguistic mind these are nonsensical notes. For the sake of illustration, let us consider the case of Richard Simon, the father of textual criticism of the Christian Scripture. He did not know a word of Hebrew. And yet, at the end of *The Preface* to his *A Critical History of the text of the New Testament* (London, 1689), he chided Christian Hebraists for their admiration of the *Masora*, and wrote: "It is a Vanity in the admirers of the Hebrew Text of the Jews, to bestow such great praises on the Massoreth, a good part of which consists in Trifles or superstitious Observations."

4. Precept, Monolatry, and Sanctity

The Tora includes a series of teachings, instructions, prescriptions, and prohibitions known as 'precepts' (מצות, sing. מצוה). A 'precept' is a contractual commitment—*not* a 'command' (see below Appendix 12). The term *azhara* (pl. *azharot*) used in Rabbinic Hebrew to indicate something disallowed by the Law, is not semantically equivalent to a 'prohibition' issued by a menacing force. As noted by R. Abraham b. ha-Rambam, *Perush*, p. 298, the root of this term is ZHR, standing for 'brilliance' and 'enlightenment.' It means 'to instruct' someone about his or her responsibilities, cf. *2K* 6:10; by "illuminating the intellectual perception, which resembles light, [just as its opposite] ignorance is compared to darkness; cf. *Ec* 2:13." Therefore, *azharot* stand not only for what the Tora outlaws, but also for what it prescribes; as per the liturgical compositions bearing this name, which include both negative as well as positive precepts.

A 'command' is an order issued by a superior force *imposing* its will on those below; see *Crowds and Power*, pp. 351–355. God did not *impose* the Law. The objective of a 'command' is 'obedience.' The Hebrew lexicon contains no term for 'obedience.' The Hebrew term comparable to 'obedience,' שמע means not only 'to hear' but also 'to understand' and 'to acknowledge'; see *Golden Doves*, pp. 29–30. Fulfillment of a 'precept' involves [i] recognition of the *contractual commitment* at Sinai-Moab and [ii] *compliance*. In a state of 'compulsion' (אונס), there cannot be either 'compliance' or its opposite 'transgression' (עברה); see *Yebamot* 53b–54a; *MT Yesode ha-Tora* 5:4; *MT Sanhedrin* 20:2; *Sefer ha-Miṣvot,* negative precept #294; cf. *Maggid Mishne* on *MT Sukkot* 8:15. The subject of a precept is at a perennial 'crossroad,' free to choose one path and reject the other; see *Dt* 30:15, 19; and cf. 11:26–28; *MT Teshuba* 3:4; 5:1–2. Hence, freedom of choice is "the great principle upon which the Law and precept (מצוה) stand" (*MT Teshuba* 5:3; see *Golden Doves*, pp. 66–69). [Here Maimonides uses *miṣva* in its double sense of 'Oral Law, instruction' and a 'duty to be performed'; see the quotation in Section IV n. 179]. On the other hand, the subject of a command is in a state of perennial *submission* and is excluded from any decision-making. He "can never stand at a cross-road, for, even if he did, it is not he who decides which road to take" (*Crowds and Power*, p. 361). Only man, in quality of being created in God's image can be subject to a מצוה, see below Appendix 24.

Miṣva involves consent and personal accountability. Therefore, although Judaism is universal and open to one and all—the first system in history to accept proselytes—it is not Catholic; i.e., it cannot be *imposed.* More accurately, pried from consent and volition, a *miṣva* equals a command. Protological man dwelt within the realm of myth, where 'reality' is the effect of a series of mental projections and displacements. At this level of consciousness, people are incapable of distinguishing between their feelings and emotions, and the outside world. A case in point is that of Adam and

Eve after eating the forbidden fruit and taking refuge "inside" (בתוך) the tree of knowledge (*Gn* 3:8, see *Homo Mysticus*, pp. 58–69), thus evading accountability and responsibility by initiating a process of 'guilt' and 'guilt-displacement' to 'an-other.' Adam blames Eve. In mimetic response, Eve blames the snake (*Gn* 3:12–13; see *Homo Mysticus*, p. 80). Protological man, too, by sequestering himself into the realm of myth, evades responsibility by denying accountability: invariably, an-other is the 'responsible.' A prerequisite for Judaism is personal accountability and responsibility. People inhabiting the realm of myth and fiction cannot grasp the distinction between a contracted duty and a command imposed by a despot. At this level of consciousness, all lines of division between a *miṣva* and a command vanish. Invariably, *miṣvot* will be misread as *commands*, and participation in the Sinaitic covenant would be pointless.

Formally, there are 613 'precepts' (מצוות). Each is a kind of 'general system principle' unfolding into a variety of fields of interests, distinct levels of consciousness, and different strata of opportunities. Together, the precepts comprise a *total system* (see Chapter 24), and could be fulfilled only collectively by "the Congregation of Jacob" (*Dt* 33:4). Thus, the Jewish people ought to serve Him in unity and harmony, as a close-knit crew, for no individual could possibly fulfill every single precept; see the remarks of R. Moses di Ṭrani, *Qiryat Sefer* (Venice, 5311/1551), Introduction, Chapter 7. Given that fulfillment of a precept presupposes acknowledgment of the *berit*, the rabbis taught that someone who had complied with a single precept—no matter whether by 'honoring one's parents,' or 'sending a bird away before taking her nestling,' etc.—"has a portion in the World to Come," since that individual has in fact partaken in the *berit*. According to the rabbis, the diversity of precepts was intended to offer an opportunity to every Jew to partake in the fulfillment of the Tora. Since it would be difficult to find a single Jew who in the course of his or her life had not fulfilled at least a single precept, the rabbis taught that "every single [member] of Israel has a portion in the World to Come" (Mishna *Sanhedrin* 10:1), i.e., she or he had *merited* salvation. This doctrine was formulated by R. Ḥananya ben 'Aqashya (2nd century), and is contained in a most popular Mishna (*Makkot* 3:17), usually recited before the *Qaddish*, when concluding the study of *Abot*. It proclaims that the great variety of precepts contained in the Tora was given because God wished "to warrant merit to Israel" (לזכות את ישראל). In *Perush ha-Mishnayot*, ibid, vol. 4, p. 247, Maimonides explained:

> It is one of the Law's fundaments of faith, that if an individual had executed [even] one of the 613 precepts of the Law, in a proper and satisfactory manner,

without associating with it some mundane designs at all, but did it for its own sake, as [an act of] love… that person has gained the rights to the life in the World to Come. R. Ḥananya teaches that the great variety of precepts ensures that during the entire course of one's life one would have had the opportunity to perfectly fulfill [at least] a single [precept].

Since a precept is, by definition, a contractual requirement, it stands to reason that an individual who is "required to fulfill a precept and executes it has more merits than one who is not required to fulfill the precept and nonetheless executes it" (גדול המצווה ועושה יותר ממי שאינו מצוה ועושה; *Qiddushin* 31a; see *Ḥiddushe ha-Riṭba, ad loc.* cols. 347–347). Conversely, someone that is not required to fulfill a precept cannot be faulted for not fulfilling that precept. Thus, the principle formulated by R. David ha-Kohen, *Teshubot ha-Radak* (Constantinople, 5297/1537), #XVII, 9, 119b: "A gentile fulfilling the seven Noahide precepts, and a woman fulfilling the [specific] precepts incumbent upon her, equal [the sanctity of] a High Priest"; cf. *Baba Qamma* 38a, and *The Mishnah of Rabbi Eliezer* (Heb.), VI, p. 121. Similarly, the rabbis taught that the Patriarchs "fulfilled the entire Tora," see *Yoma* 28b, because they fulfilled whatever God asked from them; see *Tosefta Qiddushin* 5:20, p. 299; *Tosefta Ki-Fshuṭah*, p. 986. Cf. R. Abraham Maimonides, *Perush*, p. 120. The same applies to a 'transgression' (עברה). Someone who is not a subject of the covenant cannot be charged with 'transgression' (עברה). In this respect Judaism distinguishes between 'reward and punishment,' relating exclusively to precepts (שכר מצוה); and 'recompense and chastisement' (= Ar 'עוץ') that relate uniformly to all (אין הקב"ה מקפח שכר שום בריאה; *Pesaḥim* 118b; *Baba Qamma* 38b; etc.); see R. Hayye Gaon, in *Gaonica*, ed. S. Assaf (Jerusalem: Darom, 1933), #XV, pp. 155–156; and the comments of Professor Zucker, "'*Iyyunim*," pp. 102–104.

A major consequence of the concept of fulfilling a *miṣva* is that it cannot involve the transgression of a law. Hence the rabbinic rule that "a precept which was fulfilled via a transgression" (מצוה הבאה בעברה) is without merit; see *Sukka* 30a and *MT Issure Mizbeaḥ* 5:9. There is a lively discussion in *Yerushalmi Shabbat* XIII, 3, 14a among 3rd century rabbis, concerning someone who "ate a stolen *maṣṣa*" on the night of the *Seder*, "has not fulfilled his requirement." "R. Jonah explained: A transgression (עברה) cannot constitute a precept (מצוה)." The same idea was expressed differently by his colleague, R. Yose: "A 'precept' (מצוה) cannot be constituted via a transgression (עברה)." The root of this doctrine is that God can be worshipped only according to the rules established at Sinai-Moab. Therefore, someone sinning within the Law cannot have fulfilled a precept! In the words of R. Ila, "[It is written:] '*These* are the precepts' (מצות; *Lev* 27:34; *Nu* 36:13)—if you fulfill them as they were prescribed they are precepts (מצות), and if not they are not precepts (מצות)." Cf. *Mekhilta de-R. Shim'on b. Yoḥai*, p. 139, cited below.

The preceding bears directly on the Hebrew concept of 'sanctity' (קדושה): it can be acquired only by fulfilling the precepts. Thus, "to be holy unto your God" (*Nu* 15:40), means that "holiness is acquired through [the fulfillment] of each one of the precepts" (קדושת כל המצות; *Sifre Numbers* #115, p. 127). "What does the sanctity of the precepts (קדושת המצות) mean?" asked the rabbis, "That every time that God adds another precept to Israel, He is adding to them sanctity" (*Mekhilta de-R. Shim'on b. Yoḥai*, p. 139); cf. *Guide* III, 33, p. 390, ll. 1–8.

Belief in the 'sanctity of the precepts' (קדושת המצות) constitutes a repudiation of the notion of cosmic sacrality, common to pagan humanity. "To be sacred" (*Lev* 20:7), taught the rabbis, "this is the sanctity of all the precepts" (קדושת כל המצות). Sanctity cannot be acquired through pagan rituals. Pondering on the apparent redundancy of the verse, "and you shall become sacred and will be sacred" (*Lev* 20:7), the rabbis explained: "This [the apparent redundancy, comes to teach] abstention from an alien cult. Lest you may say, 'this refers to the sanctity of all the precepts' (קדושת כל המצות) [and is not a repudiation of pagan cult]! Since it had already stated "you shall be sacred" (*Lev* 19:2)—the sanctity of all the precepts (קדושת כל המצות) was already stipulated. Then, what are you to learn from "and you shall become sacred and will be sacred? This is abstention from alien worship." (*Sifra Qedoshim* X, 2, 82b. Concerning 'alien cult,' see below Appendix 11, and "Introductory Remarks," Section III). Accordingly, Maimonides concluded that there is no semantic difference between God exhorting Israel to "be sacred" and His saying "fulfill my precepts." The same applies to terms such as 'purity' and 'impurity'; they are semantically identical to 'observe my precepts and don't transgress my ordinances'; see *Sefer ha-Miṣvot*, IV, pp. 18–19; *Guide* III, 33 and 47; and *Kuzari* III, 49. Cf. R. Abraham b. ha-Rambam, *Perush*, p. 302.

Consequently, Judaism also repudiates *jihad*-devotion, whether against others or against ourselves; see below Appendix 59. Or what amounts to the same, Judaism repudiates the *minut* ideology whereby the end justifies the means; see *Pr* 3:17 and below Appendix 55.

We can now proceed to examine a fundamental dimension of Jewish monolatry. It not only means that God is to be worshipped exclusively according to the precepts of the *berit*, but that said precepts are to be fulfilled according to the norms stipulated by *halakha* ('Rabbinic law')—

not by intuition and pious impulse! R. Judah ha-Levi explained that this postulates that the precepts are not some sort of indeterminate articles to be executed according to one's whims, but that "they have known and precise definitions" (*Kuzari* III, 49; Ar. p. 129, l. 13). The Tora is "exact" (Ar.מצ‘בוטה), with precise demarcations (*Kuzari* II, 50; Ar. p. 70, l. 14). Thus, religious devotion cannot be grounded on "your personal feeling and sagacity" (*Kuzari*; III, 49; Ar. p. 130, l. 19; cf. I, 99; III, 53), and it must be expressed within the boundaries of the precepts, i.e., "according to their definitions and stipulations" (*Kuzari* I, 79; Ar. p. 20, l. 17). This means that "diligence and fervent zeal" are not valid criteria for religion and spirituality. In fact, the sin of the golden calf (Ex 32:1–8), was not because the children of Israel worshipped another deity or worshipped an image, but because they gave free rein to religious fervor and worshipped the God of Israel with a ritual which was not specified in the covenant (see *Kuzari* I, 97; cf. ibid I, 79 and IV, 14 and 23. For a full examination of the subject, see José Faur, "The Biblical Idea of Idolatry," *The Jewish Quarterly Review* 69 [1978], pp. 1–26).

Thus, a major difference emerges between Judaism and other spiritual systems ('monotheistic religions' included) concerning the place and function of religious zeal. In Judaism fervor and personal endeavor alone do not equal 'religion'; rather, religious fervor must operate within the strict confines of *halakha*. Were one to admit that personal endeavor could serve as a spiritual criterion, then there would no longer be any grounds to differentiate between heathenism, magic, and 'religion'; see José Faur, "Two Models of Jewish Spirituality," *Shofar* 10 (1992), pp. 7–11; and *Studies in the Mishne Tora*, pp. 126–132. The main purpose of this doctrine is not to exclude pathos and feelings from worship, but to make sure that religious devotion is confined to the perimeters of the Law.

Let us point out, by way of conclusion, that the rabbis distinguished between a 'precept' (מצוה) and a 'mandatory action' that one is compelled to do under pressure (חובה); e.g., washing the finger-tips after a meal, which is done for hygienic reasons; in contradistinction to the ritual of the washing of the hands (נטילת ידים) done as a 'precept' (מצוה); see *Ḥolin* 105a; cf. *Tosafot* on *Giṭṭin* 90b *s.v.* *'im*. Because the rabbis (*Shabbat* 25b) referred to the lighting of the Sabbath candles as 'mandatory' (חובה), it was debated whether it also required a 'blessing.' For a learned analysis of this debate, see R. Raṣon 'Arusi, "*Birkat Hadlaqat ...*," *Sinai* 85 (5739/1979), pp. 55–91. Occasionally, the term 'precept' (מצוה) is used in the sense of 'a good' or 'preferred action'; see, for example, Maran, *Shulḥan 'Arukh, Oraḥ Ḥayyim* ##XXIV, 2; XC, 12; CXC, 4; etc, etc.

5. Defilement of the Hands

Concerning the rule that upon touching a Scroll of the Hebrew Scripture the hands are ritually defiled, the Mishna *Yadayim* 4:6 explains: "לפי חבתן היא טומאתן"; that is, "their impurity is a function of their high esteem" in which the Scrolls of Scripture are held; cf. ibid. 3:5; Mishna *Kelim* 15:6. To grasp the sense of this legislation, it is necessary to consider the obsession with 'sacred' objects peculiar to the protological mind. The subject has been examined by Mircea Eliade, *The Sacred and the Profane* (San Diego: Harcourt Brace & Company, 1987). Let me quote one of the pertinent passages, pp. 11–12:

> The modern Occidental experiences certain uneasiness before many manifestations of the sacred. He finds it difficult to accept the fact that, for many human beings, the sacred can be manifested in stones or trees, for example. But as we shall soon see, what is involved is not a veneration of the stone in itself, or a cult of the tree in itself. The sacred tree, or the sacred stone are not adored as stone or tree; they are worshipped precisely because they are *hierophanies*, because they show something that is no longer stone or tree but the *sacred*, the *ganz andere* [wholly other].

A pivotal point in Scripture and Rabbinic tradition is that sanctity may be acquired only through the fulfillment of God's precepts (see Appendix 4). Through touching one can acquire 'ritual impurity' (טומאה), but not sacrality! It appears that some believed that one could draw in the 'sacrality' from a 'sacred object' by touching it; see R. David Qimḥi on *Ez* 34:19 and R. Abraham ibn 'Ezra on *Ex* 28:2. When the sacred object was afar, as with the moon and other heavenly bodies, the worshipper would stretch his hand towards it, as if to kiss it, and draw in its sacrality unto himself, cf. *Job* 31:27 and R. Se'adya's Gaon *Commentary*, *ad loc*. It was alleged that Babylonian Jews would pull the hair off the escape-goat on its way to the desert on the Day of Atonement, and say to it: "Seize [my sins] and go away! Seize [my sins] and go away!" Mishna *Yoma* 6:4; see Saul Lieberman, *Tosefta Ki-Fshuṭah*, 10 vols. (New York: The Jewish Theological Seminary of America, 1955–2001), vol. 4, p. 794. *Tosefta Kippurim* 3:13, p. 245, reports that the people committing this sacrilege were Alexandrian Jews—an accusation that they vehemently rejected; see *Yerushalmi Yoma* VI, 4, 33d. On their part, Babylonian Jews replied that they were not the culprits, but the victims of Alexandrian slander, see *Yoma* 66b.

To discourage this type of devotion, the Tora declared that [even] priests engaged in preparation of the red heifer and purification water—basic elements for the purification ritual—are themselves ritually impure (see *Nu* 19:7–10, 30). Likewise, the rabbis taught that ashes of the red heifer, as well as the sprinkling-water used in the purification-rite, are ritually impure; see Mishna *Kelim* 1:1, 2; cf. *Tosefta Para* 10:1, p. 638; Mishna *Para* 4:4 and *MT Para* 5:1–7. Indeed, to make sure that the people would not believe that the priest preparing the red heifer was something of a 'pure icon,' the rabbis demanded that the priest should be in a state of (minor) impurity; see Mishna *Para* 3:6 and *MT Para* 1:14. With this purpose in mind, the Tora declared that the person leading the escape-goat into the desert—an essential procedure in the atonement ritual—is ritually impure; see *Lev* 17:26, Mishna *Yoma* 6:6. Moreover, the rabbis stipulated that he could perform the ritual while in a state of impurity; see *Yoma* 66b and *MT 'Abodat Yom ha-Kippurim* 5:21. A similar rule applied to all other sacrifices burnt outside the Sanctuary (and therefore exposed to abuse by the uneducated public); see *MT Para* 5:1–7. To dissuade the people from touching the sacrifices, it was taught that coming in touch with a sacrifice would render the person ritually impure—something that caused dread to pagans as well as Jews. This seems to have been the context of the query that the priests submitted to Prophet Ḥaggai, whether food that came in contact with the meat of a sacrifice is 'sanctified,' see *Ḥaggai* 2:12— a euphemism for 'prohibited,' see *Targum ad loc*; cf. *Targum* on *Dt* 22:9, and R. Abraham ibn 'Ezra on *Ex* 30:29. Some visitors, particularly during the holidays, were tempted to touch the sacred objects at the Temple, especially the table containing the shewbread (see *Ex* 25:23–30), representing material abundance and sustenance. To discourage this practice, the authorities at the Temple warned the public: "Beware, least you touch the (shewbread) table"; see Mishna *Ḥagiga* 3:8; *Ḥagiga* 26b; *Yerushalmi Ḥagiga* III, 8, 79d. The explanation offered by the Talmudic commentators, that the warning intended to prevent the people from defiling the table (see *Ḥagiga* 26b and commentaries) is elusive. People ritually impure were prohibited to enter the sanctuary—a rule strictly observed during the holidays by *everyone*—even those habitually lax about ritual purity; see Mishna *Ḥagiga* 3:6. Indeed, during the holiday season, "all of Israel have [the status] of colleagues (חברים)"—individuals known for their punctilious observance of purity-laws; see *Ḥagiga* 26a and *MT Ṭum'at Mishkab wu-Moshab* 11:9. Therefore, there could be no reason for assuming that someone would defile the Temple's objects. Moreover, these objects were zealously guarded by the priests, and virtually impossible to touch. It seems to me that the intention was to warn the people that *they* would be defiled by the sacred objects! Evidence for this thesis is the reading preserved in R. Ḥanan'el, *Ḥagiga* 27a, that at night the Menorah was immersed for purification purposes. According to the standard explanation it makes no sense to 'purify' the Menorah at the time that it is supposed to be lighted! Therefore, this reading was rejected; see Professor Lieberman *Tosefta Ki-Fshuṭah*, vol. 5, p. 1336. In fact, the text is authentic, not only because it was transmitted by R. Ḥanan'el, but also because it is supported by the *Tosefta Ḥagiga* 3:35, p. 304, edited by Lieberman himself! According to the *Tosefta,* the Zadokites criticized the rabbis for prescribing that the Menorah should undergo a purification ritual, crying: "Look! They are immersing the Light of the Moon!" Reference to the Menorah as the "Light of the Moon" clearly indicates that the purification-rite took place at night, not during the day. That makes perfect sense if one were to assume that purpose of 'purifying' such objects was to debunk the popular belief that these objects had some sort of magical power; cf. Radaq on *Zech* 4:2; and R. Abraham ibn 'Ezra on *Nu* 3:8; 4:20.

A similar strategy underlined the legislation stipulating that touching a Scroll of the Scripture would result in 'defilement' of the hands. The purpose was to contest the belief that a volume of Scripture is some sort of magical totem, and one could draw in 'sacrality' by touching it (or by dancing with it in frenzy) rather than by studying it. The justification offered by the rabbis that touching a volume of Scripture renders the hands impure, "לפי חיבתן היא טומאתן" (*Mishna Yadayim* 4:6*; Tosefta Yadayim,* 2:19, p. 684) means: 'their impurity is a function of the affection' professed to these objects by the unlettered public. Since the actual volumes of Scripture (rather than the content) are particularly prized by the unlettered public, (see the frenzy-dance by the analphabetic-crowds during *Simḥat Tora*), it could become the object of adoration (as in cosmic religiosity). Therefore, the rabbis declared that touching them would defile the hands. Accordingly, that legislation did not apply to the scrolls read at the Temple; see Mishna *Kelim* 15:6. In my view, the purpose of the rule stipulating that *teruma* that has touched a volume of the Scripture becomes impure, Mishna *Zabim* 5:12; *Shabbat* 13b, 14a (cf. *Megilla* 7a), was to contravene those who believed that by 'bonding together' two sacred objects their respective sacrality would be augmented.

The rabbinic strategy declaring that the above items were impure was systematically challenged by the Zadokites. Concerning the red heifer, see Mishna *Para* 3:6; and *MT Para* 1:14. Regarding the Menorah, see *Tosefta Ḥagiga* 3:35, p. 304. The same applies to the 'defilement' of hands by way of touching a volume of Scripture, see *Mishna Yadayim* 4:6–7; *Tosefta Yadayim,* 2:19, p. 684.

6. 'Depositing a Text' for Publication

The root NWḤ 'depositing' is frequently used for 'placing' something in a ceremonial way; see *Ex* 16:34; *Nu* 17, 19; *Dt* 14:28; 2*Ch* 4:8; cf. *Makkot* 18b, and *Menaḥot* 61b. Thus, the priest "placed" (והניחו, root NWḤ) the first-fruits next to the altar (*Dt* 26:31). The noun טנא describing the 'receptacle' containing the first-fruits is found as a verb in Phoenician and other Northwestern Semitic languages, and it denotes 'setting up a votive offering'; see Cyrus H. Gordon, *Evidence for the Minoan Language* (Ventnor, N. J.: Ventnor Publishers, 1966), p. 28. Likewise, "blessing" (*Ez* 44:30) and "wisdom" (*Pr* 14:13) are metaphorically "deposited" by God. In the same tenor, God settled His presence (מנוחתי, root NWḤ) at the Temple forever; see *Ps* 132:14 and cf. *Is* 66:1. Since God 'placed' His presence in the land of Israel, it is referred to as מנוחתי, see *Ps* 95:11. Moses, too, "deposited" (הניח, root NWḤ) in the Ark, the Tablets containing the Decalogue (1*K* 8:9). According to the rabbis these Tablets, "laid deposited (מונחים, root NWḤ) in the Ark" together "with the fragments of [the first] Tablets," *Baba Batra* 14b. Rather than 'resting,' the expression 1) בית מנוחה *Ch* 28:2), in reference to the Temple, has to do with 'placing,' and 'depositing' "the Ark containing God's covenant"; see 1*Ch* 28:2, cf. 1*Sam* 6:18; 1*K* 8:56; *Ps* 132:8, 14. On the basis of this connotation, the rabbis taught that the requirement to "place there" (והניחם, root NWḤ) the High Priest's ceremonial garments at the conclusion of the Day of Atonement's ceremony (*Lev* 16:23), meant that they must be *deposited away* in a protected area (גניזה); see *Pesaḥim* 26a and *MT Keli ha-Miqdash* 8:4.

Articles which were 'deposited' were to remain in place indefinitely. In the language of the rabbis: "until Elijah comes"; see *Baba Meṣi'a* 3a. Therefore, it was used for 'burial,' see 1*K* 13:31. Since articles placed in 'deposit' were not expected to be moved to another location, the rabbis taught that a vessel "that was designed to stay down" (העשוי לנחת, root NWḤ), did not have the status of a movable object, and therefore cannot become defiled, *Ḥagiga* 26b; see *MT Kelim* 3:1. Similarly, the Scriptural prohibition against removing an object from one premise to another on the Sabbath, applies only when said object had been first 'placed' (הנחה, root NWḤ) on that premise, and then removed away (עקירה) and 'placed' (הנחה) on another premise; see Mishna *Shabbat* 1:1; *MT Shabbat* 13:1. [This meets the objection against Rashi raised by *Tosafot, Sukka* 43a *s.v. veya'birennu*]. In the same tenor, out of deference, one should not 'place' other books on top of a Scroll of the Tora; see *Megilla* 27a, *MT Sefer Tora* 10:5—not simply 'put' or 'left' casually, as commonly thought. Because things 'placed in deposit' enjoy 'protection,' (מנוחה, root NWḤ) this term is used to convey a sense of inner 'tranquility,' and 'security'; see *Rut* 1:9; *Jer* 45:3; as well as 'peace,' see 1*Ch* 22:9. This is why the land of Israel, as the promised home of the Jews, is designated מנוחה, see *Dt* 12:9; cf. *Is* 28:12; *Mi* 2:10.

From the preceding it is clear why the flask of oil found after the Temple was recaptured at the end of the Maccabean revolt was assumed not to have been defiled, since it had been "deposited" (מונח) and "under seal"; see *Shabbat* 21b. On the specific connotation of the term 'להניח' in connection to phylacteries, see below Appendix 9.

7. An Academy to Police the Hebrew Language

See Section II, n. 24. It is for the reason given by Vico, that a free people ought to exercise "sovereignty over languages and letters," that I oppose the establishment of a National Academy in Israel with the authority to impose meaning and to regulate the linguistic apparatus of a people, while at the same time, perversely denying legitimacy to their linguistic and literary tradition. As a regulatory body, the 'Aqademya' cares little about the language that it is supposed to watch over. Let me point out that it is hardly possible to find a single member of the *Aqademya* that could read a section of the Scroll of the Tora without making capital errors. In fact, they consistently confuse about one-third of the consonants of the alphabet, not to speak of grave and acute syllables, all forms of *dagesh*, etc. Children exhibiting similar reading impediments in a French or English primary school are sent to remedial schools. Such an agency can acquire Orwellian dimensions when motivated by political ideologies, as in modern Israel, particularly when important segments of the media are state-sponsored. [A special tax called '*igra*' is *imposed* on every house owning a radio or TV apparatus, to pay for the state-sponsored-media—regardless of whether the owner wishes to watch the state-sponsored media or not. As with the 'Church-tax' levied in Germany and in other Christian countries on members of communities, regardless of whether they attended Church or not]. On the danger of an agency with authority to manufacture words, see Martin Buber, "To Create New Words?" in Martin Buber, *A Believing Humanism* (New York: Simon and Schuster, 1967), p. 31. The rabbis noted that when people do not exercise linguistic autonomy, justice and law are inoperative. Given that the people in the Eastern Roman Empire were not fluent in the legal and political language of the state, the rabbis (Mishna *Giṭṭin* 8:5) designated the Roman government an "unfair empire" (מלכות שאינה הוגנת). The reason for this is because the people of the area "have neither [their own] writing (*ketab*) nor [their own] language" (*Giṭṭin* 80a; cf. *Aboda Zara* 10a). In such an environment, 'law, justice, etc,' are matters of linguistic manipulation, rather than substance; see the humorous story in *Shabbat* 116a-b.

Let us consider, for the sake of illustration, one of the new terms sponsored by the 'Aqademya.' For reasons having to do with psychology rather than linguistics, it discarded the traditional nomenclature of personal pronouns, in favor of *guf* (גוף). Believing that this term is equivalent to 'person,' we have 'first *guf*,' 'second *guf*,' etc. Hebrew *guf*, however, is not a 'person.' It serves to indicate *inanimate objects*, such as 'land,' see *Baba Meṣi'a* 96a; 'fruits,' see *Ḥolin* 114b; 'a beast,' see *Menaḥot* 14b, *Temura* 9b; and an 'amorphous fetus,' see *Tosefta Nidda* 4:15, p. 645, *Nidda* 23a, b, 24a, b. In Medieval Hebrew, *guf* stood for 'substance' and 'matter' in general. A popular hymn sung at the Synagogue proclaims that "God is not a *guf*"—in the sense that He is not corporeal. The 'oversight' may be related to the anti-humanistic ideology dominating the Israeli élite, according to which, 'human' is a misnomer for a certain mass of chemical substances meant to serve the social and political machinery of the State; see Appendix 24. Another monstrosity, pointing to the dark and murky creeds lurking beneath the mind of this august institution, is using Hebrew 'קרבן' standing for 'a sacramental or votive sacrifice offered to God at the Temple', to designate a 'victim' of a crime or an accident. It takes a profoundly sick psyche to confuse the fatality of a crime or accident with an offering presented to God.

These points aside, it does not seem too much to expect that a minimal requirement to qualify for membership in such an august body would be to know how to say 'Academy' in Hebrew—rather than *aqademya*—a term never before used in Hebrew sources. Let us note that it does not appear in the first, and to a large extent still the best, *Modern Hebrew Lexicon*, by Eliezer ben Yehuda (1858–1922)—and for good reason! Cf. Section V, n. 61. An English reader may best appreciate the linguistic elegance of this august body, by considering that the exact translation of their title is, "The Academy to the Hebrew Language." In fact, the title is nothing less than a linguistic oxymoron. 'Aqademya' being a Greek term unknown in Hebrew, used to designate a 'Hebrew' institution for the purpose of promoting Hebrew! That would be equivalent to something like, "The English *Midrashiya* for the study and promotion of English"—in an English speaking country! Rhetoric aside, the main purpose of this august institution is to *alienate* Israelies from the Scripture: people speaking Modern Hebrew cannot understand a single sentence from the Hebrew Scripture.

8. Reciting a Text for Publication

When Jeremiah attempted to publish an elegy on the future destruction of Jerusalem, the first step consisted of reciting the text to his trusted scribe Barukh ben Neriya (*Jer* 36:1–4). Then, he instructed him to recite it publicly at the Temple (*Jer* 36:6, 8–9). This, Barukh ben Neriya did from the office of "the scribe, at the upper hall, from the entrance of the new gate … in the ears of all the people" (v. 10). Jeremiah's elegy was banned and not allowed to circulate, see *Jer* 36:11–26. In my view, the reason for banning its publication was not merely on account of the content, but also because Barukh ben Neriya affronted the king by bypassing the authorities, and by publishing the text directly to the general public. It is worthy of note that when the officer who permitted Barukh ben Neriya to read the text in public became aware of the content, he immediately reported the matter to the officials "sitting at the Scribe's Hall" (v. 12). The officers requested Barukh ben Neriya to withdraw the text, and advised him that he, as well as Jeremiah, had better hide (v. 19, cf. v. 26). Finally, the text was brought to the king himself, who condemned it to the fire. The removal of the text from circulation was carried out in a special ceremony. An officer read before the king three or four verses at a time, and then the king would "cut it out with a scribe's razor" and throw the piece to the flames (vv. 21–23).

Let us conclude with three additional notes. First, some officers disapproved of the king's action (see v. 25). Second, God ordered Jeremiah to write the text again. This time, however, Jeremiah did not publish the text but passed it privately to Barukh ben Neriya (vv. 28–32). According to the rabbis the text in question was *Ekha.* Since it was not published by the higher authorities of Israel, this work was included neither in the *Prophets* nor in the *Hagiography*, but as one of the "Five Scrolls," indicating later and lesser rank publication. The authorities did not forgive his behavior. That is why Jeremiah is not mentioned in the *Books of Kings*; see Joseph Klausner, "Why was Jeremiah Ignored in the Book of Kings?" In *Alexander Marx Jubilee Volume*. Hebrew Section (New York: Jewish Theological Seminary, 1953), pp. 189–203.

9. Wearing Phylacteries

A fundamental act of Jewish devotion consists in 'wearing' (Hebrew: לבש, Judeo-Arabic: *libs;* Judeo-Spanish: *vestir*) the 'phylacteries' (תפלין, singular תפלה) every weekday. One is placed on the arm and another on the forehead; see *Berakhot* 14b and *Sha'are Teshuba* #153, p. 16b. The phylactery of the arm is designated אות 'sign' (*Ex* 13:9, 16). This is not the place to launch a full-fledged analysis into Biblical semiotics. Within the limits of our subject, it would suffice to note that in Hebrew semiotics a 'sign' conveys both 'difference' and 'meaning.' More precisely: meaning through difference; see *Golden Doves*, pp. xxiv–xxv, 83. A 'sign' is either recognized or not, and it cannot be subjected to analysis or division; see *Golden Doves*, pp. 77–78. (Hence, the four sections of the Tora it contains are written on a *single* parchment, and its folder is *not* divided, see below). The phrase לאות 'for-a sign' appears three times in Scripture. The function of these signs is to identify the Jew to *others*, (the circumcision, *Gn* 17:11; the phylactery on the arm *Ex* 13:9, 16; *Dt* 11:18; and the Sabbath, *Ez* 20:12, 20); cf. R. Se'adya Gaon, *Commentary on Exodus*, ed. and tr. Y. Ratzaby (Jerusalem: Mossad Harav Kook, 1998), pp. 187–188. Cyrus Gordon, *Adventures in the Near East,* (London: Phoenix House, 1957), p. 78, noted that the 'seal' was used for identification purposes. Notably, לאות of the phylactery of the arm parallels the 'ensign' that the Jewish monarch wore attached to his arm; see *Sanhedrin* 21b and the quotation from Philo in Section III, n. 126.

The focus of this appendix is the second phylactery, to be placed on the forehead. It is designated זכרון (*Ex* 13:9), Targum: דוכרן—a 'memorandum.' As we hope to show in the following, its significance is its connection to the inner dynamics of Jewish memoranda and national archives. The forehead-phylactery is designed as a 'folder,' containing four separate compartments or wallets (בתים), in each of which is stored a different 'file' (see below). Each file must be rolled from left to right (*MT Tefillin* 2:1, 3:7, 5:6), so that one wishing to examine it could read it from beginning to end. Each roll is then tied with a leather strip, and the strip bound over with a string of hair (*MT Tefillin* 3:1, 8). [There is a picture of an ancient file from Jewish Elephantine of the 5th Century BCE: see 'rolled and sealed,' in the *Encyclopedia Judaica,* vol. 3, p. 374]. The file is then stored in one of the assigned compartments (בתים; see *MT Tefillin* 3:5). The letter *Shin* (last letter of *Qadosh* 'Holy') on the right side of the folder serves to indicate that it contains sacred memoranda—not commercial or diplomatic documentation. The four-armed *Shin* on the left side (*MT Tefillin* 3:1, 2) indicates that there are four interconnected files (something that could not be made with either the letter *Qof* or *Dalet* of *Qadosh*). The term 'אחמתא' in *Ezra* 5:2 serves to designate a royal file. This is how it is described in *Midrash Daniel wu-Midrash 'Ezra*, p. 122: "It is a type of a file where they keep letters and books." Cf. Radaq, *Sefer ha-Shorashim* on *'Ezra*, cl. 838. I take this term to be a metathesis of 'אמתחת' *Gn* 44:1, 2, (root MTḤ 'to stretch') which is a 'sack of leather'; see R. Jonah ibn Jannaḥ, *Sefer ha-Shorashim*, p. 276, and Radaq *Sefer ha-Shorashim*, cl. 406.

The nuances peculiar to the phylacteries conform to the norms regulating the writing and filing of sacred archives. Some of the divergences between these norms and those regulating a Scroll of the Tora (see *MT Tefillin* 1:16; 4:15), are clearly understood upon recalling that the Tora is a *book* designed for circulation—not an archived document. Because a duly archived file cannot be amended, neither the *Tefillin* nor *Mezuza* can be corrected; see *MT Tefillin* 1:16, 2:2. On the other hand, a Scroll of the Tora is a *book* for reading, and faults can be rectified; see *Ketubot* 19b, and *MT Tefillin* 1:16; *Sefer Tora* 7:12–13. Therefore, unlike the *Tefillin* and *Mezuza* (see *MT Tefillin* 1:6–9), the Tora must be written on a different type of parchment, with wide margins, *MT Sefer Tora* 7:4–7; and in a special format, *MT Sefer Tora* 9:1–12, etc. Although the *Mezuza*, too, is an archived file, unlike the *Tefillin*, it is exposed to the outside and needs to be periodically examined, see *MT Mezuza* 5:9; whereas the *Tefillin* does not need to be periodically examined; see *Mekhilta de-R. Yishma'el*, p. 69; *Sha'are Teshuba* #153, 16c; *MT Tefillin* 2:11; cf. *Teshubot R. Neṭruna'e Gaon*, ed. Robert Brody (Ofeq Institute: Jerusalem-Cleveland, 1994), vol. 2, pp. 405–406. This explains why it must be written differently, and on a different material than the *Tefillin*; see *MT Tefillin* 1:8–9, 12, etc.

The four files of the *Tefillin* are a memoranda of the *whole* Tora. The first file (*Ex* 13:1–10) records the *salvation* of Israel from Egypt. The second file (*Ex* 13:11–16) registers the *connection* between the Exodus and the Land of Israel: the significance of the former must be carried onto the latter. The third and fourth files establish, respectively, the corner-stone of Judaism: first, *faith* in and *love* of God (*Dt* 5:4–9); and second, *fulfillment* of His precepts (*Dt* 11:13–21). There is *nothing* in the whole Tora which is not comprehended in these memoranda. In the words of the rabbis, *Qiddushin* 35a: "The whole Tora has been placed side by side (הוקשה) with the *Tefillin*." Similarly, we find in *Sha'are Teshuba*, #153, 16b (quoting the *Mekhilta*, see below): "Whoever wears *Tefillin* it is as if the whole Tora is (active) on his lips"; including the Oral Law, see ibid., 16c, and *Yalquṭ Shim'oni, Bo,* #222, s.v. *lema'an,* vol. 2, 69c. [This source was overlooked by R. Isaac Berakha, *Berekh Yiṣḥaq* (Venice, 7523/1763), 38c]. To stress the parallel between the Tora and the phylacteries, both are to be sewn similarly; see *Makkot* 11a and *Yalquṭ Shim'oni, Bo,* #222, s.v. *lema'an,* vol. 2, 69c. The rabbis did not intend an exact parallel between the Tora and phylacteries, but to point out to a kind of symmetry between them, where one synthesizes or symbolizes the other. This critical idea was instituted in law. Judicial procedure requires that in the administration of certain oaths (שבועת הדיינים), the defendant should hold a Scroll of the Tora. If this key element is omitted, the oath is invalid and must be administered again. Could the *Tefillin* be used instead? The law varies. In a case in which the defendant is *not* a learned individual, judicial procedure requires him to hold an actual Scroll of the Tora; the *Tefillin* would be accepted only in case of an oversight. However, if the defendant is learned, judicial procedure requires him to hold only the *Tefillin*—not the Tora (see *Shebu'ot* 38b, *MT Shebu'ot* 11:11–12). The underlying principle is clear. The symmetry Tora/phylacteries is approximate; ultimately, it depends on the individual making the synthesis.

The preceding will elucidate a number of regulations about the *Tefillin.* Let us point out that the *Tefillin* may not be worn either at night, on Holidays, and on the Sabbath. This regulation makes good sense upon realizing that archives were accessible during daylight and at weekdays only. As with archives, the files of the phylactery are positioned in reference to someone *facing* them, as if that individual would want to open and examine them—not in reference to the person wearing it; see *MT Tefillin* 3:5, cf. 3:7. Consistent with the preceding, the act of placing on the phylacteries is designated, להניח (root NWḤ)—a term standing for 'placing' or 'depositing' a valued object in a sacred place for safe-keeping, see above Appendix 6. Most appropriately, the blessing *for* this act is להניח, see *MT Tefillin* 4:5, and cf. *Bet Yosef, Oraḥ Ḥayyim,* XXV, 7. By depositing the phylacteries on himself the Jew becomes a national archive incarnate. Thus, the most important memoranda of Israel are secured. We can now appreciate the regulation stating that the head-phylactery acquires its special status *after* it was duly placed on the forehead; see *MT Tefillin* 3:17. It is the individual Jew, in function of 'archive,' which is the reason for the *Tefillin's* special sanctity—not the other way around. Because the actual *body* [hence the concept of 'wearing'—*labash/libes/vestir Tefillin*] is archive incarnate, the fulfillment of this commandment requires the highest level of personal hygiene (see *Shabbat* 130a, *MT Tefillin* 4:15) and mental focusing (see *MT Tefillin* 4:14)—something not required in the performance of any other ritual. Lest the *Tefillin* be taken to be some sort of amulet, the rabbis stipulated that it is *incumbent on the individual wearing it* "to protect" it; see *Tosefta, Ḥagiga* 1:2, p. 374–375; *Sukkot* 42a; *'Arakhin* 2b; and *Tosefta Ki-Fshuṭah,* vol. 5, p. 1269—rather than expect to be protected by it! (Although, I heard of butchers wearing *Tefillin* to insure that they would incur no harm when cutting the meat.)

Circular phylacteries and amulets on the forehead were used in Ancient Egypt for magical protection, particularly among 'theosophists.' In Elias Bickerman and Morton Smith, *The Ancient History of Western Civilization* (New York: Harper & Row, 1976), after p. 50, #79, there is a picture of the bust of a theosophist from the 3rd century with a circular phylactery.

(A 'circular' headgear is still worn by the Japanese 'Yamabushi' priests). Given that this type of headgear was used for magical protection, the rabbis referred to them as *amagoza, magos*, 'of' or 'pertaining to,' a 'magician'; see Mishna *Megilla* 3:8; and Talmud *Megilla* 24b. Regarding head ornaments used for decorative purposes, see *Sha'are Teshuba* #153, 16c.

The preceding considerations explain the original matrix of the *Bar-Miṣva* ceremony. It celebrates the child assuming personal responsibility as depositary of Israel's sacred treasures. In the Sephardic tradition the ceremony is designated *libes at-Tfilllin* in Judeo-Arabic, and *vestir el Tefillin* in Judeo-Spanish—rather than '*Bar-Miṣva.*' Usually, senior members of the family will assist the child in the task of placing the *Tefillin* for the first time, thus symbolizing transmittal of tradition. Those refusing to "deposit" (מנח, root NWḤ) *Tefillin* on their "cranium"—an allusion to the head-phylactery—have failed to permit their *bodies* to act as the living-archive of Israel. Therefore, in a sense, they have "executed a transgression [against the Tora] *with their own body*" (פושעי ישראל בגופם); see *Rosh ha-Shana* 17a. Connected to this symbolism is the custom that those directly participating in the circumcision ceremony (father, *mohel* and *ṣandaq*) are to wear *Tefillin*; see R. Joseph Ḥayyim David Azulai, *Mar'it ha-'Ayyin*, (Leghorn, 5564/1804), 127c.

The details surrounding the meaning and execution of duly filed memoranda are to be supplied by the archivists (see *Est* 6:1–3); in our case, the individual wearing the phylacteries. Therefore, the phylactery of the head is symbolically associated with learning and scholarship; see *Ex* 13:9, *Yoma* 86a, and cf. *Shabbat* 13a. Some maintain that as a sign of humility, it would be appropriate for a student to wear a smaller phylactery than that of a sage; see *Teshubot ha-Geonim,* ed. R. Jacob Musafia (Jerusalem, 5727/1967), #3, 6a-b, and cf. *Matt* 23:5. Some rabbinic authorities argued that it may be construed as conceit for someone who is not a sage to wear phylacteries altogether; see *Newly Discovered Geonic Responsa*, #161, pp. 233–237. Following this trend of thought, others proposed that since a scholar is in fact a living Tora (see *Homo Mysticus*, pp. 7–8), he should not be required to wear phylacteries altogether! In evidence, a paragraph was cited from *Mekhilta de-R. Yishma'el*, p. 68. That may have been the reason why some rabbis from the Holy Land did not wear *Tefillin*; see *Newly Discovered Geonic Responsa*, #161, pp. 234–235. The authenticity of the citation from the *Mekhilta* was rejected by the *Ṭur* and *Bet Yosef, Oraḥ Ḥayyim,* XXXVIII, 6 and all subsequent authorities. On juridical principles alone, R. Samuel ben Ḥofni Ga'on (d. 1013) rejected the citation; see Abraham E. Harkavy, *Zikhron la-Rishonim*, I (Petersburg, 1880), p. 38. In fact, it is contradicted by the *Yerushalmi 'Erubin* VI, 1, 26a, establishing the principle that, "whoever is required to [study] Tora is required to put on *Tefillin*." Finally, as pointed out by R. Israel Moses Ḥazzan, *'Iyye ha-Yam*, 61a, the citation from the *Mekhilta* is faulty. The original text read: "Whoever wears *Tefillin* it is as if the whole Tora is (active) on his lips."

Historical circumstances following the Destruction of the Second Temple brought about the momentous significance of *Tefillin.* The Romans were bent not only on the physical genocide of Israel, but also on the eradication of the Tora. With this purpose in mind, after authorizing his troops "to burn and sack" Jerusalem, "on the next day," Titus "set fire to the Archives" (Josephus, *Jewish Wars*, VI, 354; vol. 3, p. 479). The Jews made a strategic decision: Roman brutality would be met with the *Tefillin*. Thus, every Jew would become the symbolic archive of Israel. It should not be surprising to discover, therefore, that the *Tefillin* became a target of Roman persecution. With special reference to the phylactery of the head, they decreed: "Whoever places (מניח) *Tefillin*, (we shall) prick out his brain" (*Shabbat* 49a; cf. *Megilla* 24b).

There is a beautiful symbolism in the rabbinic doctrine that God, too, wears the phylactery of the head (*Berakhot* 6a-b; cf. *Teshubot ha-Ge'onim,* ed. R. Jacob Musafia, #115, p. 35). The memoranda attesting to God' miracles and precepts are guarded by each Jew in his own person. Reciprocally, He, too, guards the deeds and wonders wrought by Israel throughout her long and torturous history in His 'personal archive.' That is why, the verse in God's *Tefillin* reads: "Who could compare to Israel, Your nation, a people unique in earth" (1*Ch* 17:21).

The preceding could shed light on the syntax underlying the concept of *Rosh ha-Shana.* In the Tora this Holiday is referred to as זכרון תרועה מקרא קודש (*Lev* 23:24). Here, too, the *Targum* rendered זכרון as דוכרן, 'a memorandum.' The next term (תרועה) is rendered יבבא, a 'trumpet' or 'proclamation' made at the sound of a *shofar.* The last two terms מקרא 'a call' and קודש 'to the sanctuary' specify that this is a 'summons' to appear at the קודש, 'sanctuary'. Before exploring the sense of the verse we should note that the prosodic marks (טעמים) connect זכרון—תרועה as one syntactical unit, and מקרא-קודש as a second syntactical unit. Accordingly, the sense of מקרא-קודש, intersect and compliments זכרון-תרועה, as follows: A1-B2 = B1-A2 = A1+B2. Thus: זכרון/קודש = מקרא/תרועה. The exact translation is "a memoranda" (A1) "at the Sanctuary" (B2); i.e., "a summons" (A2) "with a trumpet" (B1). In plain terms: 'A summons to be executed with a trumpet, calling to appear at the Sanctuary where the memoranda (pertaining to each individual) will be reviewed.' Precisely and to the point, the rabbis interpreted this to mean that on *Rosh ha-Shana* we are to be summoned to appear at the Sanctuary, where the memoranda registering our actions (see *Mal* 3:16; *Est* 2:23, 6:1) will be examined before the Divine Tribunal. As with all memoranda, the archivists will be called on to supply the details (see above). Hence, the motifs of 'Divine Judgment,' and 'Books of Life and Death' (see *Rosh ha-Shana* 16b), peculiar to the liturgy and pathos of the day.

10. The Autonomy of the Law

Belief in the autonomy of the Law underlies much of Biblical and post-Biblical Jewish history. Throughout the ages, the political, ecclesiastical, and judicial authorities were challenged by the people—in the name of the Law.

The episode of Ahab and Nabot (1*K*29) illustrates how in Ancient Israel, even tyrants did not claim eminent domain and recognized the supreme authority of the Law. When Nabot refused to sell his vineyard, Ahab fell into despair, not knowing what to do. The idea of using trumped up charges against Nabot came from his wife—the pagan queen Jezebel—who herself (the daughter of a Syrian king), was well acquainted with the art of judicial manipulation. Remarkably, even under those circumstances, meticulous procedure was observed. More importantly, the eventual usurpation of Nabot's property was denounced for generations as a most heinous crime (see 2*K* 9:21–26); see below Appendix 13. The Rabbinic doctrine of 'the kingdom of heaven' (מלכות שמים), Mishna *Berakhot* 2:2, usually explained in theological terms, is a *political* doctrine. It postulates that the "kingdom," i.e., the sovereignty,—"of heaven," i.e., the Law, is supreme (see Chapter 19). From this doctrine two legal principles emerge: "there cannot be a fiduciary relation in matters involving a transgression' of the Law" (אין שליח לדבר עברה), and "the orders of a superior authority and the orders of an inferior authority, whose orders shall we obey?" (דברי הרב ודברי התלמיד, דברי מי שומעים); see *Qiddushin* 42b and parallels; *MT Melakhim* 3:9; *Sefer ha-Mișvot,* positive precept, #173, p. 146; cf. *MT Me'ila* 7:2. The first formula rejects the notion that there could be a duty to act on behalf of another person in matters involving an illegal act. Therefore, neither the king nor any other authority may be obeyed in matters involving the breaking of the Law. The second formula establishes that an individual is responsible for his own actions, and cannot claim immunity on the basis that he was acting as an agent of a 'higher authority.'

The same standards applied to the ecclesiastical authorities: they, too, are under the absolute mandate of the Law. When acting outside the confines of the Law, the priesthood has no authority. The conflict between Amos and the high priest Amaziah (*Am* 7:7–17), illustrates this fundamental principle: the office of high priest was challenged at the royal sanctuary, by Amos—a common individual with no office. The point is clear: the eminence of the priesthood is the effect of the Law, and it must be measured accordingly. (This episode has been the subject of a brilliant analysis by Professor Shalom Spiegel, "Amos vs. Amaziah," in ed. Judah Goldin, *The Jewish Expression*, New Haven: Yale University Press, 1976, pp. 38–65. Cf. *Mal* 2:5–7.)

A similar incident took place during the period of the second Temple in Jerusalem. The rabbis reported a clash between the people and the high priest, who was also the king, when he deviated from a prescribed ritual (see Mishna *Sukka* 4:9). Josephus, *Jewish Antiquities*, XIII, 372, vol. 7, p. 413, described the incident as follows:

> As for Alexander, his own people revolted against him—for the nation was aroused against him—at the celebration of the festival, and as he stood beside the altar and was about to sacrifice, they pelted him with citrons, it being a custom among the Jews that at the festival of Tabernacles everyone holds wands made of palm branches and citrons—these we have described elsewhere; and they added insult to injury by saying that he was descended from captives and was unfit to hold office and to sacrifice; and being enraged at this, he killed some six thousand of them, and also placed a wooden barrier about the altar and the temple as far as the coping (of the court) which the priests alone were permitted to enter, and by this means blocked the people's way to him. He also maintained foreign troops of Psidians and Cilicians, for he could not use Syrians, being at war with them.

For the feeling of disgust that the people had for this type of high priest, in contrast to the reverence that they had for two proselytes, teachers of the Law, see *Yoma* 71b, and *In the Shadow of History*, p. 201.

The authority of the judiciary, too, depends on the Law. We have seen that if the Supreme Court of Israel issues a decision contrary to the Law, they are not to be obeyed (see Chapters 10, 20, etc; and *Studies in the Mishne Tora*, pp. 20–24.). Maimonides codified the rule that if the Jewish authorities appointed an unqualified person as judge, the appointment is worthless (*MT Sanhedrin* 4:15; cf. *MT Melakhim* 1:7). The following passage, *Yerushalmi Bikkurim* III, 3, 65d, offers a glimpse into the rabbis' view on this matter:

> [1] R. Mane (3rd century) would deprecate those [judges] that were appointed because of money. [2] R. Amme (end of 3rd century) applied to them the verse "Gods of silver and gods of gold do not make for yourselves" (*Ex* 20:23). [3] R. Joshia (3rd century) said, his *ṭallet* (mantel) is to be regarded as a donkey's back strap. [4] R. [A]shyan (3rd and 4th centuries) said: Whoever is appointed because of money, one cannot stand up [in reverence] before him or call him

> 'Rabbi,' and his mantle is to be regarded as a donkey's back strap. [5] R. Ze'ira (3rd and 4th centuries) and a rabbi were seated, when one of those who was appointed because of money passed. Said that rabbi to R. Ze'ira: 'Let us pretend that we are studying, so that we would not need to stand up before him.'

The reason that the mantles of these judges are compared to a donkey's back strap is that as a matter of distinction, the judges used a thick mantle. The point here is that just as a donkey, because of the back strap, does not feel its rider, this type of judge is not aware that he is been driven by those who had invested him with the mantle of authority.

In the matter of incompetent judges duly appointed by the Exilarch, R. Hayye Gaon (939–1038) issued the following decision:

> Concerning your query about judges that impound the beds of the poor and other objects, not in accordance with the law of the Tora, and [consequently] the creditors come and rob their houses and loot their beds and utensils which cannot be [legally] impounded, and you have no power to constrain them. Let the spirit of those judges be accursed! They are judges of Sodom! Ye Robbers and Thieves! Concerning them it is written: "You have looted the vineyard; the loot of the poor is in their houses" (*Is* 3:14). Therefore, you must disseminate the word among all your neighbors and nearby places, and disgrace them and remove them from office, since they do not care about the Tora and the words of our rabbis of blessed memory. And you, who know the law of the Tora and rabbinic statutes, organize, take council, deliberate, and bring forth from among you God-fearing men and scholars who care for the honor of the Tora, and appoint them over you. You should have no second thoughts about this matter. (*Sha'are Teshuba* #86.)

The same principle was applied to the political authorities. As per the following Geonic decision (*Newly Discovered Geonic Responsa*, #96, p. 88; cf. p. 274 [iv]):

> A king, governor, or tax-collector who sends [agents] to the Community to excommunicate for his own private needs and endeavors, either to punish or to seize Jewish money—and it is impossible not to excommunicate because of [his] coercion. All excommunications that were issued are worthless, and no one should pay any attention to them. Likewise, if an Israelite who had deposited money with a friend, and was denounced, and the king ordered that he [who received the deposit] should be excommunicated, and the confidant does not want to disclose [the deposit he received in trust] except to the heirs [as required by the law] in order to pay [i.e. the debts incurred by the deceased]: Blessing shall descend on him, and the baseless curse will not come! No one should heed to that ban and excommunication. And we must acknowledge him [the confidant] for the good [that he did], and bless him because he persisted in his faithfulness, and he is compassionate with the heirs. Concerning this man it is written, "My eyes are on the faithful of the earth" (*Ps* 101:6).

Concerning judges appointed for money, see below Appendix 58.

Throughout their long history the Jewish people remained steadfast to the principle that all forms of authority must be grounded on the Tora.

Let us review some the principles pertaining to the interpretation and application of the Law discussed in the preceding Sections. The "Tora"—comprising the total value-system of Israel—is the result of a *berit* (covenant), freely contracted by God and Israel. Specifically, the Pentateuch or Written Law is the Constitution, while the Oral Law is the *perush* representing the interpretation of the Jewish Constitution by the Supreme Court. The Mishna contains the *halakhot* 'regulations' pertaining to the Jewish Constitution, as formulated by R. Judah ha-Nasi and the Supreme Court of Israel. To apply these regulations, however, we need a "Court Ruling" (see *Baba Batra* 130b; *Horayot* 2a; *Mishne Tora, Shegagot* 12:2; 13:1; and below Appendix 48). The Talmud contains the Court Rulings of the last National Court of the Jewish people. Since after the Talmudic period there were no National Courts, there was a need for the expert opinion of *posqim* "rabbinic jurists." Although technically lacking the authority of a National Court, their codes and responsa were a kind of "General Counsel Memoranda," reflecting, but not representing, what the opinion of the National Court was (or would have been if the issue would have come before them).

A good model for the Rabbinic System is the Internal Revenue Code of the USA. The Code itself is drafted by the Congress, the legislative branch of government. In this sense, it parallels the Written Law. All income tax rules must ultimately find a source in the Code and apply the rules by its authority. In applying the Code we need to consult the "Treasury Regulations," paralleling the Mishna. The regulations, however, are not drafted by the Congress, but by the Department of Treasury (nobody knows for sure, but it is probably a part of the Executive). As with the Mishna, the "Regulations" constitute the official *perush* of the Code. To apply the Code one must consult with the "Regulations," just as one must consult the "Regulations" of the Mishna, before applying the law of the Pentateuch. In addition, there are "Court Rulings," issued by the Judiciary (not the Executive). They are similar to the Rabbinic Court of the Talmud reviewing the regulations of the Mishna. Generally, a Court will not disagree with a "Regulation," and would limit itself to resolving specific issues brought before it. For instance, "Treasury Regulations" require the taxation of "income." The Court could decide if a particular item constitutes "income" for tax purposes, but it would not rule on what is not income. For our purpose, there are also "Revenue Rulings" by the IRS (treasury) that, like the Talmudic Court, will adjudicate on specific questions submitted before it, e. g., whether an entity is a corporation or a partnership. Finally, there is the "General Counsel Memoranda" issued by the attorneys of the Internal Revenue Service. Although technically lacking authority, the memoranda, like the decisions issued by the *posqim* are practically binding, in the sense that they are an accurate description of what the Internal Revenue Service ruling will be. (In this context it would be opportune to remember that as noted by Justice Holmes, lawyering is a form of "prediction" of what the court may decide; see above Section V, n. 303).

Given that the Tora was entrusted "to the community of Jacob" (*Dt* 33:4), 'law' is not simply what the Supreme Court—or the political and ecclesiastical authorities—dictate. Thus, the Jewish Supreme Court can be found in judicial error. On this key-issue the Jewish legal system differs from other systems. By way of contrast, although the Supreme Court of the US may occasionally decide that a prior opinion was 'erroneous,' it could never be 'in error'; see "Law and Hermeneutics in Rabbinic Jurisprudence," pp. 1670–1672. Rhetorical noise aside, the Constitution is what the US Supreme Court says it is. This point was elucidated by Chief Justice Charles Evans Hughes (1862–1948)—one of the most brilliant minds to grace the Court. "We are under a Constitution," he declared—"but the Constitution is what the judges say it is." (Cited by Joseph W. Bishop, Jr., *Justice Under Fire: A Study of Military Law* [New York: Charterhouse, 1974], p. 175). A corollary to this doctrine is that although the Supreme Court may be theoretically 'erroneous' it cannot commit a judicial mistake. Given the absolute discretion of the Supreme Court, "the people," as argued by Jefferson, "will have ceased to be their own rulers, having to that extent practically resigned their government in the hands of that eminent tribunal" (see Section II n. 137). It is true that the U.S. constitutional system with its checks and balances, designed to make sure that the court does not overstep its boundaries, offers a sense of stability. However, even well-accepted constitutional principles, could—at least at the theoretic level—be subject to broad change and abrogation.

Therefore, Constitutional Law pertains more to the realm of the ethical than to the legal. Here is what Jolowicz, *Lectures on Jurisprudence*, p. 25 writes:

> *Constitutional Law* also, in so far as it relates to the composition of the sovereign, is no law. For whether a particular man, or particular body or composition of bodies is habitually obeyed by the bulk of a society, is a question of fact. Moreover, what is commonly called 'constitutional law'—meaning the principles upon which the sovereign should act—is really only positive morality, for sovereign power cannot be limited.

Modern states, too, uphold the same ideal. The objective of legal and judicial institutions is to express, and thereby uphold and defend, the wishes of the 'sovereign.' True to the ideal that might equals right, litigation is in essence a *battle* between two parties. In Rome, the source and inspiration of Western legal tradition, a trial is "in its substance a struggle, a battle in a closed arena... a shock of contending forces." Rather than justice, the task of the court is to serve as the arena of "a just duel fought out between them [the parties] in the full light of day under certain rules, which the umpire is present to enforce." (Both quotations come from M. Car Ferguson, "A Day in Court in Justinian's Rome: Some Problems of Evidence, Proof, and Justice in Roman Law," *Iowa Law Review* 46 [1960–1], p. 740). To a large extent, this is still the case in modern judicial systems, where equality before the law is not readily attainable. Invariably, the legal system will end up protecting established inequality and hierarchies; cf. "Repressive Tolerance," pp. 116–117. (The classical portrayal of this type of justice is Albert Camus, *The Stranger,* see Chapter 3 in particular). Appropriately, one may argue that modern constitutions guarantee basic human rights. Indeed they do. However, since these constitutions are neither 'eternal' nor 'divine'—as with the Jewish Law—they may be changed at the wish of the sovereign. Thus, even in the best of democracies, we must recognize the possibility of disenfranchising national minorities and undesirable individuals in a strictly constitutional manner. More to the point, since there is no formal covenant articulating the specifics of the law, in fact the Constitution is nothing more than "the persons and bodies who can amend the Constitution." Thus, the actual sovereign is the person or persons that could alter and interpret the Constitution. Clearly, the Preamble of the Constitution proclaiming, "We the People of the United States... do ordain and establish this Constitution," presupposes an authoritative body ("We the People") anteceding the legal system. This offers unlimited constitutional powers to "the People." At the same time, since the Supreme Court cannot be in judicial error, "We the people," is in fact a circumlocution for what five out of nine judges dictate.

There is one major difference between Tora—as the basic constitutive document of the Jewish Nation—and the US Constitution. The Judicial authority to interpret and review the Tora by the Supreme Court is explicitly authorized by a provision *in* the Tora (*Dt* 17:8–13). The authority of the US Supreme Court to interpret and review the Constitution is not enumerated in the Constitution, but, rather, derives from its own ruling, *Marbury v. Madison,* in which it assumes judicial supremacy in constitutional interpretation and the authority to impose its constitutional interpretations on other branches of government. The difference is huge.

The inability of Jews to assimilate to other political, religious, or legal systems is a corollary of having rejected the notion that authority is the effect of power; that is, violence.

11. Alien Cult

The Hebrew idea of monolatry—in the sense of worshipping God according to the specific terms prescribed in the covenant—stands at the basis of the Scriptural prohibition of *'aboda zara* ('alien worship'). It includes not only the prohibition against worshipping images or other deities, but also worshipping God with an 'alien worship,' i.e., with cults and rituals not prescribed in the covenant; see above Appendix 4. From this perspective, it is irrelevant whether one worships God with images or with an unprescribed cult. The rabbis stipulated that worshipping Michael, the 'ministering angel of Israel,' constitutes *'aboda zara*; see *Tosefta Ḥolin* 2:18, p. 503; *'Aboda Zara* 42b; *Ḥolin* 40a; etc. Similarly, Talmudic law classifies Christianity *'aboda zara* not because it worships images—images were introduced into Christianity after the Talmudic period—but, solely, because it worships with a cult *not* stipulated in the Sinaitic covenant; see *Studies in the Mishne Tora*, pp. 230–238.

The concept of 'alien deities' was instituted by Patriarch Jacob, who referred to pagan idols as "alien deities," (אלהי נכר; *Gn* 35:2, 4); see Se'adya's translation *ad loc.* The sense of this term will be clear upon considering that a married woman is described as 'alien' (זרה, נכריה), i.e., forbidden, not because she is evil but because she is *not* your wife; see *Pr* 2:16; 7:5. Therefore, worshipping other deities is compared to adultery; see, for example *Hoshea* Chapter 1). Although an Israelite is permitted to marry a priest's daughter, he is referred to as 'alien' (זר) to indicate that he is *not* a priest (*Lev* 22:12). Similarly, the two sons of Aaron were punished because they offered an "alien incense" (אש זרה), i.e., which God "had not ordered them" (*Lev* 10:1; cf. *Nu* 3:4; 26:61); see R. Se'adya Gaon, "Fragments," ed. M. Zucker, *Sura* 2 (1955–1956), pp. 337–338. The same term is used to proscribe priests in general from offering an "alien incense" (קטרת זרה; *Ex* 30:9). In the same vein, a 'ritual' (עבודה), which is 'alien' (זרה), is forbidden, not because it is necessarily 'evil,' but, simply, because it is 'alien' to Judaism. In the words of R. Elie Benamozegh, *Em la-Miqra*, vol. 3 (Leghorn, 1863), 41b:

> ...That truly, any type of deviation or change from the prescribed rituals and required conditions [stipulated in the Tora] is designated "*'aboda zara*," because it is in fact 'alien' (*zara*), constituting not 'worship' (*'aboda*) of the God of Israel, but worship of an alien god, or to what was fabricated (by the worshipers).

The term 'alien cult' (עבודה זרה) used by the rabbis to designate other religions (including Christianity) has been misconstrued to mean 'idolatry.' The excuse for such an interpretation is semantic assimilation (see Appendix 58), coupled with rabbinic illiteracy. Simply put, an 'alien cult' is any form of worship not prescribed by the Law. Therefore, it applies exclusively to Jews. The rabbis (*Megilla* 9b) noted that after translating the prohibition against worshipping "other gods... the sun, or the moon, or any host of heaven," the Septuagint added: "which He did not command you to do" (*Dt* 17:3). The English translation of the Septuagint "which he commanded not to do" is incorrect. Cf. *Homo Mysticus*, pp. 9–13.

Jewish regulations of *'aboda zara* don't apply to gentiles outside the Land of Israel. According to the Mishna (*Berakhot* 9:1), someone witnessing a place where idols were removed, should say: "Blessed is God, Sovereign of the Universe that *'aboda zara* has been removed *from our land*." Cf. *Sifre* #61 (3), p. 127; *Sefer ha-Miṣvot*, positive precept #185, p. 153. Let us point out that Maimonides registered the status of a pious gentile in two places. In *MT Teshuba* 3:5 he codified the rabbinic doctrine that a "pious from among the nations of the world" has a portion in the World-to-Come, i.e., he would be saved (just like a Jew), but refrained from defining 'pious.' This is consistent with the view that Judaism, although open to *all*, is *not* Catholic like Christianity and Islam; i.e., it cannot and will not impose its ideas of sanctity and devotion on the rest of the world. Therefore, Maimonides was careful *not* to define what constitutes a 'sin' for a gentile; cf. *MT Teshuba* 3:2. He defined a pious gentile in terms of the seven Noahide *miṣvot* in the section about Jewish governance and territory, concerning the status of non-Jewish residents in the Holy Land (*MT Melakhim* 9:2). The sense is obvious. An alien residing in Israel must respect Jewish standards and regulations as it would be expected from every alien to respect the laws and regulations of the host country. Support for this thesis is the fact that Maimonides included as one of these seven *miṣvot* to establish a judicial system to try capital cases (*MT Melakhim* 10:11, cf. 8:7; 9:1, 14). This could hardly be feasible outsied the land of Israel. I don't share the view of R. Abraham b. ha-Rambam, *Perush*, p. 302; cf. editor's n. 14.

The preceding is in line with the thesis that we proposed in Chapter 25, that idols and rituals branded by the rabbis as '*aboda zara* are state-sponsored (mostly representing imperial dominance over Israel). Explicitly, the rabbis excluded from '*aboda zara* "someone worshipping an object out of love or fear." (For a detailed analysis of the sources and opinions on this subject, see *Studies in the Mishne Tora*, pp. 219–230. Cf. *Homo Mysticus*, p. 10). We should note that in Antiquity the worship of alien deities was regarded as a 'civil,' rather than a 'religious' offense, in the modern sense of this term; see Albert Barnes, *The Book of Job,* vol. 1 (New York: Leavitt, Trow, & Company, 1845), pp. xxviii-xxix. In this connection I would like to quote a passage from Reverend Jonathan Mayhew, in *Seven Sermons*, reprinted in *Religion in America* (New York: Arno Press, 1969), pp. 68–69:

> It is to be remembered that Judaism was at least as much a *political* as a *religious* institution. The *Jews* had God for their immediate *king* and *lawgiver,* both in *church* and *state.* Their *civil* and *ecclesiastical* polity were blended together; and being derived from the same source, every violation of the law of *Moses* might be considered and punished as an offence against the state, in a greater or less degree: And *idolatry* being in these circumstances equivalent to *high treason*, it is not strange that a capital punishment should be annexed to it.

12. *Morasha*

Morasha is the Hebrew term for 'National Memory' (See *Introductory Remarks*, Section IV). It is mentioned twice in the Tora, once in relation to the *territory* of Israel (*Ex* 6:8; cf. *Ez* 11:15; 25:4; 33:24; 36:5), and again in relation to the *Law* of Israel (*Dt* 33:4). Although related to 'succession' it is not synonymous with 'inheritance' (*yerusha*). "In a common succession," explained the rabbis, "the living inherit the dead, but here [concerning the land of Israel], the dead inherit the living," *Baba Batra* 117a. An heir may dispose of his inheritance as he or she wishes. *Morasha* is akin to the 'fee tail estate' in Feudal England, that an heir receives with the special responsibility of keeping the estate in the family. This explains Nabot's refusal to sell his vineyard to King Ahab; see 1*K*29 and above, Appendix 10.

We are now in a position to properly evaluate the semantics of *Morasha* with respect to the Law (*Dt* 33:4). It involves transmission of said Law in perpetuity, from one generation to the other; see *Targum ad loc*. Commenting on this verse, R. Abraham ibn 'Ezra pointedly noted that the preposition -ל ('for') in 'for us' [Law instructed ל-נו, i.e., 'for us,' rather than 'to us'] should apply also to the terms '*morasha*' and to '*qehillat.*' Accordingly, the verse is to be rendered: "A Law was instructed (צוה) for us (לָנו), for (-ל) *morasha*, for (-ל) the Congregation of Jacob." He explained: "It means that it [the Law] should be conveyed in succession from one generation to the other, (each) conveying (to the next): 'This is what we have received from our Teacher Moses as heritage in our hands.'" [For a comprehensive analysis of this passage, see R. Isaac Shrem, *Be'er Yiṣḥaq* (Leghorn, 5624/1864), 152b, note #14. There are some obvious errors in the printed text of R. Abraham ibn 'Ezra's note. In my opinion the correct text should read:

תורה צוה לנו משה—זהו שישא, ויאמר דור לדור: כך העתקנו מפי משה ירושה בידינו. ויהיה למ"ד לנו מושך עצמו ואחר עמו, וכן היא: מורשה לקהלת יעקב... ויהי: מורשה—למורשה לקהלת יעקב.

Cf. Ms. Vat. Ebr. 38. Ed. Prof. Etan Levine, *Abraham ibn Ezra's Commentary to the Pentateuch*, (Jerusalem: Makor, 1974), p. 212]. A similar syntactical construction ('צוה לי, rather than 'אותי'), in the sense 'he instructed me *to say*,' is found in 1*Sam* 20:29.

To fully appreciate the niceties implicit in '*Morasha* of the Law,' let us begin by noting that the verb צוה is not semantically identical to 'command.' 'To command' implies rank and authority and the power to compel, as in a hierarchic system, when a superior officer issues an order to a subaltern. In this sense it is found only occasionally; e.g., when the *pagan king* of Aram instructed (צוה) his captains to target King Ahab (1*K* 22:31), or when King Ahasuerus issued an order (צוה) that everyone should prostrate himself to Haman (*Est* 3:2; cf. 3:10 and 8:9). In the latter case, government officials asked Mordecai why he was "transgressing the command (מצות) of the king" and refuse to prostrate himself to Haman (*Est* 3:3). Generally, however, it appears in the sense of 'instructions,' implying 'trust and confidence' that the recipient would comply, rather than 'obidience' (cf. above Appendix 4). As with parents expecting their children to comply with their instructions. Bearing the sense of 'trust,' it appears as the 'last will' of a father (see *Gn* 18:19; 50:16; *Jer* 35:6, 14, 18; 39:11); or as a 'request" from a relative (*Est* 2:10, 20), or a friend (1*Sam* 20:29), or a teacher to his disciple (*Jer* 51:59)—implying *hope and expectation* that the will or request to be fulfilled. In the same vein, it also denotes 'instruction' offered by a mentor to his disciples; see *Dt* 4:14; 6:1; *Tosefta Sanhedrin* 4:7, p. 421; *Nedarim* 37a and cf. *Jer* 51:59. In rabbinic literature, this verb is used for 'instructions' from father to children regarding how they should conduct their affairs after he passes away; see *Pesaḥim* 112 a, b; 113b; *Baba Batra* 147a. Since these kinds of instructions were usually given at the deathbed (see *Gn* 49:29; 2*Sam* 17:23; 1*K* 2:1; 2*K* 20:1; *Is* 38:1; cf. *MT Qeri'at Shema'* 1:4), in rabbinic literature this verb is also used in conjunction with a gift by a donor contemplating death (*causa mortis*); see *Giṭṭin* 66a; *Baba Batra* 151b; *MT Zekhiya* 8:2, 5, 23, etc. It appears also as a noun, in the form צוואה, for a 'deed' or a 'last will' in which the testator declares how he wishes to dispose of his properties; see *MT Sanhedrin* 24:1; *Shulḥan 'Arukh, Ḥoshen Mishpaṭ* CCCLIII, 32; etc. In reference to the territory of Israel, God, as the Executor of the heritage "instructs" (צוה) how the territory should be parceled and passed in succession; see *Nu* 34:29; 36:2; *Josh* 1:13.

In light of the preceding, it seems appropr iate to render צוה as 'conveyance' and 'transmission,' implying therefore, to 'delegate' and 'entrust' the recipients—rather than the usual rendering 'to command.' Consider, for example, the people's request "to bring the *Scroll* of the Law which Moses צוה Israel" (*Neh* 8:1; cf. ibid. 8:14). One may *command* the Law, but not the *Scroll* of the Law! A more appropriate rendition would be 'to bring in the *Scroll* that Moses had *entrusted* Israel with,' i.e., the Scroll of the Law that Moses had deposited in the national archives of Israel (see above Chapter 7). The same applies to the "precepts that Mosesצוה to the children of Israel" (*Lev* 27:34). It means: "the precepts that Moses had 'conveyed,' thus 'entrusting' Israel"—rather than 'commanding'; cf. *Dt* 4:13; *Jud* 3:4; 1*K*11:10; *2K* 17:34. Similarly, on the basis that God "ויצו" Adam (*Gn* 2:16), Maimonides concluded that Adam, as the recipient of 'the image of God' was an intelligent being, "given that one cannot convey an instruction to a beast or to someone who lacks intelligence" (*Guide* I, 2, p. 16, ll. 13–17; cf. *Saadya's Commentary on Genesis*, p. 274 and editor's n. 363). However, one can certainly give a 'command' to a beast and machines; see above Chapter 24, and "Performative and Descriptive Utterances in Jewish Law," pp. 112–114. That is why God did not 'ויצו' to the "big fish" to swallow Jonah (*Jonah* 2:1).

If we are to come to grips with the full sense of 'צוה' it would be important to take note that together with the sense of 'trust' this verb denotes also 'the responsibility incumbent upon the recipient to fulfill the trust and to convey it further' to the nation f Israel. About Joshua it was written: "There was not a word that Moses had entrusted (צוה), which Joshua did not read (קרא) before the Congregation of Israel" (*Josh* 8:35). Joshua did not "read" something "commanded" to him, but something which Moses had *entrusted* him to 'convey' to the people. In this manner, the Scripture teaches that Joshua was a trustworthy executor of whatever Moses had entrusted (צוה) him; see *Josh* 8:31; 11:15; and cf. *Dt* 34:9. R. Abraham ibn 'Ezra's interpretation is clearly stated in *Ps* 78:5: "For He established a testimony in Jacob, and a Law He appointed in Israel, which He entrusted (צוה) our fathers, that they should make known to their children." The double sense of 'trust/conveyance' of 'צוה' is fundamental to the Hebrew concept of 'Law': it factually depends on *conveyance* to, and *trust* in, future generations, rather than the might of an army or a police force. Thus, the responsibility incumbent upon each generation not to betray the trust of their parents, see 2*K* 21:8.

To sum up, *Morasha* is a *national* pledge by Israel, with respect to their *territory* and their *Law*. Specifically, it implies the solemn responsibility of keeping this double trust in the domain of Israel; and *conveying* it in *trust* to the next generation as fiduciaries of the original *Morasha*, in perpetuity. Hence, the double sense of the verb 'צוה.'

13. Becoming a Single Body

Halakha regards a husband and a wife as a single body; see *Berakhot* 24a; *MT Qeri'at Shema'* 3:18; cf. *Bekhorot* 35b. "A man," the rabbis taught, "should love his wife [at least] as his own body"; *Yebamot* 62b and *Sanhedrin* 76b. They are also regarded as a single person. Therefore a man cannot testify against his wife for the same reason that he cannot testify against himself, given that this would constitute self-incrimination; see *Sanhedrin* 9b–10a. Conversely, the bill of divorce is designated כריתות (see *Dt* 24:1, 3), 'cutting'—as if 'tearing a single body' and rendering it into two parts. At a corporeal level, sexual relations establish a special link between the parties; e.g., a man having sexual relations with a woman in a state of menstrual impurity will acquire the woman's status; see *Lev* 15:24 and Mishna *Kelim* 1:5. Consider also *Soṭa* 3b, where sexual contact involves after death communion between the parties. It should be noted that the verb דבק is *not* connected with sexual activity, see *Dt* 4:4; 10:20; 11:22; 30:20; *Rut* 1:14, etc. Eventually, this type of pathos evolved into what Judah described as two souls "attached" (קשורה) to each other; see *Gn* 44:30 and *Targum ad loc*. It culminated in the principle expressed in *Lev* 19:18 to love our fellow-human as ourselves. (This is not to be confused with the narcissistic love expressed by inquisitors, missionaries, and preachy lunatics of both religious and secular persuasions).

The Jewish people, too, are regarded "as a single body and a single soul." Therefore, if "one of them were to sin, all of them are chastised" (*Mekhilta de-R. Shim'on b. Yoḥai*, p. 139). Cf. Section III, n. 152.

14. Gideon and Washington

'Apotheosis' and the 'deification' of rulers pose the greatest danger to political freedom and democracy. There is little doubt that the concept of sovereignty, reflected in the monarchy and modern dictatorships, whether from the left or the right, involves the deification of the ruler. Concerning the deification of rulers, see *Mekhilta de-R. Yishma'el, Masekhta de-Vayyassa'*, p. 17, where it proposes that the rebels wishing to appoint a "chief" to guide them back to Egypt (*Nu* 14:4), were seeking a leader that could eventually appropriate the spirit of the idol and act as a deity. The rebels reasoned: "It seems to us that no one remained alive in Egypt. Let us take on a chief, and we will make for ourselves an idol and it [i.e., the spirit dwelling in the idol] will come down and rest over [i.e., incarnate] our chief, and we will return to

Egypt." Cf. *Mekhilta de-R. Shim'on b. Yoḥai*, p. 102; Rashi and *Em la-Miqra* on *Nu* 14:4, vol. 4, 43a-b; R. Se'adya Ga'on, *Perush* to *Daniel,* p. 70.

In a question addressed to R. David b. Abi Zimra, *Teshubot Radbaz*, 2vols. (Warsaw, 5642/1882), Part IV, vol. 2 (#187 = 1258), a case was presented to him concerning a preacher who maintained that those who worshipped the golden calf had previously worshipped Moses as a god. The rabbi concluded that the preacher was wrong but nonthelss he did not warrant excommunication. With all due respect, I believe that the preacher was making a valid point, particularly in light of the rabbinic sources cited above. Only people believing that Moses incarnated the spirit of God would believe that the same spirit could be transferred and incarnate a statue and then another leader. The Pope, as *incarnation* of God's Word when acting *ex Cathedra*, is the most powerful exposition of this political ideology—certainly, much more successful than the institution that the late Emperor Hirohito (1901–1989) represented. Rev. Jonathan Mayhew, too, saw the close relation between belief in the "divine right of kings" and the "fabulous and chimerical" doctrine of "transubstantiation." See Section III, n. 301.

The danger of these ideas was clearly perceived by Washington and the Founding Fathers. It was their spiritual fortitude that prevented this sort of ideology from taking root in America. I believe that the reason that George Washington had such strong reservations about accepting the presidency was his concern that the office of the presidency might be linked to his military victory. Many thought that Washington was the 'logical' candidate, simply, because he defeated the English. Washington, who was a profoundly religious man with deep roots in the Hebrew Scripture, needed to be convinced that his military victory was *not* the principal reason for his election as president. The "Brumidi's Fresco" illustrates how real the danger of apotheosis was.

15. The Concept of *Galut*

The four constitutive points underlying the *concept* of *Galut* were developed by the Prophet Ezekiel. They are: [a] the corruption of Jewish political leadership. The misery befalling Israel was not the result of some recondite fate lying in the realm of the mysterious (as mystics and corrupt politicians preach), but the consequence of incompetent leadership (see Chapters 8, 13, 19, 22, 34). [b] In such a situation, there is a need to assume *individual responsibility* for one's fate, adhere to the requirements of the Law (see

Chapters 18, 20, 22), and ignore the counsel of a fundamentally boorish leadership. [c] This will result in the national redemption of the people (see Chapters 11, 36–39). [d] In the end, this strategy will culminate in the rebuilding of the Temple in Jerusalem and the full restoration of the nation Israel (see Chapters 40–48).

16. By Virtue of Conquest

The right of the 'English Crown' to possess territories by virtue of conquest is fully acknowledged by the US Supreme Court, and serves as the basis for American sovereignty over the territories and lands previously occupied by Native Americans.

In a decision rendered on March 10, 1823, "Johnson and Graham's Lessee *v.* William McIntosh," 21U.S. 543, 5L.Ed. 681, 8 Wheat. 543 (1823), at 12–13, we read:

> Thus has our whole country been granted by the crown while in the occupation of the Indians. These grants purport to convey the soil as well as the right of the dominion to the grantees. In those governments which were denominated royal, where the right to the soil was not vested in individuals, but remained in the crown, or was vested in the colonial government, the king claimed and exercised the right of granting lands, and of dismembering the government at his will ... In all of them, the soil, at the time the grants were made, was occupied by the Indians. Yet almost every title within those governments is dependent on these grants ... It has never been objected to this, or to any other similar grant, that the title as well as possession was the Indians when it was made, and that it passed nothing on that account.

Cf. ibid. 21 US 543 at 592–605.

In the US, the Congress is the Sovereign, and therefore the absolute owner of the land. In a ruling, The Tee-Hit-Ton Indians *v.* United States 348 US 272, 75S. Ct. 313, 99 L. Ed. 314, 1955. at 279, we read:

> After conquest they were permitted to occupy portions of territory over which they had previously exercised "sovereignty," as we use the term. This is not a property right of occupancy which the sovereign grants and protects against intrusion by third parties but which right of occupancy may be terminated and such lands fully disposed of by the sovereign itself without any legally enforceable obligation to compensate the Indians.

For our purpose it is significant to note the view of Senator Plumb, cited ibid at 293:

> I do not know by what tenure the Indians are there nor what ordinarily characterizes their claim of title, but it will be observed that the language of the *provisio* I propose to amend puts them into very small quarters. I think about 2 feet by 6 to each Indian would be the proper construction of the language 'actually in their use or occupation.' Under the general rule of occupation by a white man, that would be a tolerably limited occupation and might possibly land them in the sea.

It is worthy of note that this decision was rendered *after* the landmark decision (Brown *v.* Board of Education) on February 7, 1955 barring racial discrimination from Public Education.

The theory of 'conquest,' awarding European nations the right to take possession of the territories of Native Americans, is grounded on the theory of *occupatio* (and 'discovery') in Roman law. In a nutshell, it means that something which was never the subject of ownership (*res nullius*) belongs to the first person taking possession; see Henry Maine, *Ancient Law*, pp. 144–147. Native Americans were not regarded as fully human, and therefore America was regarded as unpopulated; see my "Jews, *Conversos,* and Native Americans: The Iberian Experience," *Review of Rabbinic Judaism* 3 (2000), pp. 95–121. For an extensive and well-documented study, see Steven T. Newcomb, "The Evidence of Christian Nationalism in Federal Indian Law: The Doctrine of Discovery, *Johnson v. McIntosh,* and Plenary Power," *New York University Review of Law and Social Change* 20 (1992–1994), pp. 303–341. A more or less similar doctrine was put forward by Henry Wheaton, *Elements of International Law*, ed. with notes by George Grafton Wilson (Oxford: Clarendon Press, 1936). According to this illustrious legal scholar the Native Americans were a "dependent nation," and must be regarded as a "ward" incapable of managing their personal affairs. By a "dependent nation," I presume that he meant that "A tribe is not a 'foreign State,' within the meaning of the Constitution, for the purpose of suing in the Federal Courts." Here is what he writes in #38 p. 50:

> They were a domestic dependent nation; their relation to us resembles that of a ward to his guardian; and they had an unquestionable right to the lands they occupied, until that right should be extinguished by a voluntary cessation to our government.

His position is not clear. A ward retains title of his property but cannot make any contracts respecting said property. Accordingly, it would be instructive to learn by which legal theory could the Native Americans have "extinguished by a voluntary cessation" their rights? Elsewhere, Henry Wheaton, *International Law* (literal reproduction of 8th ed., 1866,

London: Humphrey Milford, 1936), p. 587 wrote: "That discovery gave an exclusive right to extinguish the Indian title of occupancy, either by purchase or by conquest." Rhetoric aside, since their human status was not actually acknowledged their ancestral lands were in fact never theirs. The purpose of dislodging or purchasing land from Native Americans was to "extinguish," i.e., 'to absorb' the 'title' from their lands. Again, quoting Wheaton, p. 51:

> Whenever the republic has bought out an Indian tribe, and induced it to remove from a section of country, the act has always been 'extinguishment of the Indian title' upon the lands of the United States.

This is what he wrote, p. 51:

> The Indian tribes have only a right of occupancy. Their possession was held to be so nomadic and uncivilized character as to amount to no more than a kind of servitude or lien upon the land, chiefly for fishing and hunting: the absolute title being in the republic.

This view is reflected in a Supreme Court ruling, *The Tee-Hit-Ton Indians v. United States* 348 US 272, at 293, citing 15 Long. Rec. 530, that, "Permissive Indian occupancy may be extinguished by Congress in its own discretion without compensation." However, "Generous provision has been willingly made to allow tribes to recover for wrong, as a matter of grace, not because of legal liability." (Cf. ibid. at 279). *The Tee-Hit-Ton Indians v. United States* 348 U.S. 272, 75 S. Ct. 313, 99 L. Ed. 314 (1955), p. 293:

> It is to be presumed that in this matter the United States would be governed by such considerations of justice as would control *a Christian* people in their treatment of an *ignorant and dependent race.* (Italics added)

It has been generally assumed that extinction of the Indian title required an act of Congress. This, however, was not to be the case. In 1986, some members of Missiquoi Abenaki Tribe in Vermont were fishing without a license. In their defense, they argued that since they were fishing in their ancestral home, they were not required to obtain a license. Moreover, their rights were never extinguished by Congress. The local Judge decided in their favor. However, the decision was appealed by the State of Vermont, and the State Court overturned the lower courts decision, ruling in favor of the State. (*Country of Oneida v. Oneida Indian Nation*, 470 U.S. 226, 247 (1985); (*State v. Elliot* 616 A. 2d 210 [Vt. 1992], *cert. denied.* 113 S. Ct 1258 [1993]). See Joseph William Singer, *Entitlement* (New Haven: Yale University Press, 2000), pp. 181–190.

Two other doctrines derive from the preceding: (i) 'Eminent Domain,' according to which the Fifth Amendment is interpreted as a tacit recognition of the Government's power to take private property for public use; and (ii) 'Sovereign Immunity,' establishing that no suit can be instituted against the Sovereign without its consent. The latter is predicated on the logic that the 'King can do no wrong,' or what amounts to the same, that there can be no legal rights against the authority that makes the law. In simpler words: might is right and not the other way around. See the following Appendix.

17. Private Property

The idea of private property as an institution *immune from government intervention* is exclusively Jewish. It was proclaimed by God at Sinai, when He declared: "Thou shall not steal" (*Ex* 20:12). It is of paramount importance to note that it was proclaimed in the desert, *outside the perimeters of government and settled society.* Therefore it is not a *privilege* awarded by the Sovereign to his faithful subjects, a privilege that the Sovereign could withdraw or condition. The standard idea of 'property,' as ultimately dependent on the sovereign, renders "Thou shall not steal" meaningless. In fact 'sovereign' and 'private ownership' are two mutually incompatible concepts. John Locke was quite aware of this pivotal point. The following is a quotation from his "Second Treatise of Government," *Two Treatises of Government*, #194, p. 395:

> Their *Persons* are *free* by a Native Right, and their *properties*, be they more or less, are *their own, and at their own dispose*, and not at his; or else it is not property. Supposing the Conqueror gives to one Man a Thousand Acres, to him and his Heirs for ever; to another he lets a Thousand Acres, for his life, under the rent of *l.* 50 or *l.* 500 *per Ann*. Has not the one of these a Right to his Thousand Acres for ever, and the other during his Life, paying the said Rent? And hath not the Tenant for Life a *property* in all that he gets over and above his Rent, by his Labour and Industry, during the said term, supposing it be double the Rent? Can any one say, The King, or Conqueror, after his Grant, may by his Power of Conqueror, take away all, or part of the Land from the Heirs of one, or from the other, during his Life, he paying the Rent? Or, can he take away from either the Goods or Money they have got upon the said Land, at his pleasure? If he can, then all free and voluntary *Contracts* cease, and are void in the World; there needs nothing to dissolve at any time but Power enough: And the *Grants* and Promises of *Men in power*, are but Mockery and Collusion. For can there be anything more ridiculous than to say, I give you and yours this for ever; and that in the surest and most solemn way of conveyance can be devised: And yet it is to be understood, that I have Right, if I please, to take it away from you again to Morrow?

Concerning the doctrine that the Sovereign has absolute dominion over the lands of the country by right of Conquest, Locke wrote in the "Second Treatise of Government," *Two Treatise of Government*, #193, p. 395:

> But granting that the *Conqueror* in a just War has a Right to the Estates, as well as Power over the Persons of the Conquered; which, 'tis plain, he *hath* not: Nothing of *Absolute Power* will follow from hence in the continuance of the Government. Because the Descendants of these being all Free-men, if he grants them Estates and Possessions to inhabit his Country (without which it would be worth nothing) whatsoever he grants them, they have, so far as it is granted, *property* in. The nature whereof is, that *without a Man's own consent it cannot be taken from him.*

On the relation of 'property' to 'sovereignty,' see Morris R. Cohen, "Property and Sovereignty," *Cornell Law Quarterly* 13 (1927–1928), pp. 8–30. For some valuable insights on the concept of 'property,' see Laura S. Underkuffer, "On Property: An Essay," in Elizabeth Mensch and Alan Freeman eds., *Property Law: International Library of Essays in Law and Legal Theory* (New York: New York University Press, 1992), vol. 1, pp. 414–417. See above Appendix 16.

18. Equality before the Law

Early in human history, tribal organization consisted of people living under the same chief. Sir Henry Summer Maine, *The Early History of Institutions* (Port Washington, N. Y.: Kennikat Press, 1966), p. 69 writes: "In some cases the Tribe can hardly be otherwise described than as the group subjected to one chieftain." A more common form of tribal organization, centering on families, was based on the belief that all members of the Tribe descended from a common ancestor. Roland de Vaux, *Ancient Israel*, vol. 1, p. 4 writes: "A tribe is an autonomous group of families who believe they are descended from a common ancestor. Each tribe is called by the name or surname of that ancestor." And *ibid.* p. 5: "What unites all the tribesmen, then, is this blood-relationship, real or supposed; they all consider themselves 'brothers' in a wide sense." This element was particularly dominant in the Indo-European world. Maine, *ibid.* p. 66, wrote: "If a man was not of kin to another there was nothing between them. He was an enemy to be slain, or spoiled or hated, as much as the wild beasts upon which the tribe made war, as belonging indeed to the craftiest and cruelest order of wild animals. It would scarcely be too strong an assertion that the dogs which followed the camp had more in common with it than the tribesmen of an alien and unrelated tribe."

In the Near East tribal organization widened to include people not thought of as physically descendent from the same ancestor. De Vaux, p. 6, noted: "Individuals, too, can be incorporated into a tribe either by adoption into a family ... or through acceptance by the sheikh or the elders." Eventually both notions of tribe and family blended. Links could be established through blood and obedience.

Concerning the *alien*, the *enemy*, and the *guest*, we read in *Indo-European Language and Society*, p. 294: "In short, the notions of enemy, stranger, guest, which for us form three distinct entities—semantically and legally—in the Indo-European languages show close connections... This cannot be understood except by starting from the idea that the stranger is of necessity an enemy and correlatively that the enemy is necessarily a stranger. It is always because a man born elsewhere is *a priori* an enemy that a mutual bond is necessary to establish between him and the EGO relations of hospitality, which would be inconceivable within the community itself... In the same way, in the early history of Rome, the stranger who becomes a *hostis*, enjoying *pari iure cum populo Romano*, legal rights equal to those of the Roman citizen."

Outside of Israel, the idea of *ethnical* equality before the law came late, even among advanced societies, enjoying a progressive judicial system. This could be shown from the "Chinese Exclusion Act," promulgated in the not too distant past. "The USA Act of Congress, Chinese Exclusion Act," May 6, 1882. *U. S. Statutes at Large*, vol. XXII, #14, p. 58 says:

> That thereafter no State court or court of the United States shall admit Chinese to Citizenship; and all laws in conflict with this act are hereby repealed.

For the above and other comparable cases; see the valuable monograph of Milton R. Konvitz, *The Alien and the Asiatic in American Law* (Ithaca, N.Y.: Cornell University, 1946).

In the year 1839, the schooner 'Amistad' carrying a cargo of slaves recently brought from Africa dropped anchor on the coast of Connecticut. The Spanish government argued that since they were Spanish property they should be returned to Cuba. President Van Buren agreed. However, in February 1841 the US Supreme Court ruled that they had been kidnapped and had been transported illegally, and were therefore free. Let it be noted that the rights of runaway slaves seeking asylum were already stipulated in *Dt* 23:16. It is worthy of attention that at the same time, in the Dred Scott decision of 1857, the Supreme Court ruled that no black—whether a slave or free—could be a US citizen since his ancestors were brought into the country as slaves. As a non-citizen, Scott did not have the right to sue in a Federal Court and was to remain a slave.

19. Ṭ'M

In Aramaic, the Semitic root Ṭ'M stands for an executive order; see *Dan* 3:29; 4:3; 6:27, and the corresponding translation of R. Se'adya Ga'on, *Perush* to *Daniel*, pp. 72, 76, 119; see also *Ezra* 4:19; 5:3, 17 and *Midrash Daniel and Ezra*, pp. 41, 43, 121. In Hebrew, the usual sense of this root is 'taste' and 'food'; although, as noted by R. Jonah ibn Jannaḥ, *Sefer ha-Shorashim, s.v. ṭa'am*, p. 182, it is also used in the sense of 'counsel' and 'deliberation'; see *Ps* 34:9, *Pr* 31:18, *Job* 12:20. Both senses of 'taste' and 'deliberation' indicate a primary, conclusive knowledge.

The Aramaic טעמא is widely used in the Talmud. When applied to *halakha* it stands for the basic premises and 'conceptual gist' of the law. The טעמא of a *halakha* was not explicit. Rather, it was expected that students and scholars would construe on their own the טעמא of the *halakha*. We are informed that as part of training his students, R. 'Aqiba would encourage them to step forward and present a different *טעם* for the *halakha* under discussion; see *Tosefta Zabim* 1:5, p. 676 and the quotation in Section IV, n. 102. The ability to construe the טעמא of the *halakha* is an absolute prerequisite to qualify someone to pass an legal opinion on the subject under consideration. Explicitly, the rabbis barred disclosing the *טעם* of a *halakha* under discussion; see *Sifra* 75c, quoted above in Section V, n. 320. This is why, when issuing a legal decision, the court did not disclose the *טעם* of their decision, unless it was requested by the guilty party, see *Sanhedrin* 31b. The upshot of this rule is that someone not knowing the *טעם* of a legal decision cannot use it as a precedent and apply it to a new case; see *Baba Batra* 130b–131a, quoted in Section V, n. 321. For that reason, R. Abraham Maimonides disqualified a decision given by a judge since he failed to demonstrate that he had understood the conceptual gist of the *halakha*; see *Teshubot R. Abraham b. ha-Rambam*, #98 quoted below, Appendix 65. This is exactly what Maimonides meant when he wrote that legal demonstration (ראיה) consists in knowing "to expose why a legal authority concluded thus"; see *Iggerot ha-Rambam*, vol. 2, p. 441, quoted above Section V, n. 328. See below Appendices 48 and 69.

20. Malicious Erudition

Edward Gibbon was heir to the learned studies of the antiquarians and the philosophic historians of the Enlightenment, such as Jean-Baptiste D'Alambert (1717–1783) and Voltaire. From some of them he also learnt how "to blend malice and erudition"; see A. D. Momigliano "Gibbon's Contribution to

Historical Method," in his *Studies in Historiography* (New York: Harper & Row, 1966), pp. 40–55, especially p. 43. He was also heir to the virulent anti-Jewish and anti-Judaism mood of classical anti-Semites, from Apion, Tacitus, and Cicero in Antiquity (see above Chapter 37), to Voltaire, Rousseau and the rest of the Enlightenment's *philosophes* (cf. Chapter 12 and the quotation from Maine, Section III, n. 23). Here are a few examples taken from *The Decline and Fall of the Roman Empire*, XV, vol. 1, p. 383: "The Jews, who, under the Assyrian and Persian monarchies, had languished for many ages the most despised portion of their slaves." They are "an ungrateful race" (p. 385), and "unsocial people" (p. 386). Indeed, they are so hateful, that they constitute a distinct human species:

> The sullen obstinacy with which they maintained their peculiar rites and unsocial manners seemed to mark them out a distinct species of men, who boldly professed, or who faintly disguised, their implacable hatred to the rest of human-kind. (p. 384)

Concerning Christian misanthropy, see below Appendices 21 and 24. However, as Gibbon kindly explained, Christian intolerance is no fault of its own. Although it managed to overlook upwards of ninety-eight percent of Judaism, unfortunately, "The inflexible and, if we may use the expression, the intolerant zeal of the Christians, derived, it is true, from Jewish religion" (p. 383). Jewish history (in contradistinction to the civilized societies of *europaischen Menschentums*) is nothing but a "sanguinary list of murders, of executions, and of massacres, which stain almost every page of the Jewish annals" (p. 392). Jewish resistance to Hadrian was "desperate fanaticism" (p. 390), and consequently, illegitimate. By contrast, Hadrian's massacre of almost the entire Judean population, including women and children—the biggest known genocide in human history—(see Chapter 40), was nothing more than "the rights of victory"; although, Gibbon had to admit, these rights were exercised, "with unusual rigor" (p. 390). Jewish faithfulness to the Tora is the effect of their peculiar "obstinacy" (pp. 384, 388). Their rituals consist of "useless and obsolete ceremonies" (p. 389). By opposition, the Christian rite—I presume he had in mind the Eucharist where the faithful consume the flesh and blood of their Savior—is "a pure and spiritual worship" (p. 388), see below Appendix 23. With the power of a *superstes* (see *Introductory Remarks*, Section IV, n. 2), Gibbon *knew* exactly how people all over felt about Jewish rituals. Here is what he writes in p. 387:

> They still insisted with inflexible rigour on those parts of the law which it was in their power to practice. The peculiar distinction of days, of meats, and a variety of trivial though burdensome observances, were so many objects of

> disgust and aversion for the other nations, to whose habits and prejudices they were diametrically opposite.

By way of contrast, let us see what Philo wrote on the same topic in *Moses* II, 13, *Philo*, vol. 6, p. 459–461:

> We may fairly say that mankind from east to west, every country and nation and state, shew aversion to foreign institutions, and think that they will enhance respect for their own by shewing disrespect for those of other countries. It is not so with ours. They attract and win the attention of all, of barbarians, of Greeks, of dwellers on the mainland and islands, of nations of the east and west, of Europe and Asia, of the whole inhabited world from end to end. For, who has not shewn his high respect for that sacred seventh day, by giving rest and relaxation from labour to himself and his neighbours, freemen and slaves alike, and beyond these to his beasts? For the holiday extends also to every herd, and to all creatures made to minister to men, who serve like slaves their natural master. It extends also to every kind of tree and plant; for it is not permitted to cut any shoot or branch, or even a leaf, or to pluck any fruit whatsoever. All such are set at liberty on that day, and live as it were in freedom, under the general edict that proclaims that none should touch them.

Philo also mentioned the fact that multitudes of non-Jews came to celebrate the translation of the Septuagint together with the Jews; see quotation in Section IV, n. 24. One only can wonder why the people in Colonial America, as well as in India, Africa, etc., did not make similar celebrations for the *Magna Carta*?

One could argue that Gibbon's 'malicious erudition' was tactical. Since he had blamed the spread of Christianity for the collapse of the Roman Empire, he had to malign Jews and their religion, lest he would be accused of being 'pro' Jewish—a blemish too heavy to bear in the enlightened society of 18th century Continental Europe. On his anti-Christian views, see Shelby Thomas McCloy, *Gibbon's Antagonism to Christianity* (London: William & Norgate, 1933). I propose that his malice was rather substantive. A major point of Gibbon's was the link between the spread of Christianity and the collapse of the Roman Empire. In our terms, the "Two-Realm Governance" solution proposed by Christianity and accepted by the Caesars (see Chapter 26), suffered a sudden reversal. This was fundamental to Gibbon's ideology, "that history changes by revolutions rather than by slow evolution" ("Gibbon's Contribution to Historical Method," p. 49). In our case, the revolution was brought about by Christianity. "At the same time, Gibbon brought into special prominence, as Voltaire had done, that the Christians joined hands with the Barbarians to destroy the Empire," wrote Momigliano, ibid. p. 48. This was a brilliant move, destined to further expand Christianity and consolidate Church power.

As those experienced in the art of commerce know, a key element in negotiation is the availability of alternative suppliers to force your provider to acquiesce to your terms. The triumph of the Barbarians and the subsequent fragmentation of the Roman Empire into countless and deeply antagonistic territories provided the Church with a large number of suppliers. By contrast, once Judaism was declared unfit for human consumption, Caesars of all denominations found themselves with no alternative suppliers to negotiate with. (Julian's 'universal toleration' was an attempt to find new suppliers. It was, however, too little, too late; see *Decline and Fall*, XXIII). 'Secularism'—and all forms of political and intellectual ideologies—are intended to provide alternative suppliers to the Caesars of the world. Gibbon understood this well. Rather than presenting an 'objective' picture of the past, Gibbon presented a 'history' designed to promote a peculiar ideology close to his own mind and ethos. Again, quoting Momigliano, p. 49:

> Thus his *Decline and Fall* is both a complex and vivid picture of the Middle Ages from a *certain point of view and unique self-portrait of the eighteenth-century mind.* (Italics added)

Lest some may want to consider the legal and political system of the Hebrew Scripture and the Jews, as in Colonial America at the time (see Chapter 36), it was imperative to repeat the same anti-Semitic litany for all to hear. 'Jewish' danger was greater in England where, as shown by W. B. Selbie, "The Influence of the Old Testament on Puritanism" was supreme. It was incumbent upon Gibbon, in quality of *europaischen Menschentums* (see Momigliano, pp. 44–48), to defame the Jews and their religion; in the name of honor and common decency.

A marginal note. For the sake of fairness, let us note that Christian betrayal of Roman Caesars on behalf of barbarians is perfectly legitimate according to *minut*-ethics where the end justifies the means; see below Appendix 55. In simple terms: if the Church could be *Verus Israel*, why barbarians could not become *Sacrum Romanun Imperium Nationis Germanicae*? Cf. Appendix 30.

21. Why we should all strive to be Illiterate

The Pauline ideal is for all to be illiterate, "for the letter killeth, but the spirit giveth life" (*2Cor* 3:6). According to *minut*-hermeneutics, Moses' veil symbolizes the blurred, obscure character peculiar to the written text: "even unto this day, when Moses [i.e., the Tora] is read, the veil is upon their heart" [i.e., of the readers] (2*Cor* 3:15, cf. vv. 7, 13–14). To free humanity from writing, Jesus was nailed to the cross. Thus, "Blotting out the handwriting of ordinances that were against us [= the Scriptural precepts], which was contrary to us, and took it out of the way, nailing it to his cross" (2*Col* 2:14). The "veil" covering Moses' face, remained "untaken in the reading of the Old Testament [*diatheke,* i.e., the Tora]," but was "done away in Christ" (2*Cor* 3:14), allowing, as per Greek ideality, for the truth to shine forth (cf. 2*Cor* 3:16–18). Jesus' truth is superior to the Tora because it "is written not with ink, but with the Spirit of the living God; not in tables of stone, but in the fleshy tables of the heart" (2*Cor* 3:3). This posits, as per Greek analphabetic ideality (see Chapter 2), that the written word hinders 'the truth.' Since this surreal 'truth' is not easily communicated to people in a different psychological mood, misanthropy enables its possessor to dismiss 'the others' as inferior beings questioning 'the obvious' (leading, thus, to the de-humanization of the 'other,' see Appendix 24). Without hatred, this brand of truth would turn into a harrowing nightmare of self-delusion. See Appendix 22.

The "illiterate people" (עם הארץ) constituted a class unto itself based not on birth or economic status, but on their attitude towards education and life style; see the learned work of George F. Moore, "The Am-ha-Arez (The People of the Land) and the Haberim (Associates)," in F. J. Foakes-Jackson and Kirsopp Lake eds., *The Acts of the Apostles* (*The Beginning of Christianity*), vol. 1 (London: Macmillan, 1920), pp. 439–445. The "illiterate people" discussed in *Pesaḥim* 49b, are not merely unlettered men, but people repudiating the Book on behalf of theological analphabetism. "Greater is the hatred that illiterate men (עמי הארץ) profess towards the disciples of sages," remarked the rabbis, "than what the (pagan) nations profess against Israel." In my view, they were the early Judeo-Christians forming Jesus' Crowd.

22. Purloining an Ass for Christ: Freedom *without* Law

There is something more than symbolic in the fact that the Christian Messiah is portrayed as entering Jerusalem on a purloined ass, to show his fulfillment of the prophetic vision of 'a just and righteous' Savior. *Matt* 21:2–3 relates how Jesus sent two of his disciples to dispossess an ass on his behalf, in his capacity as 'King' of the Jews'; see *Leviathan,* XX [106], p. 259. This is in line with Jesus' doctrine to "Render unto Caesar the things which are Caesar's" (*Matt* 22:21), thus validating the tax-collectors practice to dispossess property from the legitimate owner without due process; see below Appendix 60. As with Jesus, donkeys were seized by tax-collectors without much ado; see Mishna *Baba Qamma* 10:2. Compare this with Moses, *Nu* 16:15 who would not "seize" a single donkey from anyone; see *Targum*, R. Se'adya, and Rashi *ad loc*; cf. 1*Sam* 12:3. In defense of Jesus' behavior, we may argue that since "the Son of man hath the power on earth to forgive sins" (*Matt* 9:6), he could surely exercise His prerogative of mercy on Himself and His followers and relieve Himself and His followers from any crimes and disabilities—as a pagan Rex could; see above Chapter 26. According to the doctrine that "the Son of man hath the power on earth to forgive sins," salvation is a matter of personal whim, rather than justice. To this we should add Jesus' temperament, always in ire, cursing and threatening with dire consequences those who would not concur with him. An obvious reference to this kind of behavior is a passage in *Abot* 5:19 contrasting "the disciples of Abraham" with "the disciples of Balaam, the wicked." Balaam, too, was a prophet, but in contradistinction to Abraham, his 'blessings' were valued mainly because of the magical threat of his curses, see *Nu* 22:6. (Indeed, it is difficult not to gain the impression that the public that Jesus addressed was more affected by fear of his curses than by the bliss of his blessings). On the association 'Balaam/Jesus,' see the version of *Sanhedrin* 39b cited by R. Ḥanan'el, *ad loc.* I believe that the passage in *Mekhilta de-R. Yishma'el,* p. 221, that upon hearing of the Theophany at Sinai "all the kings of the nations of the world went up to consult with Balaam," is an allusion to Paul who furthered the strategy of threats and curses in the promotion of spiritual salvation. Surely, his doctrine about the 'Law' was balsam to pagan authorities, since by abrogating the Tora Paul was in fact giving free rein to totalitarian governments. On the identification 'Balaam/Jesus,' see *Christianity and the Talmud*, pp. 64–78.

Concerning the Paulian doctrine of Freedom *without* Law, see Chapter 12. It equals Freedom *via* Submission. In *Eph* 5:21–25 we read:

> Submitting yourselves one to another in the fear of God. Wives, submit yourselves unto your own husbands, as unto the Lord. For the husband is the head of the wife, even as Christ is the head of the church: and he is the saviour of the body. Therefore as the church is subject unto Christ, so let the wives be to their own husbands in every thing. Husbands, love your wives, even as Christ also loved the church, and gave himself for it.

The incarnate *logos* is the Spirit, that is, freedom *from* the Law: "and where the Spirit of the Lord *is*, there *is* liberty" (2*Cor* 3:17). Those that are "led" by the Spirit, Paul assured his audience, "are not under the

Law" (*Gal* 5:18). Accordingly, the *logos* displaces—in legal terminology, abrogates—the Law: "For the Law came through Moses," explained John, "but grace and truth came through Jesus" (*Jn* 7:18). Cf. "The Rich Man's Salvation," in *Clement of Alexandria* (Loeb Classical Library), VI, 939 P., pp. 283–287. The abrogation of writing came with Jesus' death, "Blotting out the handwriting of ordinances that were against us [= the Scriptural *miṣvot*], which was contrary to us, and took it out of the way, nailing it to his cross" (*Col* 2:14; cf. 1:13–14). The blood 'blotting' writing was that very blood that would "deliver" mankind "from darkness," i.e. alphabetic reasoning, and thereby bring "redemption" and "forgiveness of sins" through analphabetic spirituality (*Col* 1:13–14). According to this theory, the purpose in Jesus' death was analphabetic freedom or what amounts to the same freedom from the alphabet. By abrogating the circumcision, Paul was in fact urging a renunciation of the covenant that God made with Patriarch Abraham (*Gn* Chapter 17): thus formally breaking all ties with the alphabetic God of Israel. See *Gal* 5:1–5 and Section III, n. 275

23. Ingesting Jesus

There is some irony in the fact that Jewish dietary laws are derided by the rationale that "Not that which goeth into the mouth defileth a man" (*Matt* 15:11; see ibid. 12–20; *Mk* 7:15; cf. *Acts* 10:10–16; 1*Cor* 8:8). At the same time, salvation is gained by ingesting "that which goeth into the mouth," i.e., the Eucharist. No wonder that Reverend Mayhew regarded "transubstantiation" as "fabulous and chimerical"; see above Appendix 14, and Section III, n. 301. The whole idea of 'swallowing' another and of being 'swallowed' by another is typical of sado-masochist tendencies, common to individuals who have lost self-esteem; see *Escape from Freedom*, p. 180. On the magical character of the Eucharist, see Morton Smith, *Jesus the Magician*, pp. 122–123. For a modern testimonial on the subject, see Pope John Paul II, "On the Mystery and Worship of the Eucharist," in ed. Austin Flannery, O. P. *Vatican Council II* (Collegeville, MN: The Liturgical Press, 1982), pp. 64–92. Cf. Section III, n. 67.

In *Ec* 10:12, King Solomon points out to two different approaches in which an individual may address another person. "The words of a wise-man's mouth (פי) are gracious (חן)," that is, they generate mutual cordiality and sympathy—essential for carrying on a *meliṣa*-discourse, in which both parties stand horizontally *vis á vis* the other; see Chapter 46. By way of contrast, "the lips (שפתות) of a deceitful-person will swallow him up"—

thus, excluding the possibility of speech between two subjective parties; see Chapter 3. Within such a context, the only possible relationship is that of superior/inferior, whereby the the superior incorporates the other into his body. Or what amounts to the same, the inferior must annihilate his/her own personality to be swallowed by the superior. There is a minor linguistic detail worth noting. The words of the wise-man are uttered by his "mouth," in the singular. By contrast, the words of a deceitful speaker come out of his "lips," in the plural. Implying duplicity; see above Section I, notes 92 and 131.

24. Extreme Dichotomy

The Christian doctrine of "Two-Governances" is a spin-off of the "Splitting of the *Logos*," inaugurating Greek philosophical thought; see José Faur, "Splitting of the *Logos*," *New Vico Studies* 3 (1985), pp. 85–103. In turn, the 'Splitting of the *Logos*' is a spin-off of the polytheistic *Weltanschauung* peculiar to *europaischen Menschentums*, where the universe is divided into neatly compartmentalized sections, having absolutely nothing to do with one another. At the intellectual level, this led to what Ortega y Gasset called "The Barbarism of Specialization"; see *Golden Doves*, p. 153 n. 81. By positing the doctrine of "Two-Governances" at the center of Western intellectual and spiritual life, Christianity was in fact sanctioning a course of thought which, at the very least, disallowed for humanism, Biblical or otherwise; see *In the Shadow of History*, pp. 33–34. An example of this sort of extreme dichotomy is the philosophy that views the human 'other' as void of spirituality and individuality; see *In the Shadow of History*, pp. 4–8. This is conceptually connected to the materialistic ideology positing man as a cog in the large political and social machine of the State. Concerning this philosophy, very real in our own times, Ludwig von Bertalanffy, *General System Theory*, pp. 52–53, wrote:

> Man is not only a political animal; he is, before and above all, an individual. The real values of humanity are not those which it shares with biological entities, the function of an organism or a community of animals, but those which stem from the individual mind. Human society is not a community of ants or termites, governed by inherited instinct and controlled by the laws of the super ordinate whole; it is based upon the achievements of the individual and is doomed if the individual is made a cog in the social machine. This I believe, is the ultimate precept a theory of organization can give: not a manual for dictators of any denomination more efficiently to subjugate human beings by the scientific application of Iron Laws, but a warning that the Leviathan of organization must not swallow the individual without sealing its own inevitable doom.

25. Erasing the Memory of 'Amaleq

A fundamental dimension of Israel is its National Memory. It is on this basis that political judgments are achievable. When National Memory is discarded or fails to elicit a response, Israel ceases to function as an autonomous political entity, and national disasters follow. The role of Jewish National Memory is evident in the case of 'Amaleq, Israel's political arch-enemy. They were the earliest terrorists on record. What made their attack particularly heinous was that, (a) it was unprovoked, since Israel was passing through the desert, and not through their territory; (b) it was sudden, against unsuspecting travelers; and, (c) it was carried out against the "weak and infirm," who could not defend themselves, rather than against the army (*Dt* 25:17–18). As we shall see in what follows, these facts, rather than mere 'ethnicity' are the defining elements of *'Amaleq*.

The Tora did not specify the atrocities perpetuated by 'Amaleq; rather, they were entrusted to the National Memory of Israel. Jews are required to "remember" what 'Amaleq did (*Dt.* 25:17), and to "erase the remembrance (זכר) of 'Amaleq" (*Dt* 25:19; cf. *Ex* 17:14). The conflict must be carried on from generation to generation (*Ex* 17:16). Usually, this is understood in ethnical terms. This understanding is unacceptable. Clearly and unambiguously the Tora mentions "the *remembrance* (זכר) of 'Amaleq"! According to the rabbis, after King Sennacherib invaded the Near East, the original natives of the region were deported and replaced with others. Therefore, the present inhabitants of these areas could no longer be identified with the national entities mentioned in Scripture. See Mishna *Yadayim* 4:4; *Tosefta Qiddushin* 5:4, pp. 295–296; *Tosefta Yadayim* 2:17, pp. 683–684. For additional sources and an in-depth discussion of the subject, see *Tosefta Ki-Fshuṭah, Nashim*, pp. 972–974. Therefore, it is impossible to identify the ethnicity of any of the ancient inhabitants of the region. (Maimonides applied this principle to *all* people of the region, see *MT Issure Bi'a* 12:25; *Melakhim* 5:4, and Radbaz' note *ad loc.*) Thus, on technical grounds alone it would be impossible to identify any one person or people with the original inhabitants of the region. If so, how could Jews be expected to keep on fighting the Amalekite enemy "from generation to generation"? The question is particularly poignant in light of the fact that after having lost contact with 'Amaleq for over 500 years, Jews in Persia were able to identify Haman—the proverbial 'Jew-hater'—with 'Amaleq (see *Esther* 3:1, 10, etc.). What was the basis for this identification?

The correct meaning of the "remembrance" was given by R. Isaac Abul'afya (1824–1910), *Pene Yiṣḥaq*, vol. 6 (Jerusalem 5668/1908), *Shabbat Zakhor*, 41a. He called attention to the fact that the Scripture charged Israel to erase "the *remembrance* (זכר)"—never the *seed* (זרע)—of 'Amaleq! What was intolerable about 'Amaleq was their inhumanity against unsuspecting travelers; particularly, marking the weak and infirm as the preferred target. The remembrance of *'Amaleq* has little to do with ethnicity, but with a level of inhuman behavior that cannot be tolerated, no matter what. This type of threat faces Israel "from generation to generation." Because Israel had registered in her National Memory the atrocities committed by *'Amaleq*, she is charged with the double responsibility of identifying and erasing *the remembrance* of *'Amaleq*. The Jews in Persia were able to identify Haman with their proverbial enemy, because in their National Memory his activities and ideology reminded them of *'Amaleq*: it was a matter of behavior, not merely genealogy or nationality. After a detailed analysis of the sources, R. Abul'afya, concluded:

> From the preceding we have learned that a people who became infamous (because of the manner in which they conducted their attack against the Jewish people) were designated *'Amaleq*. This (identification) may take place even in our own days, when people that are ethnically mixed (and cannot be identified ethnically as 'Amaleq)...At any rate, once that they are identified as *'Amaleq*, because of their behavior they are one and the same with *'Amaleq*, and to eradicate them will constitute, in fact, erasing the name of 'Amaleq.

This point is implicit in the rabbinic tradition declaring that the descendants of Haman taught Tora to the Jewish people (*Giṭṭin* 57b). If *'Amaleq* is a matter of genealogy, the rabbis should have put them to death, rather than give them teaching positions; cf. *In the Shadow of History*, pp. 200–201.

The preceding could help us resolve a halakhic puzzle. An absolute stipulation to classify a Scriptural assignment as a precept (*miṣva*) is that, at least in theory, it could be fulfilled in perpetuity (*Sefer ha-Miṣvot,* III). To wit, although sacramental sacrifices are not offered today, nonetheless they qualify as precepts (*miṣvot*) since they could be offered when the Temple is rebuilt. Now, if to erase "the remembrance (זכר) of 'Amaleq" meant some sort of 'ethnic cleansing,' then once executed, it could never be fulfilled again. (Maimonides attempts to cope with the problem, in my view unsuccessfully, see *Sefer ha-Miṣvot,* positive precept #187. The same problem applies to the precept to destroy the seven Canaanite nations—once it is properly fulfilled, it could not be fulfilled again). On the other hand, identification of *'Amaleq* in terms of behavior and the memories that it evokes, rather than ethnicity, permits the fulfillment of this *miṣva* in perpetuity.

A final note: there may be several valid interpretations on how to identify and proceed to erase the "memory of 'Amaleq." 'Ethnic cleansing,' however, is not one of them.

26. 'Prophets/Scribes' and the National Archives of Israel

The *Targum* to the *Prophets* translates 'prophet' (נביא), when not accompanied by a personal name, 'scribe, scribes' (ספר, ספריא); see 1*Sam* 10:11; 19:20; 2*K* 17:13; *Is* 3:2; 9:14; 29:10; *Jer* 29:1. The same applies when it appears together with *kohen, kohanim*; see 2*K* 23:2; *Is* 28:7; *Jer* 14:18; 23:11; 26:16; *Zech* 7:3; Is 28:7; *Ekha* 2:20. Support for this tradition may be seen in the frequent association of 'prophet' (נביא) with 'writing' in the *Book of Chronicles*, see 1*Ch* 29:29; 2*Ch* 9:29; 12:15; 32:32; cf. 13:22; 26:22. It is in this connotation that 'prophet' (נביא) is used in *Abot* 1:1: "Moses ... conveyed the Tora to Joshua ... and the elders to the prophets (נביאים)." As I proposed in *Golden Doves*, pp. 14–15, 124, 'Tora' in the above passage is a reference to the legal tradition kept in the national archives. In my view, the original sense of the title 'prophet' (נביא) that in Medieval Ashkenazic tradition was given to some of the sages was not that of the Biblical 'prophet,' as commonly understood, but of 'scribe,' 'archivist'; i.e., 'guardian of tradition'; see, however, Abraham Heschel, "Inspiration in the Middle Ages," in *Alexander Marx Jubilee Volume*, Hebrew Section (New York: The Jewish Theological Seminary of America, 1950), pp. 175–236. Maimonides, too, in his "*Introduction*" *MT*, ll. 47–48, stated that "the head of the court or the *prophet* of that generation would write for himself a summary of the legal traditions, which he had learned from his teachers, and then teach them orally"; see above Chapter 30.

Similarly, R. Se'adya Gaon wrote that before the exile these traditions were "supervised and safeguarded by the king and priests, particularly at the time of the prophets"; *Sa'adya's Commentary on Genesis*, p. 186 (Ar. p. 15). Professor Zucker's translation, "kept in their memory" is inaccurate. Although the Arabic root ḤFT could be used in the sense of 'remembering,' ḤRṢ conveys 'to watch, to safeguard,' as per archives, rather than to remember.

I would like to translate here a passage of R. Elie Benamozegh about the National Archives of Israel and their relation to the Oral Law. Commenting on *Ex* 18:13, in *Em la-Miqra* vol. 2, 51a, he wrote:

> There is little doubt that prior to the appointment of judges, Moses judged alone, as mentioned in the Tora. Thereafter, Moses would sit to adjudicate only difficult cases. The same applied to all the judges that came throughout the generations; as with Debora to whom the children of Israel would come for judgment. In general, it was the same with all the laws and rules that our judges adjudicated throughout the ages [those difficult cases that would be

resolved by the highest judicial authority]. It is unwarranted (to assume) that some record would not have been kept in the midst of the nation. Where would you find a nation that would not register the legal decisions of its judges in every single case, in addition to its written history? Rather, it would be safe to assume that when (a new) case which had not been adjudicated previously, came before Moses, and which in turn he had to present before God, as was the case of Zelophehad's daughters [see *Nu* 27:1–11], (that the case had been properly recorded by the Court). Many more such cases came up in every generation, [i.e.] new questions about which there were not to be found a clear statement in the Scripture [= *Dinim Mufla'im*], and which were resolved by the prophets and elders [of the time] according to accepted procedures—these constitute the Oral Law. Thus, one may learn about the existence of (the Oral Law), as with as much validity and reasonable evidence, as with *mores geometrico*.

27. *Yeshiba*

In its original sense *Yeshiba* stood for a 'session' of the judicial authorities. (The name *Yeshiba* 'seating' reflects the fact that at these meetings the 'seating' arrangements were regulated by strict procedure; see *Tosefta Sanhedrin* VII, 8–9, p. 426; *Horayot* 13b; cf. *Baba Batra* 120a and *Pesaḥim* 119a). It is one of the principal National Institutions of Israel. Members of the *Yeshiba* were duly appointed with the consent of the public; see *Sifre Bemidbar* #92, p. 93; *Sifre Debarim* #13, p. 22. Because the school was an integral part of the court, sometimes it is difficult to ascertain whether '*Yeshiba*' refers to the court proper or to the school; see for example, Mishna *Yadayim* 3:8; 4:2; *Sifre* #321, p. 370. Another institution of higher learning was the *Bet-Midrash*. However, unlike the *Yeshiba*, it was not attached to the court and was not a national institution. On the relation of the *Yeshiba* to 'ordination,' see *Studies in the History of the Sanhedrin*, pp. 208–212. For *Yeshiba* in the sense of 'School of Higher Learning,' see *Ta'aniyot* 8a; *Mo'ed Qaṭan* 16b; *Nidda* 70b; and *Derekh Ereṣ* 2:8, p. 94. The term *Yeshiba* was also used to designate a special 'session' arrainged to deliberate some scholarly matters; see *'Erubin* 26a, *Ketubot* 103b, *Baba Qamma* 16b; or public policy; see *Yoma* 28b, and *Perush ha-Mishnayot, Bekhorot* 4:4, vol. 5, p. 245. This term passed into the *Koran* in the form *majlis* (58:12) from the root *jalasa* ('to seat')—an exact translation of Hebrew *Yeshiba*; see Abraham Shalom Yahuda, "A Contribution to Qur'an and Hadith Interpretation," in *Ignace Goldziher Memorial Volume,* part I (Budapest, 1948), pp. 290–292.

28. *Perush*, *Be'ur*, and *Peshaṭ*

In *Qiddushin* 49b 'Tora' is associated with מדרש תורה; i.e., 'exegesis.' There were several styles and various functions attached to exegesis. *Be'ur* stands for 'elucidation,' 'clarification'; see *Sifre* #5, p. 13. This term is connected to באר 'well,' from where water flows (unlike בור 'pit' which collects water from the rain; see *Yalquṭ Shim'oni, 'Eqeb* #873, vol. 1, 298d; and R. Abraham ibn 'Ezra on *Lev* 11:36). Since to tap water from a well one needs 'to dig,' this term was associated with 'perforating' a hard surface. By association, it was also used for 'engraving' an inscription on stone (*Dt* 27:8; *Hab* 2:2); see J. L. Palache, *Semantic Notes on the Hebrew Lexicon* (Leiden: Brill, 1958), s.v. *be'er*, p. 9. On the semantic association of באר to the act of 'inscribing/ chiseling' on stone, see *Soṭa* 35b. Given that 'digging' (to make a well) and 'chiseling' (a stone) involves perforating a hard surface to bring up its content (water, law); and given that legislators 'engrave' the new rules on stone, the *Targum* to (*Nu* 21:18) associated 'באר' in "a well (באר) was dug by the princes, it was perforated by the nobles of the nation, with their scepter and with their staves"—with 'legislation.' Thus, it rendered *with their scepter and with their staves*, as "*the scribes* (ספריא) *with their staves*"; cf. R. Se'adya Gaon *ad loc*. In the same vein, the *Targum* rendered the verb באר (*Dt* 1:5) as "explaining the teaching of the Tora" (אולפן אוריתא); cf. R. Se'adya *ad loc* and *Sanhedrin* 34a. In this precise sense Maimonides uses this term at the head of each Section (הלכות) of the *MT*. After giving a list of the Biblical precepts to be examined he concludes with the following sentence: "And the *be'ur* of all these precepts (will be presented) in the following Chapters."

For some interesting insights into this matter, see R. Elie Benamozegh, *Mabo le-Tora she-be-'al-Pe*, ed. R. E. Zini (Jerusalem, 5762/2002), pp. 28–42.

Perush stands for something 'separate' from the common and the general, warranting, therefore, 'specification' and 'notification'; see *Targum* to *Dt* 21:17. Accordingly, to be binding a *perush* warrants 'judicial instruction,' see *Targum* on *Dt* 17:8; and 'promulgation'; see *Vayyiqra Rabba*, I, 10, vol. 1, pp. 24–25; *Shir ha-Shirim Rabba* II, 1, 4, vol. 2, 14d; III, 1, 4, vol. 2, 19c. Cf. *Tosefta Ki-Fshuṭah*, vol. 8, pp. 699–702; *Hellenism in Jewish Palestine*, pp. 200–202; and *A Dictionary of Greek & Latin Legal Terms*, s.v. *diatagma*, pp. 79–81.

Perush is construed on the basis of the *general* sense of the phrase; see Mishna *'Aboda Zara* 1:5; cf. *Tosefta Demai* 1:8, p. 63; *Baba Qamma* 11:1, 2, p. 58; *Baba Meṣi'a* 1:19, p. 66; *Baba Batra* 9:2, p. 160, etc. Therefore, one would need to say: "I heard explicitly" (שמעתי בפרוש), Mishna *Shebi'it* 6:5, 6; *'Orla* 1:7, etc. to indicate that although he was not repeating the words verbatim, he was transmitting the actual sense of the phrase. Invariably, *perush* refers to a *formulated* text. To place the locus of a *perush*, the sages (*Sifre* #40, pp. 83–84) would ask: "Where is it to be found, the explicated text of this matter (פרושו של דבר)?" Although it mostly concerns Scripture, occasionally *perush* is used in connection to oral texts; see Mishna *Nedarim* 2:4 and *Sanhedrin* 7:5. On the identification of 'Oral Law' with the *perush* of the 'Written Law'; see the Geonic *responsum*, in A. E. Harkavi, *Ḥadashim gam Yeshanim* (Jerusalem: Karmiel, 5730/1970) (II, p. 72), p. 368.

On *peshaṭ*, see *Shabbat* 15a; *'Aboda Zara* 8b; *Ḥolin* 135a; *Yerushalmi Sanhedrin* I, 1, 18a, etc. where *peshaṭ* involves 'familiarity,' 'general consensus.' Hence the expression "a prohibition that was accepted [*pashaṭ*] throughout Israel" (פשט איסורו בכל ישראל); see *'Aboda Zara* 36a; *Ḥolin* 135a. This root appears in the sense of 'usual,' 'frequent,' 'habitual'; see *Midrash Tanḥuma* (Constantinople, offset reproduction by Makor: Jerusalem, 1971), 30b. The association of *peshaṭ* with the 'plain' or 'grammatical' sense of the text was introduced by medieval commentators of Scripture. The rabbis, however, were not concerned with grammar or philological data. In fact, the rabbis classified as *peshaṭ* explanations that have nothing to do with the 'literal' sense of the verse; see, for example, *'Erubin* 23b; *Yebamot* 24a; *Ketubot* 111b; *Sanhedrin* 100b; *Zebaḥim* 113a; *'Arakhin* 8b, 32a, etc. Rather, *peshaṭ* has to do with "stretching" (*pashaṭ*) the scroll containing the text to be expounded (see Appendix 41). Thus the expression "whereto is this text *pashuṭ*?"—in the sense: "where does [the verse] apply"; see *Vayyiqra Rabba*, XVI, b, vol. 2, p. 351. Occasionally, when an explanation had been thoroughly assimilated into the text, the verb 'read' (קרא) is used; see *TY Berakhot* III, 1, 6c.

The term *peshiṭa*, in the Babylonian Talmud refers to "the explanations given by teachers (in the classroom) to their students—the type of explanations that every [student] was not required to learn by heart and to include in the *gemara*" [lesson, see below Appendix 48], but later on, the teachers found it necessary to incorporate [that explanation] into the *gemara*" (*IShG*, p. 63). Although the term *peshiṭa* is frequently used in seboraitic editorial notes, the expression itself originated in the tannaitic expression *pashuṭ hu lan*, in *Vayyiqra Rabba*, XI, 6, vol. 1, p. 227; cf. *pashṭa lan*, *Baba Qamma* 47a, 62a.

For further material and analyses, see *Golden Doves*, pp. xvii, 12, 136–137; José Faur, "Basic Concepts in Rabbinic Hermeneutics," *Shofar* 16 (1997), pp. 1–12; idem "Retórica y hemenéutica: Vico y la tradición rabínica," in ed. E. Hidalgo-Serna, *et al*, *Pensar Para el Nuevo Siglo,* vol. 3 (Napoli: La Cittá del Sole, 2001), pp. 917–938; and above Section IV, n. 226.

29. Pappus b. Judah

He was a Jewish sage flourishing in the 1st century C.E. and variously cited in Tannaitic and Talmudic sources. Although his name is spelled in a variety of forms (פפיס, פפייס, יהודה בן פפוס, פפוס בן יהודה) they all allude to the same Pappus b. Judah, the protagonist of the story we examined in Chapter 39; see *A Commentary on the Palestinian Talmud*, vol. 1, p. 410. He testified before the rabbis on an assortment of halakhic issues; see Mishna *'Eduyot* 7:5 (= *Nazir* 3:2), and *Nazir* 16a. In one case, he testified about the ritual meal of a sacrifice in which he participated together with his family at the Temple, see *'Eduyot* 7:6 (= *Temura* 3:1), and cf. *Rosh ha-Shana*, 6a. He also testified together with R. Joshua, Mishna *'Eduyot* 7:6; *Tosefta 'Eduyot* 3:1, p. 459; *Sanhedrin* 2:13, p. 418; and with R. Judah b. Betera, see *Beṣa* 29b. The fact that a view which he reported (שמעתי) is duly registered in Mishna *Sheqalim* 4:7, confirms that his reputation was well established among the sages.

His behavior, however, was considered eccentric and unbecoming; see *Yerushalmi Berakhot* II, 9, 5d. (The same story, however, is attributed in *Baba Qamma* 81b to R. Judah b. Qanusa). The manner in which he treated his wife served as an example, "Of someone that saw a fly standing inside his cup [but not touching the drink] threw it, and (refused) to drink from it. Like Pappus b. Judah, that shut the door before his wife and left" (*Tosefta Soṭa* 5:9, pp. 178–179; cf. *Tosfeta Ki-Fshuṭah*, vol. 8, p. 661). More to our point, he seemed to share some of the Gnostic ideology peculiar to early Christians, positing some kind of Primeaval Adam (or *Protanthropos*); see *Mekhilta de-R. Yshma'el*, pp. 112–113; *Bereshit Rabba* XXI, 5, vol. 1, pp. 200–201, and editor's n. ibid. Cf. *Shir ha-Shirim Rabba* I, 9, 10d; and *AdRN*, A, XXVII, 42a. At the same time, he was critical of Moses and Israel, while commending the gentiles; see *Mekhilta de-R. Shim'on b. Yoḥai*, p. 131; cf. *Mekhilta de-R. Yshma'el*, p. 194 and *Sanhedrin* 94a. This may explain his policy of seeking accommodation with the Romans.

30. *Verus Israel*?

See above Chapter 42, and *Golden Doves*, p. 15. Cf. R. Saul Levi Mortera, *Gib'at Sha'ul*, II, p. 13; and R. 'Azarya de Fijo, *Bina le-'Ittim*, vol. 2, p. 82. A person who has been the victim of identity theft could empathize with Jewish agony over the Christian claim of *Verus Israel*. The rabbis compared this to a man who witnesses someone impersonating him and then on the basis of the pretended identiy proceeds to rape his wife; or that he claims ownership over his property and then proceeds to expel him from his domicile. Similarly, *cristianos viejos* would rape Native American women while having their husbands tied under the bed; see José Faur, "Jews, *Conversos*, and Native Americans: The Iberian Experience," *Annual of Rabbinic Judaism* 3 (2000), pp. 95–121. On the psychological process whereby the murderer usurps the personality of the victim and appropriates his name, see Jorge Luis Borges, "La forma de la espada," *Ficciones*, pp. 491–495, a beautiful metaphor for *Verus Israel*. In *converso* tradition the 'sword' is a code-term for 'the cross,' given that both have the same form.

To properly understand Church claim of *Verus Israel*, and its subsequent attitude towards Jews and Judaism, we should bear in mind that theological blabber aside, the Church was organized as a *corpus* or 'corporation of Christ' or *Christi*, in the model of Roman commercial corporations (see Chapter 29). The success of the Church is the result of its excellence in the art of hostile takeover. The claim *Verus Israel* was part of its bid to takeover 'Israel.' The bid, however, was rejected by the 'board': the shareholders rather suffer agony and martyrdom, than to accept the new management. As a result, even the Judeo-Christian communities originally formed around Jesus and his disciples were ignored by the new corporation: the Church Fathers regarded Jesus' original disiples, their companions and families, as heretics! There was a good reason for that. By rejecting the original bid, Jews prove themselves 'perfidious,' i.e., unwilling to submit to hostile takeovers. Therefore, it would be wise not to trust a Judeo-Christian as well; only those of pagan background could be *Verus Israel*! That will explain the preeminence of Paul over James and Peter, and the Church's efforts to *erase every trace* of the *early* Christian Community in the Holy Land. This could explain the fact that *St Peter's Basilica* was not built upon the Apostle's tomb, as claimed by the Church, but over a pagan cemetery. Accordingly, it would be unrealistic to expect the Church to try to become *Verus* Judeo-Christian—by honoring the original Judeo-Christian communities in the Holy Land—before pretending to be *Verus* Israel. As those acquainted with the art of hostile takeovers will tell you, there would be no remission of sins, earthy or otherwise, for the board and shareholders that have refused to cooperate fully with the new managment.

A marginal note. The attitude of the Church towards the original Judeo-Christian communities was similar to its attitude towards the Roman Empire. As historians teach us, Christians joined forces with the Barbarians to destroy the Empire. In its place was created the *Sacrum Romanun Imperium Nationis Germanicae*, bringing enlightenment, liberty and peace to European society until modern times. Cf. above Appendix 20.

31. *Remez*

Remez, a term widely used in rabbinic literature, stands for a 'gesture' or non-verbal 'sign' made to communicate. For example, signals made to a deaf-mute person, see Mishna *Giṭṭin* 5:7, *Tosefta Yebamot* 13:7, p. 49; or by a husband unable to speak, 'signaling' that he wishes to divorce his wife; see *Tosefta Giṭṭin* 5:1, p. 263; *Yebamot* 120b, etc. It is commonly (but not exclusively) used to indicate a gesture made in visual contact by the eyes (for example, 'winking' at someone, as in Arabic); see *Yoma* 19a. It also stands for an 'encoded' term or a word used not as a linguistic symbol, but in the place of a non-verbal 'signal,' suggesting something outside the semantic field of the sentence. Accordingly, a *remez* may be suggested by a full or defective spelling of a word; see *Shabbat* 103b; cf. *Teshubot Geonim Qadmonim* #79, 23b and *Kelale Shemu'el*, 5d; or by the general impression, gained from a peculiar style or construction of a verse; see *'Aboda Zara* 25a; *Zebaḥim* 115b; *Menaḥot* 76b; etc. *Remez* cannot be treated as speech. Although 'written,' it functions as an *extensional* sign, outside its semantic field. Like a non-verbal 'riddle' or 'cryptogram,' it requires 'decoding' and 'unraveling,' rather than linguistic 'interpretation.' Therefore, it should not be taken as a kind of word-puzzle (as per 'כל שמות הנרמזים באותיותיו ובפסוקיו').

Given the non-linguistic character of a *remez*, it cannot, by definition, be linguistically explicit; see *Sanhedrin* 10a, *Ḥolin* 42a, etc. Consequently, since the 613 *miṣvot* were "said" (נאמרו) to Moses (*Makkot* 24a), implying speech and verbal communication, a *remez* cannot be in and of itself a *miṣva* (but at most, a *detail* in a *miṣva*); see *Sefer ha-Miṣvot*, III, p. 16 (contrary to Ramban ibid.). Neither could it be decoded on the basis of *sebara* (which is essentially linguistic); see *Yebamot* 54b, but only via rabbinic promulgation. Thus, we find that rabbis enacted a series of *halakhot* on the basis of a *remez* in Scripture; see *Mo'ed Qaṭan* 5a, *Yebamot* 21a, *Nedarim* 39b, *Qiddushin* 80b, *Sanhedrin* 21b, 46b, 83b; etc. We can understand now why if a sage reports a law that is not explicit in Scripture, it is assumed that it has been 'suggested' somewhere by a *remez*. In such a case the sages proceed to ask where in Scripture it was 'suggested' (היכא רמיזא); see *Megilla* 2a, *Sanhedrin* 81b, etc. The Geonim, too, justified certain rituals on the basis of a *remez* preserved in their tradition; see *She'iltot, Bereshit*, I, vol. 1, p. 12; *Sha'are Teshuba* #31, 13a. *Remez* pertains to *dinim mufla'im*. Since its resolution is not based on linguistic considerations, it is up to the legislative authorities to determine whether the law or rule promulgated on the basis of a *remez* is to be regarded as 'rabbinical' or 'scriptural.'

The keys and general system of the *remez*-technique were taught by the sages during the Second Temple to advanced students. For our purpose, let us point out that the *derashot* or homilies in *Sifra* and *Sifre* were designed to identify the *loci* in Scripture encoding (רמייזא) some of the *halakhot* contained in the Mishna. Concerning this fundamental aspect of rabbinics, R. Sherira Gaon, *IShG*, p. 39 reported:

> *Sifra* and *Sifre* are the *derashot* of Scripture and (pointing) to the *hilkheta* (Aramaic for *halakha*) is encoded (רמייזא) in the Scripture. Originally, during the Second Temple, (and) in the rabbinic period, they would teach (תני, i.e., via oral tradition) this method to them (their disciples).

See *Golden Doves*, p. 97.

The famous thirteen rules of rabbinic hermeneutics, widely discussed but rarely understood, are the principal keys designed to unravel the *remez*. Referring to the *curriculum* of the traditional rabbinic academies, Maimonides (*MT Talmud Tora* 1:11) wrote that it included three sections: the study of Scripture, the study of oral tradition, and a special section, 'Talmud' whose purpose was to train the student, to

> ... understand and comprehend the relation between the final conclusion of a subject [as promulgated by the rabbis] to its beginning [the *remez*], and (learn how) to draw one thing from the other, and match up one thing to the other, and understand the rules of hermeneutics that expound the Tora, until he could grasp the foundation of these rules of hermeneutics, and how such matters, as 'prohibited and permitted,' that he had previously learned from oral tradition, were derived. This process is what is designated 'Talmud.'

According to Maimonides, the above three-part curriculum should be followed in the formative stages of education. However, after having mastered the system, a scholar should devote his efforts "only to Talmud, in accordance with his mental scope and intellectual maturity." (*MT Talmud Tora* 1:12)

Finally, we should note that *remez* can allude to *halakhic* material, see *Sifre Bemidbar* #116, p. 132; or to some basic doctrine; see *Sifre Debarim* #329, p. 379. It may also encode esoteric material, in which case its identification and development follows a special methodology (see *Homo Mysticus*). Given that the original connotation of *remez* is a 'gesture,' at times certain stories in the Talmud (or Scripture) must be understood, not as a *linguistic narrative*, but in terms of *imagery*, functioning as a 'signal'; see *Teshubot ha-Ge'onim* (Harkavy) #244, p. 121; *Teshubot ha-Ge'onim* (Musafia) #115, 35a. To gain a better appreciation of the *remez*-methodology, it would be helpful to consider what Cyrus H. Gordon, *Riddles in History* (New York: Crown Publishers, 1974), pp. 53–54, wrote about the usage of language among the ancients:

> Our contemporaries have split the atom, reached the moon, and brought color TV to the common man. The ancients, all through historic times (i.e., since 3000 B.C.), were not less talented than today's population, but they often expressed their intelligence in different ways. They manipulated language so deftly that it often takes the modern scholars a long time to grasp the presence, let alone all the subtleties, of ancient riddles.

In particular, ancient man indulged in the design of clever cryptograms and riddles. The Scripture may serve as a good model for this usage of language. In the words of Professor Gordon, *Riddles in History*, p. 55:

> To understand how the ancients actually felt about the sophisticated uses of language, we must turn to the old texts themselves. The Proverbs of Solomon 1:6 states that the function of an education is "to understand a proverb and clever saying: the words of the wise and riddles." For the sages it was not enough to handle plaintext. Plain language is for plain people. The elite must also master riddles and cryptograms, and grasp the deeper meaning subtly concealed beneath the surface meaning.

See *Guide*, "Introduction" and I, 31. On the rabbis' predilection for riddles, see *Yerushalmi Demai* VII, 7, 26c, and the comment of R. Jacob Ḥajez, *'Eṣ Ḥayyim* (Verona, 5408/1648), Introduction, 5a.

In a well researched and beautifully written book, Marcel Danesi, *The Puzzle Instinct: The Meaning of Puzzles in Human Life* (Bloomington: Indiana University Press, 2002), thoroughly examined what he described as "the puzzle instinct" in man.

> The puzzle instinct is, arguably, as intrinsic to human nature as are humor, language, art, music, and all the other creative faculties that distinguish humanity from other species. (*The Puzzle Instinct*, p. 208)

Of particular interest for the understanding of the *remez* methodology in the rabbis and in Maimonides' *Guide* is that puzzles "are solved primarily by a form of insightful thinking that the philosopher Charles Peirce called *logica utens*" (ibid.). Danesi concluded his work with these powerful words:

> Hopefully, I have shed some light on how the puzzle instinct, in its own miniature way, has guided us, and continues to guide us, in our search for an answer, whether real or imagined, to the most vexing puzzle of all—the meaning of life. (ibid. p. 235)

Summing up some of the ideas discussed above. The rabbis believed that in addition to *peshaṭ* or *sensus communis*, the Scripture and rabbinic literature contain encoded messages, the *remez*. As it were, in addition to the divine message conveyed from the mouth of the Almighty as *qabbala*, there were special points communicated via His divine Countenance, which those closer to Him could discern and eventually unravel. The solution (rather than the method) is rendered in a *derasha*, introducing the *halakha* or legal rule to the general public. Some of the clues, however, contain *sod* or esoteric material. The methodology by which to identify this material and unravel its content is a principal concern of Maimonides' *Guide*.

On the difference between *remez* and *asmakhta* see Appendix 33—contrary to the view proposed in *Yad Mal'akhi* #202 and *Ohel Yesharim*, '*He*' #44. On the difference with *Derekh Qeṣara*, see Appendix 34. For a learned study on *midrash*; see Mayer Gruber, "The Term *Midrash* in Tannaitic Literature," in ed. Rivka Ulmer, *Discussing Cultural Influences* (Lanham: University Press of Ametica, 2007), pp. 41–58.

32. *Qabbala* and *Halakha*

To gain a proper understanding of these terms it would be necessary to consider three principles connected with *halakha*. First, it depends on *qabbala* 'authoritative transmission'; see Mishna *Pe'a* 2:6; *Giṭṭin* 6:7; *Abot* 1:1; '*Eduyot* 1:6; 8:7; *Tosefta Pesaḥim* 4:13–14, p. 165; *Sanhedrin* 6:2, p. 424; *Yadayim* 2:16, p. 683. The root QBL is common to other Semitic languages. Principally, it connotes 'frontal, face to face,' 'opposite to one another.' In Arabic it is used to designate the direction in which the faithful faces in prayer (for Moslems: Mecca; for Jews: Jerusalem), and also for 'kissing.' In Aramaic it stands for 'confrontation,' and therefore 'complaint.' It appears in Scripture as 'opposite' (in space: *Ex* 26:5; 36:12; etc.; but in rabbinics also in time, see *Bekhorot* 57b); for 'greeting' (1*Ch* 12:18), and 'in the presence of' (2*K* 15:10). It also denotes 'acceptance' (*Job* 2:10). It is used for formal 'acceptance,' involving understanding and commitment (*Pr* 19:20; *Est* 9:23, 27). In this latter sense, *qabbala* of *halakha* involves 'frontal reception' from an authority, as Moses at Sinai (*Abot* 1:1). In the process of *qabbala* the student was expected to face and pay close attention to the teacher's lip movements in order to make sure that he was hearing correctly; see *Horayot* 12a, cf. *Ḥolin* 137b. When R. Dime, *Shabbat* 145a, wanted to reassure Abayye that the report he was transmitting was authentic, he invoked *Job* 19:27: "My eyes saw and not a stranger." Adding: "from the lips of R. Jeremiah I heard," the report in question; i.e., he saw it coming out of his lips. Accordingly, "When someone is transmitting an authoritative lesson (שמועה), "he should picture in his mind the image of the author of that tradition as now standing before him" (*Yerushalmi Sheqalim* II, 7, 47a), cf. *Golden Doves*, p. 87. When a student recited the lesson before his teacher, the teacher moved his lips in harmony with the student, signifying consent; *Yerushalmi Berakhot* II, 1, 4b, etc. [In Judeo-Arabic the verb *qarri*, from Hebrew QR', denotes this type of supervision]. That is why, even after death, "Every disciple of the sages, when an authoritative lesson (שמועה) is pronounced in his name in this world, his lips move smoothly in the tomb," *Yebamot* 97a. For a glimpse on the faithfulness and tenacity with which the students guarded the lessons they heard from their teachers, see *Nidda* 36b–37a. Cf. *Yad Mal'akhi* #663, 169a-b.

Not all students were qualified to face the teacher. Some were only permitted to stand behind the teacher (see *'Erubin* 13b, reporting that R. Judah the Prince only saw "the back of R. Me'ir." R. Ḥanan'el *ad loc.*, explained that at the time he was not qualified to sit in a front row).

The connotation of *qabbala*/'kissing' (as in Arabic), is evident in the *Targum* to *Song* 1:2, rendering "He (God) would kiss me with the kisses of His lips," as: "... and [God] taught the Six Orders of the Mishna and Talmud." This idea was encoded in a point raised by R. Joshua, that "דדיך" in *Song* 1:2 is to be read in the plural, not in the singular (Mishna *'Aboda Zara* 2:5). Accordingly, the standard translation, "For thy *love* (דדיך) is better than wine," is wrong. If "דדיך" is in the plural, as per R. Joshua's teaching and the Masora reading, then we should translate: "For *those who love* Thee are better than wine"—being an allusion to the teachings of sages and scribes in charge of conveying the oral tradition. Hence the homily stressing that the teachings of sages and scribes are more beloved "than the wine of Tora" or Scripture itself; see *'Aboda Zara* 35a; *Yerushalmi Berakhot* I, 4, 3b, and parallels. Cf. also *'Erubin* 21b and *Sanhedrin* 88b. For a different interpretation, see Sh. Na'e, "*Ṭobim Dodekha Me-Yayyin*," (Heb.), in *Studies in Talmud and Midrashic Literature* in *Memory of Tirzah Lifshitz* (Jerusalem: Bialik Institute, 2005), pp. 411–434.

Therefore *halakha* stands for authentic tradition (*Tosefta Ḥagiga* 3:33, p. 393; *Ketubot* 6:6, p. 76; *Qiddushin* 5:4, p. 295; *Zebaḥim* 1:8, p. 480); indicating 'an accepted norm' (see Mishna *'Erubin* 4:8, *Baba Meṣi'a* 5:8, *Sanhedrin* 11:6, *Menaḥot* 4:3; *Tosefta Ta'aniyot* 2:5, p. 331; *Yebamot* 1:9, p. 2; *Baba Qamma* 6:5, p. 22; *Sanhedrin* 3:9, p. 420; *'Eduyot* 2:7, p. 458). The status of a *halakha*, however, is not a matter of history but of law; to be awarded by the judiciary, not by historians; see *MT Mamrim* 1:1.

A legal position may be put forward as a *din*—'a view arrived at through judicial analysis,' or as a *halakha*—'authoritative transmission.' A duly acknowledged *halakha* must be accepted, whereas a *din* could be challenged (see Mishna *Yebamot* 8:3; *Keritot* 3:9; cf. *Nazir* 7:4). Whether a legal position is a *halakha* or a *din* is a matter to be decided by the judiciary. Prior to being settled, there could be controversy on the subject (see *Tosefta Ṭebul Yom* 1:10, p. 685), and it could be treated as a regular *din* (see *Tosefta Nazir* 5:1, pp. 141–142; *Ohalot* 4:14, p. 601). When the status of a legal view is challenged, the case may be submitted to a vote and the majority opinion prevails (see Mishna *'Eduyot* 1:5, 6; *Tosefta Ḥagiga* 2:9, pp. 383–384; cf. Mishna *'Eduyot* 5:7). However, once that the matter has been settled by the court and awarded the status of *halakha*, it cannot be challenged on the basis of *din* (cf. Mishna *Pe'a* 4:1, 2; *Giṭṭin* 6:7; *'Eduyot* 8:7). That is why *halakha* is often used in the sense of 'established norm' (see Mishna *Pe'a* 3:6; *Shebi'it* 9:5; *Yebamot* 4:13; *Baba Qamma* 3:9; cf. *Targum* on *Gn* 40:13 and *Pseudo-Jonatahn* on *Gn* 40:13, 43:33 and *Dt* 12:27, etc.).

It is clear now why rejecting a *halakha* equals 'heresy' (כפירה); see *Tosefta 'Oqaṣin* 3:13, p. 689. The following incident illustrates the gravity of the matter. Once R. 'Aqiba challenged his teacher, R. Eleazar, while he was in the process of transmitting a *halakha*. The incident is depicted as follows: "his [R. 'Aqiba's] teacher, R. Eleazar, was in the process of teaching him a *halakha*... and he [R. 'Aqiba] dissented with him (כפר בו) during the argument (דין)" and was admonished for it" (see *Yerushalmi Pesaḥim* VI, 4, 35c; *Sifre Zoṭa, Bemidbar*, #XII, p. 243; *Pesaḥim* 69a; and *Yerushalmi Ki-Fshuṭo*, p.478; cf. *'Aboda Zara* 46b and Mishna *Nazir* 7:4).

To question the integrity of the transmission of a *halakha* is tantamount to rejecting the authority of the sage that transmitted it. When the rabbis decided to call for a special session to settle a matter which it had been previously transmitted by R. Eleazar as *halakha le-Moshe mi-Sinai*, it was with the intention to publicly repudiate his authority (Mishna *Yadayim* 4:3); see *Ḥagiga* 3b and *Perush* R. Ḥanan'el *ad loc*. On one occasion, after a legal dispute, one of the parties discovered that the view he was proposing was in fact a *halakha*, and therefore reported it as such; see *Baba Meṣi'a* 23a. By contrast, a *din* could always be challenged and a dissenting opinion would be duly noted.

Since the status of a *halakha* depends on the court, sometimes this term is used in the sense of 'legal decision' (see *Tosefta Sanhedrin* 6:6, p. 424; 7:1, p. 425; *'Eduyot* 1:4, p. 455; *Para* 7:4, p. 636; cf. *Miqve'ot* 4:6, p. 656); or for 'the strict legal meaning,' in contradistinction to the moral aspect of a precept; see *Tosefta Baba Meṣi'a* 3:14, p. 76. Not every *halakha* would be implemented; see Rab in *Shabbat* 12b; *'Erubin* 7a; *Beṣa* 28b; *Baba Qamma* 30b; *'Aboda Zara* 37b; *Menaḥot* 36b. (For further analyses see R. Judah Rozanes, *Mishne le-Melekh* on *MT She'ar Abot ha-Ṭum'a* 19:1, s.v. *wu-mashe'amar*). Samuel maintained that the entire last Chapter of tractate *Nidda* was *le-halakha* but not for *ma'ase* 'to be implemented'; see *Yerushalmi Berakhot* II, 6, 5b. (Conversely, some rules were put into practice as *halakha le-ma'ase* although not formally *halakhot*; see *Ketubot* 56a). This is why, the sages distinguished between *halakha* and *halakha le-ma'ase*; see *Baba Batra* 130b; *Yerushalmi Giṭṭin* V, 4, 47a; cf. *Horayot* 2a.

For the purpose of the present discussion it is important to emphasize that the authenticity and dependability of *qabbala*, and its corollary, *halakha* is not a matter of 'memory.' Rabbis, whether in their initial educational stages or as advanced teachers, were prone to memory lapses and distortions; see Rabban Yoḥanan b. Zakkai, *Tosefta Ohalot* 16:8, p. 614. On occasion, two outstanding sages would report contradictory accounts of the same lesson that they heard together from their teacher, each ready to take an oath that his version was correct, and not that of his colleague. Later sages would attempt to reconcile between them and try to find some justification for their disagreement; see, for example, *Yebamot* 32a–33b; *Ketubot* 57a and Rashi *ad loc s.v. amar*. The fullest account and justification of most such cases are found in *Yad Mal'akhi* #663. However, no justification for forgetfulness and memory lapses is really necessary. Consider the following passage in *Shebu'ot* 26a:

> When R. Kahana and R. Ase stood up from the lesson given by Rab, one would say: 'I swear: This is what Rab said.' And the second would say: 'I swear: This is what Rab said.' When they would come to Rab he would agree with only one of them. Then the second would say: 'Did I swear falsely?' (And Rab) would reply: 'Your heart had coerced you'!

See below Appendix 45. What makes *qabbala*, and its consequent *halakha*, 'infallible' is that it was recognized as such by the judiciary. Occasionally, a testimony reporting a tradition would be accepted as authentic, in so far as it makes legal sense, but not as *qabbala*; as per *Yebamot* 67a:

> זו עדות העיד ר' יוסי מפי שמעיה ואבטליון, והודו לו. אמר רב אשי: מי קתני וקבלו? 'והודו לו' קתני: דמסתבר טעמיה!

Concerning memory inexactness and misrepresentation, see the articles edited by Daniel L. Schacter, *Memory Distortion* (Cambridge, Mass.: Harvard University Press, 1995), particularly in part IV. On the different connotations of this term, see Chapters 49, 57.

33. *Halakha le-Moshe mi-Sinai*

There is a special group of *halakhot* classified by the rabbis as 'A *halakha* of Moses from Sinai' (הלכה למשה מסיני); see Mishna *'Eduyot* 4:3; 8:7, *Tosefta Sukka* 3:1, p. 266; *Yadayim* 2:16, p. 683. It is a major rabbinic concept. In a sense, "the entire Tora," including the oral tradition, is "*halakha* of Moses from Sinai"; see *Nidda* 45a; and cf. *'Arukh*, s.v. *mad* (1); R. Judah ha-Levi, *Kuzari* III, 21, pp. 128–130; "Introduction," *Perush ha-Mishnayot,* vol. 1, p. 16. Not all of these *halakhot* were originally designated as such. An opinion could have been registered in the Mishna as a *halakha* without any qualifications (see Mishna *'Orla* 3:9), and upon consideration the Talmudic authorities would classify it as 'A *halakha* of Moses from Sinai' (הלכה למשה מסיני); see *Baba Batra* 12b; *Yerushalmi 'Orla* III, 7, 63b; *Qiddushin* 37a; *MT Ma'akhalot Asurot* 10:10; *Perush ha-Mishnayot*, *'Orla* 3:9, vol. 1, p. 415. In the "Introduction" to *Perush ha-Mishnayot,* vol. 1, pp. 18–19, Maimonides recorded a list of most of the cases that were classified as 'A *halakha* of Moses from Sinai.' According to Maimonides, these *halakhot* have two characteristics. First, they have no legislative basis in the text of the Tora, i.e., they were neither 'encoded' (*remez*; see Appendix 31) in the text, nor can they be justified by judicial reasoning (דין), or rabbinic exegesis. Therefore, they could not be included in the lesson on the Tora. For purposes of mnemonics, a teacher would 'append' (אסמכתא) these *halakhot* to a term of the Tora; see "Introduction," *Perush ha-Mishnayot*, vol. 1, pp. 18–19; R. Isaac Bar-Sheshet, *Teshubot ha-Ribash* #294. However, since these attachments would not be included in the lesson, they could not be disseminated through regular channels. Rather, they 'floated' around and were occasionally forgotten; see *Yoma* 80a; *Yerushalmi Pe'a* II, 6, 17a, cf. *Shabbat* I, 4, 3d. Ideally, if one could, "then one should string a tradition (שמועא) up to Moses, but if one cannot (then he should) confirm either the earlier [source] or the later [source]"; see *Yerushalmi Shabbat* I, 2, 3a. Because the *halakhot* that were 'floating' around could be easily dismissed as unimportant, R. Johanan warned scholars: "If you come in contact with a *halakha* and you do not know its source (= 'טיפוס'-*typos;* cf. Mishna *Ketubot* 1:9), don't dismiss it. Many *halakhot* that were given to Moses at Sinai, were thereafter placed in the Mishna" (*Yerushalmi Pe'a* II, 6, 17a; *Ḥagiga* I, 8, 76d). Hence, the need to corroborate these types of *halakhot* and reinforce their status.

The *halakhot* that were designated as 'of Moses from Sinai" are those that although [i] have no connection with the text of Scripture, and [ii] although their chain of tradition cannot be fully determined, were, nonetheless, confirmed by the rabbinic authorities as authentic. Once established as 'of Moses from Sinai,' it would be improper for a later sage to try to find some 'support' for it in Scripture; see *Zebaḥim* 110a. Maimonides maintained that once a *halakha* had been classified as 'of Moses from Sinai,' the matter was settled and its status could not be contested. We have seen above (Appendix 32) that the status of a *halakha* is a judicial matter. This applies also to a *halakha le-Moshe mi-Sinai*. Its status is a matter of law—not of 'history'! Prior to gaining the status of *le-Moshe mi-Sinai*, a *halakha* could be contested (see for example *Yerushalmi Pe'a* I, 1, 15a; *Ḥagiga* I, 2, 76b; etc.). We should note that Maimonides distinguished between two classes of traditions attributed to Moses. One "about which there could not be any controversy at all" ("Introduction," *Perush ha-Mishnayot* vol. 1, p. 20; cf. *MT Melakhim* 12:2); or what amounts to the same: "about which there never was [registered] a controversy" (*MT Mamrim* 1:3). Second, a *halakha le-Moshe mi-Sinai* "about which there is no controversy" ("Introduction," *Perush ha-Mishnayot* vol. 1, p. 16)—in the present tense! Before the court renderes a decision, a *halakha* has no standing. The rabbis reported that when a party presented a view not derived from Scripture, but claimed "thus I have received (קבלתי) from my teachers," the matter must be submitted to the Supreme Court for a decision (see *Tosefta Pesaḥim* 4:13–14, p. 165; *Sanhedrin* 7:1, p. 425; *Sanhedrin* 88b; *MT Mamrim* 4:1; cf. Mishna *'Eduyot* 5:7, *Perush ha-Mishnayot*, vol. 4, pp. 322–323).

The status 'of Moses from Sinai' does not imply that the *halakha* in question had been pronounced by Moses, but, rather, that although the chain of transmission cannot be fully traced, it has been confirmed as authentic, as if it were a *halakha* given by Moses at Sinai. Consider, for example, the law about levying tithes from lands in Moab and Amon, having the status *halakha le-Moshe mi-Sinai* (Mishna *Yadayim* 4:3). The law itself is actually rabbinic; therefore, as proposed by R. Shimshon (12th century), it means that the law is authentic "as if it were a *halakha* given by Moses at Sinai" (*Perush ad loc*); cf. *Perush ha-Mishnayot 'Eduyot* 8:7, vol. 4, p. 336. Similarly, according to the original version in *'Erubin* 4a-b (preserved in *MT Miqve'ot* 1:12 and R. Menaḥem Me'iri, *Bet ha-Beḥira ad loc*, p. 21), a rabbinic rule establishing "that a tarnish, covering most of the body, constitutes a legal impediment" for a ritual bath, "even though (the person in question) is not troubled by it," was reported as a *halakha le-Moshe mi-Sinai*. R. Ḥanan'el on *Sukkot* 6b referred to that particular *halakha le-Moshe mi-Sinai* as "a rabbinic decree" (גזרו). In fact, the expression *halakha le-Moshe mi-Sinai* is used in Geonic literature as synonymous to 'authentic, reliable,' and 'lucid and unambiguous'; see R. Ḥanan'el on *Berakhot* 64a (*Perush*, p. 145); *'Arukh*, s.v. *mad* (1); *Oṣar Ḥilluf Minhagim*, ed. B. M. Lewin (Jerusalem: Makor, 1972), p. 32; R. Ḥanan'el in his *Perush* to *Berakhot*, p. 145a, etc. In sum, as explained by Maimonides, *Teshubot ha-Rambam*, vol. 2, p. 632:

> ... that even a matter which is *halakha le-Moshe mi-Sinai* is designated 'from the Scribes,' given that nothing is 'from the Tora,' unless it is explicit in the Tora ... or something that the sages have declared to be from the Tora, of which there are only three or perhaps four cases.

The preceding meets the objections raised by R. Solomon Rafael Judah Leon Templo, *Massekhet Halakha le-Moshe mi-Sinai* (Amsterdam, 5494/1734), 3a, 5a, etc.; see the response of R. Ḥiyya ha-Cohen de la-Ara, *Mishmerot Kehunna* (Amsterdam, 5508/1748), 56b–57b; and *Studies in the Mishne Tora*, p. 32.

In conclusion, for Maimonides, the Geonim, *et al*, *Halakha le-Moshe mi-Sinai* is a special type of tradition, which cannot be verified by standard procedure. Nonetheless, it has the status of settled law and and it is legally binding; e.g., *MT Qiddush ha-Ḥodesh* 5:1–2; cf. *Mishmerot Kehunna*, 56a. The same applies to Scriptural texts; e.g. such as the 'Scroll of Esther' that is "from Sinai," see *Yerushalmi Megilla* I, 5, 70d; and *Rut Rabba* IV, 5 (33d); and cf. *Golden Doves*, p. 190 n. 28. Put in contemporary terms, *halakha le-Moshe mi-Sinai* is somehow analogous to a Constitutional amendment (e.g., the Bill of Rights in the U.S.), added to the Constitution by the Court, and not subject to repeal by any subsequent panel of the Court.

The same applies to the expression "Truly, it was said" (באמת אמרו) in rabbinic literature (see Mishna *Kil'ayim* 2:2, etc, etc.), which is usually treated as a *halakha le-Moshe mi-Sinai*; see Rashi on *Nazir* 54b, *s.v. be'emet*. It is an authentic tradition, whose chain of transmission could not be verified by standard procedure. It is nevertheless authentic, as "if it were a *halakha le-Moshe mi-Sinai*"; see *Perush*, R. 'Obadya, on *Terumot* 2:1.

34. *Derekh Qeṣara*

Derekh Qeṣara or 'succinct style' refers to the 'concise' and elliptical 'style' of the Mishna in which density (rather than clarity) is a major concern; see *Golden Doves*, pp. 90–94. Originally, this expression meant 'a shorter path' than the ordinary; see Mishna *Ketubot* 13:7*;* *Shebu'ot* 2:3; Rashi on *Shebu'ot* 14b s.v. *o sheba.*; or a shorter astronomical orbit, *Rosh ha-Shana* 25a; *Yerushalmi Rosh ha-Shana* II, 6, 58b; *MT Qiddush ha-Ḥodesh* 17:23. It is one of the hermeneutical rules applied metaphorically to the text of

Scripture; see *Yalquṭ Shim'oni*, *Noaḥ* #55, vol. 1, 14c; *Shemini* #537, vol. 1, 158c, *s.v. ve-el haḥasida*; cf. *Sifra, Emor*, X, 13, 5, 95b, where it is stated that the Scripture spoke "succinctly" (בקצרה). This principle has been recognized by the great Biblical commentators. On a 'shortened idiom' (קיצור דיבור), see Rashi on *Ez* 42:2; R. Abraham ibn 'Ezra on *Ps* 52:2; for the more common 'succinct style' (לשון קצרה), see Rashi on *Gn* 29:14; 39:14; *Ex* 10:5; *Ez* 27:14; R. Abraham ibn 'Ezra on *Ec* 10:18; on דרך קצרה, see Rashi on 37:1; R. Abraham ibn 'Ezra on *Gn* 3:17; 6:16; 18:25; etc., etc.; Radaq on *Josh* 9:21; 1*Sam* 12:8; 1*K* 7:15; 2*K* 7:2; *Ps* 21:13, etc., etc; for 'a shortened verse' (מקרא קצר), see Rashi *Gn* 41:13, 49; 48:1; *Ex* 22:22; 32:32; *Nu* 14:21; 22:32; etc.; Radaq *Josh* 9:21; 20:6; *Ju* 2:3; 1*Sam* 10:21, etc. In *The Mishnah of Rabbi Eliezer* (Heb.), I, 9, pp. 20–21, 'succinct style' is counted as one of the hermeneutical rules to be applied in the development of *aggada*, particularly to those elements requiring expansion and further elucidation. Some Talmudic passages were regarded as elliptic, and were interpreted accordingly; see R. Isaac Alfasi, *Teshubot* #286; Rashi on *'Aboda Zara* 9a s.v. *ve-'i*; *Shebu'ot* 5b s.v. *mi*; Riṭba on *Sukka* 2a s.v. *sukka*; cf. *Perush ha-Mishnayot, Abot* 5:14, vol. 4, p. 463.

A fundamental principle in Geonic tradition is that the Mishna was redacted in a 'succinct style' (דרך קצרה); see *IShG*, pp. 28–29; and cf. ibid. pp. 17, 26–27, 36, 58. Maimonides, too, alluded to the 'succinct style' of the Mishna; see "Introduction," *Perush ha-Mishnayot*, vol. 1, p. 34. This style was adopted by him in the redaction of the *MT* (see "Introduction," l. 152, cf. *Iggerot*, vol. 2, pp. 441, 442, 448) in his *responsa*, see *Teshubot ha-Rambam*, vol. 2, p. 634; and in his correspondence, see *Iggerot*, vol. 2, p. 454.

35. God's Mystery (סוד)

The Hebrew term for 'mystery' (סוד) stands for 'assembly'; as with a 'forum' where a deliberative group convenes to examine matters of common interest; something akin to the 'assembly' of canon law and legislative bodies. The discussions held within the *Bet Midrash* were confidential and treated as *sod*, closed to the general public. Pupils violating this confidence were expelled; see *Sanhedrin* 31a. And cf. Mishna *Sanhedrin* 3:7; R. Isaac Alfasi, on *Sanhedrin* 31a; and the comments of R. Joseph Al-Ashqar, *Mirkebet ha-Mishne*, ed. Jacob Shpigel (5753/1993), on *Abot* 6:4, p. 318.

Teachers were cautioned to exercise discretion when exposing delicate matters; see *Yerushalmi Aboda Zara* II, 4, 41d (the printed text is faulty), the correct text is quoted by R. Ḥanan'el on *'Aboda Zara* 35a. It admonishes the teacher: "You may immerse yourself in the words of the Tora, only before upright and honest students." On the association *sod*/*halakha*, see *Tosefta Yadayim* 2:16, p. 683 and *Ḥagiga* 3b. Obviously, the statement by R. Johanan, that "God contracted the covenant with Israel only on account of the oral matters," *Giṭṭin* 60b is aimed to contravene the Christian notion that a 'covenant' with God could be established merely by appropriating the text of the Scripture without regard for the oral tradition of Israel; cf. Section IV, n. 120. For the association *qabbala*/'kissing,' see Appendix 32.

36. *Seder*

In Jewish literature the Aramaic root SDR may include legal topics, e.g., the six *SeDaRim* of the Mishna. It may also include liturgical themes, as in *SiDduR* or 'Prayer Book,' to be developed by the precentor at the Synagogue; see, for example, *Berakhot* 13a, 34a; *Rosh ha-Shana* 35a. Hence, we have the Passover *SeDeR* where the participants gather to develop the theme of the Exodus; see Section III, n. 21. The term SiDRa which is commonly used to designate the weekly portion of the Tora, probably included the Aramaic version (as *Neophyti* 1) or similar exegetical material (otherwise, it would not have made any sense to have Rab repeat the *sidra* so many times; see *Yoma* 87a-b, and cf. *'Aboda Zara* 19a). The Arabic *tatlawaha'a*, root WLY, 'to adjoin, to place next,' used by R. Se'adya Gaon to translate the Biblical term *tasim* has a similar connotation; cf. *Targum* and R. Se'adya on *Dt* 4:44. Maimonides, too, used this Arabic term in the same technical sense; see, for example, "Introduction," *Perush ha-Mishnayot*, vol. 1, p. 2. On the association of the Hebrew *sima* with the Aramaic *sedura*, see *'Erubin* 54b.

Talmudic Academies counted with a special instructor, *sadrana*, see *Pesaḥim* 105b and cf. *Yerushalmi, Horayot* III, 8, 48c (cf. below Appendix 41). His task was to *mesadder*, 'expose the *halakhot* in their proper order and sequence'; see *Tosefta Zabim* 1:5, p. 676. The same applies to the SeDaRim of the Mishna, see *Beṣa* 16b and *Ta'aniyot* 8a; the *gemara,* see *Yoma* 14b; and the *aggada*, see *Megilla* 27a, *Berakhot* 10a, *'Erubin* 21b, etc. (In the Arabic of the Jews from Syria, *sidr-al-ḥammam* indicates the ceremonial arrangement made for the bridal ritual bath. In contemporary Synagogues of congregations from Damascus and Aleppo, *messadder* is the official in charge of designating who will lead in the various sections of the services, and who will go up to read the Tora). Part of the responsibilities of the Talmudic *sadran* was to invite students to attend the lecture; see *Kalla Rabbati* IV, 14, p. 263. He would also repeat the class to the students, see *Yoma* 15a. The "head of the *sidra*" occupied an important position, once held by no lesser a figure than Rab; see *Ḥolin* 137b. In the *Yerushalmi*, *sidra* stands for the building containing the 'synagogue' or 'place of study'; see *Shabbat* VI, 2, 8a; IX, 2, 12a; XIX, 1, 16d; *Pesaḥim* I, 1, 27b; *Sheqalim* V, 4, 49b, etc. In Samaritan dialect, *sidra* stands for "assembly"; see *Yerushalmi Ki-Fshuṭo*, p. 104. Concerning the title *resh sidra* in the Talmud (*Ḥolin* 137b) and in Geonic literature, see Abramson, *Be-Merkazim*, p. 107. Maimonides, "Introduction," *MT*, l. 170, expressed the hope that the *halakhot* in his *Mishne Tora* would be "*SeDuRim* fluently by heart." For an extensive discussion of the different connotations of this term, see Moshe Assis, "On the *Sidra*," (Heb.) *Annual of Bar-Ilan University* 30–31 (2006), pp. 353–372.

37. The Four Levels of Instruction

In *Mekhilta, Mishpaṭim,* p. 246 we read:

> *These are the laws* (*Ex* 21:1). R. 'Aqiba asked: what is the purpose of *These are the laws*?—because elsewhere it was written [i] "*Speak* to the people of Israel, and *say* to them." One may think that it would suffice to *say* [these laws] to them only once. How can it be known that one is to repeat them twice, thrice and four times until they learn them? To clarify this point the Scripture teaches: [ii] "And *teach* it [the Law] to the children of Israel" (*Dt* 31:19). May one assume that it would be sufficient if they learned [these laws] (once) and they need not to go over them again? To clarify this point the Scripture teaches: [iii] "*put it in their mouths*" (*Dt* 31:19). May one assume that it would be sufficient if they knew how to repeat [these laws] without understanding them? To clarify this point the Scripture teaches: [iv] *These are the laws* (*Ex* 21:1)—present [these laws] to them as a well-set-out-table (שלחן ערוך), accessible to all! Similarly, it says: "You were *taught* so that you would *know*" (*Dt* 4:35).

Cf. "Hebrew Introduction," *Perush ha-Mishnayot*, vol. 1, p. 1; Rashi on *Ex* 34:32; and R. Abraham Maimonides, *Perush,* pp. 304, 486. The above exegesis is developed around the pronoun 'these' (אלה), which is interpreted as a deictic pronoun, pointing at something standing right in front of the speaker. On this type of pronoun, see José Faur, "*Ma ben ḥamor ze le-ḥamor ha-hu,*" *Sinai* 76 (1975), pp. 189-192.

In *Sifra, Beḥuqotai*, X, 8 (12), 122a we read:

> ...*That God put between Him and the people of Israel.*—Moses had the merits of being appointed emissary (שליח) between Israel and their Father in Heaven.

> *In the hand of Moses at Mount Sinai.*—It teaches that [i] the (text of the) Tora was delivered—(together with) [ii] its *halakhot,* [iii] *nuances* (דקדוקיה) [iv] *and explanations* (פרושיה)—to the hands of Moses at Sinai.

Cf. ibid. X, 13 (8), 127b; and *AdRN* A, I, p. 1.

The above exegeses reflect the fact that Rabbinic Academies conducted classes at *four* levels, see *'Erubin* 54b. At the first level, the instructor taught the students the 'order' (סדר), that is, the string and progression of the text, ("and say to them"); cf. "Introduction," *Perush ha-Mishnayot*, vol. 1, p. 2. Probably, the סדרנא was the tutor in charge of this program, see above Appendix 36. At level two ("and teach it") the student was expected to 'know' (see Maimonides, ibid. Ar. תעלים 'be familiar'). The purpose of the third level was for the student to become fluent in the subject ("*put it in their mouth*") and acquire a scholarly comprehension of the subject (Maimonides, ibid. Ar. תדריס 'study'). The fourth level concerned critical understanding ("You were taught so that you should know"). According to Maimonides, ibid. this refers to the Ar. תפסיר 'explanation,' which is equivalent to the Heb. פרוש, see above Appendix 28. Such an "explanation should include all the elucidations" (Maimonides, ibid.).

These four levels correspond to knowledge [i] of the text of the Tora together with "[ii] its *halakhot,* [iii] the *nuances* [iv] *and the explanations* (פרושיה)" mentioned in the *Sifra*; see Section IV n. 123 and cf. "Introduction," *Perush ha-Mishnayot*, vol. 1, p. 7. Similarly, *Sifre* #335, pp. 384–385 advised the student that after hearing [i] "the words of the Tora"—the exposition of the Oral Law—one should [ii] "put his heart" in the lesson, as well as [iii] "his eyes," [iv] "and his ears"; cf. Appendix 32 and "Introduction," *Perush ha-Mishnayot*, vol. 1, p. 2. The rabbis associated 'nuances' of the Tora (דקדוקי תורה) with the need to employ metaphors in the classroom; see *Shir ha-Shirim Rabba* I, 8, s.v. *shir*, p. 4.

38. Teaching Tora in Public

Teaching the Tora in public is equivalent to publishing a judicial tradition. Accordingly, only faculty members were authorized to teach "Tora in public"; see *Rosh ha-Shana* 25b; *Giṭṭin* 57b; cf. *Megilla* 6a, *Sanhedrin* 96b and *AdRN* A, VI, p. 29; *Midrash Tehillim* I, 18, p. 18. On the merits of teaching Tora "in public" (ברבים), see *Shir ha-Shirim Rabba* I, 9, vol. 2, p. 4. This type of instruction is different than someone "gathering an assembly in public" and teaching Tora before them, *'Aboda Zara* 18a; or conveying to them "a word about Tora"; see *Shir ha-Shirim Rabba* I, 8, vol. 2, p. 4;

IV, 1 (11), p. 55; *Midrash Mishle*, VIII, 35, p. 60. Only ordained scholars could deliver "instructions" (הוראה) about laws and regulations; see *Sanhedrin* 5a-b; *Nidda* 24b; *Perush ha-Mishnayot, Bekhorot* 4:4, vol. 5, pp. 242–245.

The Mishna is the first composition dealing with the Oral Law for the explicit purpose of "teaching it in public" (*MT* "Introduction," ll. 46–47).

39. *Shone*: Rehearsing and Conveying *Halakha*

This verb stands for 'rehearsing a formulated text.' Occasionally, it may refer to the text of Scripture; see *Tosefta Shabbat* 13:1, p. 57; or the *perush* of the Tora, cf. *Qiddushin* 49a and Riṭba *ad loc* s.v. *'al menat*. The expression "*shone* two books," *Sifre, Debarim* #306, p. 339, may allude to the *Sifre* (pl. Aramaic for 'books'), i.e., the *perush* of two books, *Numbers* and *Deuteronomy*, rather than the text of Scripture. Mostly, however, this verb is used for the recitation of *halakha*. See Mishna *Ta'aniyot* 4:4; *Abot* 3:7; *Tosefta Berakhot* 2:12, p. 8; *Shebi'it* 2:13, p. 173; *Kil'ayim* 1:2, p. 203; *Baba Qamma* 7:13, p. 32; *Zebaḥim* 2:17, p. 483; *Ḥolin* 2:9, p. 502, etc; cf. *AdRN* A, XVIII, p. 67; *Megilla* 28a; *Sanhedrin* 68a; etc. *Shone* was used to denote both the conveyance and the study of *halakha;* see *Sifre Debarin* #127, p. 185–186; *Megilla* 26b, 28b; *Soṭa* 22a; cf. *Sanhedrin* 68a. It may apply to the recitation of a *halakha* from the Mishna, see *Ḥagiga* 9b, etc., or *Tosefta*; see *Midrash Tanḥuma, Teṣavve*, VI, vol. 2, p. 99. Mastering *halakha*, involved intense training; see *Tosefta Ohalot* 16:8, p. 614 and *Para* 4:7, p. 633. This is why, *shone* is associated with 'sitting'; see *Megilla* 21a and *Golden Doves*, pp. 186–187. This type of instruction was usually conducted at the *Bet Midrash*; see *Shabbat* 30b; *Pesaḥim* 107a; *AdRN* B, III, p. 14, etc.

On *shone*, in contradistinction to *qore* 'to read from Scripture,' see *Berakhot* 4b; and cf. *Massekhet Derekh Ereṣ* 4:5, ed. Michael Higger (Brooklyn, N.Y.: Moinester Publishing, 1935), p. 115.

40. *Megillat Setarim*

On *megillat setarim*, see *Shabbat* 6b, 96b; *Baba Meṣi'a* 92a. This term has been mistranslated as 'a secret scroll,' in which case it should have been *megillat seter* or *megillat nisteret*; see *Iyye ha-Yam*, 113a–114b and *Golden Doves*, p. 109. Rather, *setarim* means 'private,' 'confidential,' e.g., *ṭum'at setarim*, in *Pesaḥim* 85a, etc. *Megillat setarim* is nothing more than a 'private file, not for general circulation'; see *Golden Doves,* pp. 108–111 and Section IV n. 108. This is exactly the sense of the Geonic *responsum*, *Geonica*, vol. 2, p. 319 that "*megillat setarim* contains legal decisions (הלכות פסוקות) as if it was a book of *halakhot*, but is not like the Talmud that is available to all"(i.e., a published work), and that is why it is called *megillat setarim.*" (With all due respect, Professor Ginzberg's interpretation, ibid. p. 295, is not accurate). These scrolls were found in the archives (*be* = *bet*, cf. IV n. 98) of R. Ḥiyya, a scholar famous for the quality of the archival material in his possession, see *Iyye ha-Yam*, 114b; *Shir ha-Shirim Rabba* VIII, 1 [2], p. 77; *Qohelet Rabba* II, 1 [8], 7c; VI, 1 [2], 17a; XII, 1 [7], 30b.

41. The Publication of Oral Texts

In rabbinic literature the verb *galle* (גלי) stands for "removing a seal and uncovering" (גלי) a hidden object; see *Giṭṭin* 68a; *Midrash Tehillim* LXXVIII, 12, p. 352. In the same vein, it is also used for 'divulging' (גלי) something to a friend, see *Nidda* 66a; or expressing formal consent to a neighbor for usage of the premise on the Sabbath, see *'Erubin* 26b. A familiar expression in the Babylonian Talmud, "God had elucidated" (גלי רחמנא), means 'exposing' an ambiguous feature or a factor in the law, rather than leaving it to inference; see *Pesaḥim* 75a, etc. Therefore, I propose that *galle* (גלי) in *Horayot* 13b, stands for the 'publication' of a text, which hitherto had circulated privately; cf. above Appendix 40. The rabbis (*Horayot* 13b) recount that two members of the *Yeshiba* planned to show that R. Simeon ben Gamliel was not fit to serve as president. According to the standard text they planned to challenge his leadership by requesting of him "to publish" (גלי) *'Oqaṣin*— a tractate unbeknown to him. To prevent a public humiliation, a sage "went" to the archives, found said tractate, sat under R. Simeon ben Gamliel's study, "stretched" (*pashaṭ*) it (the tractate), that is opened up the scroll, *garas* (chanted, i.e., in a fast pace used to memorize the text; cf. *Golden Doves*, p. 183 n. 58), and then *tane* (a longer chant used to examine and ponder about the meaning of the text). To alert R. Simeon ben Gamliel that he was trying to convey an urgent matter, the sage went on and again "*garas*" and then "*tane*" the text for a second time. By the following morning, when an official request was presented to R. Simeon ben Gamliel to "to publish" (גלי) said tractate, he was ready. The verb *pashaṭ* 'to stretch' was used to denote the opening and unfolding of a 'scroll'; see *Yerushalmi Shabbat*

XVI, 1, 15c; *Ekha Rabbati*, IV, 20, p. 53; *Midrash Tanḥuma, Ki-Tissa,* XIX, p. 119; and *Yad Rama* on *Baba Batra* 160a, s.v. *geṭ*. It should be noted, that the sage alerting R. Simeon ben Gamliel, *garas* and *tane* the text twice, but he only "stretched" it (*pashaṭ*) once, since, as mentioned, this verb refers to the opening of the scroll, which he had to open only once.

The reading 'גלי' in the standard edition of the Talmud is not found in some mss, e.g., *Paris* 1337; or in Levine's edition, *IShG*, p. 25; instead of which they read: 'פתח תנא/פתח תני.' This reading is also found in *Teshubot ha-Ge'onim*, ed. R. Nathan Coronel, p. 15. However, in ms *Munich* 95, and in the Constantinople ed. of *IShG*, noted by Levine ibid, n. 11, we find 'גלי.' I am inclined to believe that the standard edition bears the original version. To begin with, the expression 'פתח תנא/פתח תני' is *not* Talmudic and is found nowhere else in rabbinic literature. Probably, a later copiest of *IShG* thought that 'גלי' would be difficult for the average reader to understand, and change it for the easier 'פתח תנא/פתח תני.' Support for our interpretation is the statement, *'Erubin* 53a: "Because Judeans published the tractate (גלו מסכתא), their studies (תורתן) stay solid in their hands." Namely, the fact that they published the text that was taught, making it available to everyone to further study and review it, made it possible to master the tractate and not to forget it in the course of time; see *R. Nissim Gaon*, ed. Shraga Abramson (Jerusalem: Mekize Nirdamim, 1965), pp. 133–134, and below Appendix 58.

The idea of *publishing* the text, before proceeding to analyze it, underlies the method for teaching Talmud at the traditional *Yeshiba*. As it was reported by R. Sherira Gaon, *IShG*, *Liqquṭṭim*, V, p. xxviii:

> (Before) every *Kalla* meeting we assemble the teachers (אלופים) and sages (of the *Yeshiba*) and enunciate (גורסים) [that is with the correct pronunciation and intonation] the tractate (to be studied) at the *Kalla*. And we further publish (מגלים) another tractate [that will be studied in the next *Kalla*]. (See Appendix 53).

The purpose of publishing (מגלים) in advance the tractate to be studied at the *Kalla* meeting, was to ensure that the prospective students would be learning the correct text, see section V, n. 56; rather than memorizing a faulty "student's vernacular version" (שיטפא דתלמידאי תרביצאי), see Section V, n. 27. On these sort of versions, see *Teshubot Ge'onim Qadmonim*, ed. David Cassel (Berlin, 1848), #78, 23b (= *Oṣar ha-Ge'onim, Berakhot*, #318, p. 113); #81, 26a; *Teshubot ha-Geonim ha-Ḥadashot*, #97, p. 98; and the editor's note *ad loc*, citing ibid #98, pp. 101–102; #149, p. 205; *Oṣar ha-Ge'onim, Berakhot*, #244, p. 88; *Ba-Merkazim*, p. 131, etc.

I would like to mention, in passing, that a similar method was used in Sephardic and Oriental *Yeshibot* until recently. The teacher would first enunciate (גורס) the text of the lesson. Next, the text would be repeated by an advanced student acting as his assistant (equal to the Talmudic *sadrana*? Cf. above Appendix 36). After that, it would be recited over again and again by the entire class, until all the nuances of pronunciation and intonation were mastered. Only then would the teacher begin to explain and analyze the text. That was the method by which the writer of these lines was initiated into the study of Talmud. Later on, I had the opportunity to learn that the same method had been used in other such schools (with the exception of *Porat Yosef*, which was never representative of the Sephardic tradition, Talmudic or otherwise. Their contempt for the study of Scripture may serve as an indicator). For a glimpse on the traditional Sephardic *Yeshibot*, see José Faur, "*Hora'at ha-Talmud ba-Masoret ha-Ḥinnukhit ha-Sfaradit*," *Shebile Ḥinnukh*, 35 (1975), pp. 177–178.

The root GLH in the sense of 'publication' is found in *Jer* 32:11, 14, in reference to an "open bill of sale" (*sefer ha-galui*) certifying the purchase of land by Prophet Jeremiah. On the basis of *Baba Batra* 160b, Rashi *ad loc.* explains *ha-galui* as a bill,

> …which it had been certified by the Court, on the basis of [having verified the signature] of the witnesses. Moreover, the judges wrote and signed an authorization, which in effect was the certification of the bill. Unveiling (*galui*), and thereby publishing, the matter in case the witnesses would die.

R. Se'adya Gaon used *Sefer ha-Galui* as the title of one of his works (ed. Abraham E. Harkavi, St. Petersburg, 1892), standing for "Open Letter," i.e., a work that may be read and quoted by all. (The same applies to *IShG*, *Liqquṭim*, IV, p. xxvii: אגרת פתוחה; and "שתי אגרות פתוחות" in *Ba-Merkazim*, p. 98: see ibid. pp. 43, 95, 96, 174). R. Joseph Qimḥi (c.1105-c. 1170), too, entitled one of his works *Sefer ha-Galui* (Berlin, 5247/1877). In the sense of "official publication," *galui* is used in *Est* 3:14; 8:13 (LXX: *ekthentes*). The document in question was an official "edict" (Aramaic version: *diatagma,* a loan term from the Greek; see *A Dictionary of Greek and Latin Legal Terms in Rabbinic Literature*, pp. 79–81, 210), requiring 'oral promulgation' to become effective; see above Appendix 28. It should be pointed out that the *Targum Sheni,* on 3:14 has *itgelle*. Finally, in *Megilla* 3b, when God reproached Jonathan ben 'Uzziel for publishing the Targum to the *Prophets*, He said to him: "Who *gilla* my secrets to the public."

For a different interpretation of *galle*; see Professor Shraga Abramson, *Perush R. Ḥanan'el la-Talmud* (Jerusalem: Vagshal, 5755/1995), p. 114; and *R. Nissim Gaon*, p. 134 n. 7.

42. TQN (תקן)

Scripture states that King Solomon "*TiQqeN* (תקן) many proverbs" (*Ec* 12:9). This verb is commonly used in rabbinic literature in the sense of 'instituting' a statute; see *Baba Qamma* 82a, etc. Consequently, a properly instituted 'ordinance' or 'statute' is designated *TeQaNa* 'תקנה.' Occasionally the verb is used for 'establishing' a public institution, *Shabbat* 33b. More significantly, and in the light of its Scriptural sense, it was used for 'establishing' an 'authoritative text'; see for example, *Berakhot* 48b. God, too, *TiQqeN* the Tora for Israel; see *Bemidbar Rabba*, XIV, 11, 61d. According to *Midrash Tehillim* XIX, 2, 82b, Moses did the same with respect to the liturgy. The rabbis (*Yebamot* 64b) report that R. Judah ha-Nasi *TaQqiN* "the Mishna" (תקין מתניתין). A similar expression (תקין הא מתניתא) was used in *Horayot* 13b. R. Sherira Gaon used the same verb to indicate the 'authoritative text' of the Mishna; see *IShG*, pp. 17, 36, 41, 50; cf. "Introduction," *Sefer ha-Mafteaḥ*, 3a. For *TiQqeN* in the sense of 'editing, publishing,' see the *responsum* in *Geonica*, vol. 2, p. 28. Liturgical expressions, such as '*le-TaQqeN* (לתקן) the world with the Kingdom of God,' do not mean 'to fix,' as per popular wisdom, but 'to organize, to establish firmly'; cf. *Dan* 4:33. I would like to call attention to the fact that in the Yemenite liturgy we have: '*le-TaKkeN*' (לתכן), "to be firmly established,' as in 2*Sam* 20:31; *Ps* 96:10, etc.

The Hebrew *mashal* (root MShL) usually translated as 'metaphor,' and 'proverb,' is connected to *moshel* 'ruler, legislator,' because the ideal government, as per *Ec* 12:9, governs by issuing 'aphorisms' (including both the idea of 'metaphor' and 'proverb') to guide the people. In this sense *mashal* is an 'analogy that governs,' best understood in the light of Justice Cardozo's remark, concerning the two forms of legal analogies, *The Paradoxes of Legal Science*, p. 8:

> The one searches for the analogy that is nearest in point of similarity, and adheres to it inflexibly. The other, in its choice of the analogy that shall govern, finds community of spirit more significant than resemblance of externality.

"This process of reasoning from the sample to the whole species," noted Justice Cardozo, ibid. p. 9, "is induction." Given that the *halakha* of the Mishna, too, serves as an 'analogy that governs,' this was, precisely, the method applied by the rabbis in their interpretation of the Mishna. We can now better appreciate the fact that R. Sherira Gaon used this verb not only in reference to the authoritative text of the Mishna, but also to indicate the *norms* that were 'established' by the editor of the Mishna by which to decode the text of the Mishna; see *IShG,* pp. 52, 53. It may be of some interest to note that Spanish speaking Sephardim translate *halakha*, when referring to a paragraph of the Mishna, as 'aphorism' and 'apothegms.' The proximity *tiqqen*/aphorism-aphtogems/*mashal* may explain the traditional 'chanting' of *halakha* (as chanting a *mashal* and an edict or *teqana* when proclaimed by the herald), see *Tosefta Ohalot* 16:8, p. 614; *Para* 4:7, p. 633; *Sanhedrin* 99b; *Megilla* 32a, etc. This is the place to remind the reader that the Mishna was chanted with a special melody; see *Golden Doves*, p. 96. This tradition was preserved in some communities in the Sabbath services, and in the recitation of *Abot* in the weeks between Passover and Shabu'ot.

43. The Introduction of the Monetary System in Rabbinic Tradition

The rabbis attributed the introduction of the monetary system to Patriarch Jacob; see *Shabbat* 33b; cf. *Em la-Miqra*, vol. 1, 71b–72a; 108b–109a. It is important to take note that the rabbis, *Shabbat* 32b used the verb *TiQqeN* to describe the establishment of the monetary system, the same verb used for the publication of the *Mishna*; see Appendix 42. In this respect, for the rabbis, as with Aristotle, banking and bank transactions were architectonic models for the exchange and evaluation of knowledge and ideas; see *Golden Doves*, pp. 142–145.

Both conceptually and linguistically, Hebrew 'coin' (*maṭbea'*, root ṬB') is connected to a 'signet' used to 'impress' on wax or clay (cf. Mishna *Sanhedrin* 4:5: טובע... מטבעות). On the relationship of 'signet' to 'coins,' see George Macdonald, *Coin Types* (Glasgow: James Maclehose and Sons, 1905), pp. 43–45. In the Ancient Near East, seals were used as early as the fourth millennium; see Cyrus H. Gordon, *Adventures in the Nearest East*, p. 78, which "tantamount to its owner's signature." Cylinders were pierced down the middle and suspended on a cord around the neck, see ibid. p. 79. Attention should be drawn to the fact that the signet served to identify the party in question; see *The Economy of Literature*, p. 33, and provided the 'symbol' of a transaction, ibid. p. 34—as we find with "the seal and thread" in the story of Judah and Tamar, *Gn* 38:18, 26.

Therefore, 'coin' (מטבע) was stood for 'pattern, structure'; see *Golden Doves*, pp. 138–142. In rabbinic tradition the human soul is God's "seal" (Mishna *Sanhedrin* 4:5); cf. "Allegorical Interpretation," I, 43–55, *Philo*, vol. 1, pp. 177–183; "The Posterity and Exile of Cain," 98, vol. 2, p. 383; "On the Giants," 66, vol. 2, p. 479; "Noah's Work," 18–20, vol. 3, p. 223, etc. For some background literature, see Wolfson, *Philo*, vol. 1, p. 75. Hence, the idea of archetypes in Philo and rabbinic tradition. Finally, it should be pointed out that according to both the rabbis and Philo, God's seal equals "truth," see *Shabbat* 55a; Philo, "Noah's Work," 18, vol. 3, p. 223. Therefore, it is subject to forgery and falsification; see *'Aboda Zara* 54b; Philo, "The Worse Attacks the Better," 35–40, vol. 2, pp. 227–233, etc.

44. Oral Law

See *Shabbat* 31a; *Yoma* 28b; *Berakhot* 5a. On the differences between *Tora shebi-Khtab* and *Tora shebe'al-Pe*, see R. Moses di Ṭrani, *Qiryat Sefer*, vol. 1 (New York, 1953), Introduction, Chapter 2; *Iyye ha-Yam*, 8d–10a; Saul Lieberman, *Hellenism in Jewish Palestine*, pp. 83–99. On their legal status, see *Golden Doves*, pp. xxv-xxvi. For an overview of their content and general history, see *Judaism*, vol. 1, pp. 234–280.

The expression *Tora she-be'al-pe* is not found in the *Yerushalmi*. It appears only three times in the Babylonian Talmud: in *Yoma* 28b, *Giṭṭin* 60b, and *Qiddushin* 66a. The *barraita* in *Shabbat* 31a is Babylonian; see *AdRN*, A, XV, p. 60, from whence this tradition originates. The expression 'two Toras' (שתי תורות) in *Sifra, Be-Ḥuqqotai,* X, 8 (12), 122a and *Sifre* #351, p. 408, connoting one written Law and another oral Law, is late. It would be well to remember that both these works were edited by Rab; see "Introduction," *MT* I. 66, and brought to the Holy Land by one of his disciples; see *Yebamot* 72b, cf. *Shebu'ot* 41b. In the citation from R. 'Aqiba (*Shebu'ot* 29a), 'תורות' stands for the plural of 'precepts'—not of 'Law.' In *Tosefta Ḥagiga* 2:9, p. 384 and *Soṭa* 14:9, p. 238, 'שתי תורות' stands for 'dissension'—not 'two Laws." Cf. *Yerushalmi Sanhedrin* I, 4, 19c.

In *Giṭṭin* 60b, the idea of 'two Laws,' one written and another oral is associated with R. Johanan's circle, Tiberias late 3rd and beginning of 4th century; see Appendix 45. It was introduced by R. Judah b. Naḥmani in a homily, referred to as '*darash*,' 'exposed.' The sense of this term is 'presentation to the general public,' rather than to members of the *Yeshiba*; see R. Jonah ibn Jannaḥ, *Sefer ha-Shorashim*, p. 114 in the name of R. Samuel ben Ḥofni Gaon; cf. Harkavy, *Zikhron la-Rishonim* III (1880), p. 25. This may explain why this idea was not recorded in the *Yerushalmi*. There is an allusion to this concept in *Yerushalmi Pe'a* II, 6, 17a; again, connected to R. Johanan's circle. The references to 'two Laws' in the *Midrash* are late; most probably coming from R. Johanan's circle. Let us point out that the homily in *Giṭṭin* 60b and *Temura* 14b about the "two Laws," reported as from '*Debe R. Yshma'el Tana*,' are *not* from R. Ishmael. As noted in *Kelale Shemu'el*, s.v. *masoret*, 10a, a tradition reported as *Debe R. Yishma'el Tana* is not authoritative. It means: '*someone* from the school of R. Ishmael has reported.' (In contradistinction to *Tana Debe R. Yishma'el*, meaning: 'it was reported by the school of R. Ishmael. This meets the objections raised by *Tosafot Pesaḥim* 5a *s.v. dibre*; cf. *Yad Mal'akhi*, p. 164).

The preceding runs contrary to the view of Abraham Rosenthal, "Tora she-'al pe," in eds. Moshe Bar-Asher and David Rosenthal, *Meḥqerei Talmud*, vol. 2 (Jerusalem: The Hebrew University, 1993), p. 448 n. 5.

45. Writing the Oral Law

The sources and principal ideas on the subject were developed by R. Israel Moshe Ḥazzan, *Iyye ha-Yam*, 76a–119b, to which this study is much indebted. For reasons too painful to be spelled out here, many distinguished scholars writing on the subject 'borrowed' most of their material and ideas from this sage, without due acknowledgement. There is one worthy exception; see Professor Y. Sussman, "*Tora she-be-'al Pe*," *Meḥqerei Talmud*, vol. 3, part I (2005), pp. 209–384.

The 'prohibition' against writing the 'Oral Law' is the invention of medieval commentators and modern scholars, with no basis in rabbinic texts. It would suffice to point out that *none* of the early codifiers registered such a prohibition (Maran, refers to it casually in *Shulḥan 'Arukh, Oraḥ Ḥayyim* #49:1 and #53:14; cf. *Kesef Mishne* on *Tefilla* 12:8). In this regard, attention should be called to R. Ḥayyim Abul'afya, *Miqra'e Qodesh* (Izmir, 5482/1722), 124a-b who concluded that this 'prohibition' could not possibly be Scriptural. (In his *Yishrash Ya'aqob*, Izmir 5489/1729), 91b, he registered the view that it is indeed a Scriptural prohibition, and accordingly raised a question which was left unanswered. Although this work was printed seven years later, it does not necessarily represent the later views of this sage. A careful reading of both these works will show that they were written more or less at the same time. It is rather obvious that the view proposed in *Miqra'e Qodesh* is a *consequence* of the question that he posed in *Yishrash Ya'aqob* and it therefore represents his final conclusion.)

We may therefore ask: what could the rationale of such an injunction be within the cultural perimeters of the 'People of the Book'? The question is particularly poignant upon noticing that the possibility of memorizing the entire rabbinic corpus belongs to the realm of myth (see *Iyye ha-Yam*, 101a; and above Appendix 32). It was designed to beguile the credulous, rather than instruct. The Chief Editor of the Talmud, referring to mortals like himself and his colleagues, noted how difficult it was to retain the sacred texts: "[Our efforts] in regard to forgetfulness is like pressing down mustard seeds with a finger" (*'Erubin* 53a). R. Ḥanan'el, *ad loc.* (*Perush*, p. 117b) explained:

> As when someone presses his finger on mustard seeds and the like and makes a dimple, but upon lifting his finger the dimple fills up immediately. The same applies to us, no sooner do we complete a (Talmudic) Tractate and commence another that we forget the previous (tractate). (Cf. *'Arukh* s.v. *eṣba'*)

See above Appendix 32.

In the long history of Jewish scholarship, there is only one single individual about whom it is possible to verify on the basis of his writings—not on the basis of fables by legendary pundits—that he had a total mastery of the entire rabbinic corpus. That individual is Maimonides, who represents the finest rabbinic memory in history. (This view was confirmed to me by the finest rabbinic memory known to me, the late Professor Saul Lieberman). Here is what Maimonides had to say about the likelihood of knowing the Talmud by heart, in his "Introduction," *Perush ha-Mishnayot*, vol. 1, p.48: "It is not within human faculty for any man to know the entire Talmud by heart." In a letter addressed to R. Pineḥas, a judge in Alexandria, Maimonides disallowed the possibility of knowing the rabbinic corpus by heart, *Iggerot*, vol. 2, p. 444:

> ... since there is no man on earth with the power to remember the entire Babylonian Talmud and the *Yerushalmi* as well as the three *Barraitot* [*Tosefta*, *Sifra*, and *Sifre*; see *Golden Doves*, p.96] which are the bases of the law.

Cf. *MT Talmud Tora* 1:10.

Ḥagiga 3a reports a story about two mute students at the time of R. Judah ha-Nasi. Upon their recovery it was discovered that they had mastered the major rabbinic collections, including "Talmud." It should be recalled, however, that at the time our 'Talmud' had not yet been compiled (see below Appendix 48). Even if conceding, for argument's sake, the possibility of a legendary mastermind surpassing the Chief Editor of the Talmud and his colleagues, how could a non-genius memorize what Maimonides declared to be humanly impossible? (There is no evidence that Talmudic students were gifted with supernatural memory. To ensure that the Tora "would not be forgotten from Israel," R. Ḥiyya would have "recited the Six Orders" of the Mishna to six children, probably because it would have been difficult to find a single student that could remember the entire Mishna; see *Baba Meṣi'a* 85b. Students and scholars had to work hard to prepare the Mishna, see *Ta'aniyot* 8a and cf. *Ḥagiga* 9b, and memorize the lecture; see *Berakhot* 28a, *Pesaḥim* 72a, *Megilla* 7b, *Baba Qamma* 117a. The lessons they studied needed to be reviewed periodically, lest they would be forgotten; see *Berakhot* 38b, *Pesaḥim* 68b, *Ḥolin* 86b, *Keritot* 27a; cf. *Golden Doves*, p. 96. Failing to review regularly, the student would forget his studies, see *Shabbat* 147b. Finally, the public was not impressed by someone who could rattle off by memory a rabbinic text and not know what he was saying; see *Soṭa* 22a. R. Johanan, *Shabbat* 114a said that a young scholar "that could respond to any question that he was asked, even in the tractate [that was being studied presently] in the *Kalla* session (see above Chapter 48), may be appointed as a public leader. If only in a single tractate, [he could be appointed] to a local position; if in the entire curriculum, [he could be appointed] to the *Yeshiba*'s Faculty." (For an analysis of that passage, see *Sefer ha-'Ittim*, pp. 246–248). Remarkably, such a scholar was not required to know by heart the entire rabbinic corpus! Similarly, what sages of the rank of R. Isaac Alfasi expected from students was to be familiar with basic rabbinic texts and ideas. With this goal in mind, sages throughout the ages produced different compendia of the Oral Law to help students become conversant with the laws. See Maimonides, "Introduction," *MT* l. 170, where he expressed the hope that his work could help the students to have the *halakhot* sufficiently well "organized" (סדורים), so that they could be easily cited—not quoted—by heart. The correct translation of the "Introduction," *Sefer ha-Miṣvot,* p. 3, is: "to facilitate the memoriztion by heart, some of it [the *MT*] to someone who so wishes."

More to the point, the rabbis never declared that it was 'forbidden' (אסור) to write the Oral Law. We read in two places in the *Babli* (but not in the *Yerushalmi*!): "written words you may not (אי אתה רשאי) say them by heart; oral words you may not (אי אתה רשאי) say them in writing." Before proceeding to analyze the content of this statement, let us point out that "you may not" (אי אתה רשאי) is not synonymous with 'forbidden' (אסור). Rather, it stands for 'improper' (אינו רשאי; see Mishna *Berakhot* 7:4); 'inappropiate' (Mishna *Berakhot* 1:4; cf. Mishna *Berakhot* 5:4; see *Yebamot* 7a, *Nazir* 34b, *Sanhedrin* 53a, *Zebaḥim* 49a, etc.)—but it does not denote a formal 'prohibition' (אסור). Often it appears as an instruction given by a higher authority (God, the Law, the judiciary) when addressing members of the court; see *Tosefta Sanhedrin* 1:8, p. 415, *Sanhedrin* 6b–7a, *Yerushalmi Sanhedrin* VII, 4, 24c; or in a judicial directive addressed by the court to the general public, *Tosefta 'Aboda Zara* 2:1, p. 462; *Mekhilta, Mishpaṭim,* (*Masekhta di-Nziqim*) I, p. 248; III, p. 259; (*Masekhta di-Khaspa*) XIX,

p. 319; *Mekhilta de-R. Shim'on b. Yoḥai*, p. 146; *Pesaḥim* 51a, *Giṭṭin* 88b; *Nedarim* 15a, *Qiddushin* 18a, etc. We hope to show that the meaning of 'אי אתה רשאי' in our case is the same as in the rule concerning the status of a parchment on which it was "written the *Hallel* or *Shema'* for a child to study, (that) although he is not permitted (אינו רשאי) to do (so), (nonetheless) they defile the hands," i.e., they have the status of a canonically valid text; see *Tosefta Yadayim* 2:11, p. 683 and *MT She'ar Abot* 10:9.

We will now proceed to examine the above statement. Let us begin by noting the symmetrical construction of the sentence: [a] "written words you may not say them by heart, [b] oral words you may not say them in writing," whereby a/b stand parallel to one another. Thus, if from [b] one were to conclude that it is forbidden to write oral words, then by symmetric logic it should follow [a] that it would be forbidden to quote Scripture unless read from a canonically written text—a patent absurdity! To circumvent this and similar difficulties it has been suggested that this 'prohibition' applies only "when officiating for others so that they could fulfill their religious obligation" (*Tosafot, Temura* 14b s.v. *Debarim*). It would then follow that if someone *is* officiating in the Synagogue on behalf of the congregation, he should recite the *Shema'*-prayer, as well as other material coming from Scripture, from a canonically written scroll (see *Ta'aniyot* 28a). However, the rabbis reported that the High Priest at the Temple in the Day of Atonement recited orally a section of the Tora (Mishna *Yoma* 7:1). Likewise, during the *Ma'amadot*-Services carried on by laymen at the Temple, portions of the Tora were recited by heart; see Mishna *Ta'aniyot* 4:3. For a brief description of these services, see Henry Malter, *Treatise Ta'anit* [Philadelphia: The Jewish Publication Society, 1978], p. 210, n. 230).

In the light of these and similar problems, exceptions were proposed (and further exceptions to the exceptions), with no textual basis; thus rendering the above rabbinic statement a case of whim, rather than a principle. In truth, this matter involves a fundamental methodological question. The attitude of offering offhand, dysfunctional explanations to avoid challenging texts, prevalent in some rabbinic and scholarly circles, is not helpful. The result is general disorientation, rather than instruction. For a rundown of the standard 'explanations,' see *Tosefta Ki-Fshuṭah*, vol. 3, p. 202. The presumption of a personal 'obligation' to read or to hear the reading of the Scroll of the Tora is without basis either in the Talmud or the classical codifiers; see José Faur, "*'Aliyat Qaṭan li-Qro ba-Tora*," *Studies in Memory of the Rishon le-Zion R. Y. Nissim*, vol. 1 (Jerusalem: Yad ha-Rab Nissim, 5745/1985), pp. 123–133. There is, however, a *miṣva* to read the *Megilla*, which is part of Scripture. Explicitly, the Mishna *Megilla* 2:1

stipulates that if someone had recited it by heart and not from a properly written scroll, he had not fulfilled the *miṣva*. Yet, when the rabbis inquired what the justification for such a rule was, they were offered some exegesis (*Megilla* 18a). Now, if there was in fact a 'prohibition' to recite the Scripture by heart, why did the rabbis not justify the above rule by citing the principle, "written words you may not (אי אתה רשאי) say them by heart"?

It is an indisputable fact that rabbinic material was written and studied. The *tanna* was proverbially known for "spelling the words in full"; see *'Aboda Zara* 9a, b and *'Arukh* s.v. *sefer* (2). In the *Sifra* (Codex Assemani LXVI), with super linear vocalization (it was completed copying in the year 1123), the copyist registered: 'end of *megilla*' (pp. 66, 128, 250, 287, 311, 335, 413; occasionally he also registered the end of one *megilla* and the beginning of the next (see pp. 335–336, 468), indicating, thereby, that the text was copied from scrolls. R. 'Aqiba, too, rehearsed (*shone*) the lessons by the light of a fire, *AdRN,* A, XII, p. 29, indicating, thereby, that he was reading from a written text. Likewise, the rabbis taught "that the moon was specially created for *girsa*," *'Erubin* 65a, indicating that students rehearsed their lessons from written material. We have mentioned before (Appendix 41) the case in which a sage obtained a copy of a tractate *'Oqaṣin* and "stretched" (פשט) it before he recited it, indicating that the tractate was written in a scroll. In addition to *Megillat Setarim* (see above Appendix 40), and *Megillat Ta'anit* (see *Golden Doves*, pp. 102–103), we are informed about a scroll known as *Megillat Ḥasidim* quoted favorably by the rabbis (*Yerushalmi Berakhot* IX, 5, 14d; *AdRN* B, XXVI, p. 52). The rabbis reported about private "note-books" (פינקס) written by sages; see *Shabbat* 156a; *Yerushalmi Ma'aserot* II, 3, 49d, and *Iyye ha-Yam*, 114b. Jewish authorities sent epistles from Israel to their coreligionists in Babylonia, informing them about judicial decisions; see *Shabbat* 115a, *Baba Batra* 41a, *Sanhedrin* 29a, *Shebu'ot* 48b, and *IShG*, pp. 89–90. Rab penned a question to R. Judah ha-Nasi, "between the thread-stitches" of a scroll, *Ketubot* 69a; see *Iyye ha-Yam*, 79b. By specifying that the threads were made of cotton (חיטי), the rabbis were teaching that the scroll did not contain Scripture (cf. *Megilla* 19a-b), but rabbinic material. Moreover, as noted in *Iyye ha-Yam*, 114a, the Talmudic expression, "he went out, he searched, and found" (נפק, דק ואשכח) describes a sage finding a hitherto unknown tannaitic text (*Zebaḥim* 58a, *Ḥolin* 6a, 31b). Likewise, the expression, "he came [to the *Yeshiba*] bringing in hand a tannaitic text" (אתא ואתי מתניתא בידיה; see *Shabbat* 19a, 145b; *Baba Qamma* 42a; *'Aboda Zara* 50a, b; etc, etc.), indicates that there were reliable archives containing rabbinic material. Occasionally, a sage finding a reliable tannaitic text would certify it before presenting it at the *Yeshiba*. Thus, the expression, "he arrived (at the *Yeshiba*) holding a tannaitic text in his hand" (אתא, ואייתי מתניתא בידיה), *Shabbat* 19b, 145b, *Sukka* 54a, *Beṣa* 26b, *Yebamot* 57a, 58a, *Soṭa* 24b, *Baba Qamma* 42a, *'Aboda Zara* 50a-b, *Ḥolin* 68b, *Bekhorot* 17a, *Nidda* 5b, 21a-b.

The rule "written words, you may not (אי אתה רשאי) say them by heart; oral words, you may not (אי אתה רשאי) say them in writing," is first mentioned in *Giṭṭin* 60b. It appears at the head of a three-string homily (a/b/c) [= דרשה משולשת] on the verse "… Write for thee these (אלה) words, for on the basis of these (אלה) words, I am contracting a covenant with you" (*Ex* 34:27). The three homilies were brought together to highlight the pre-eminence of oral tradition. Homily (a)—which is the main subject of this analysis—was said by R. Judah b. Naḥmani (3rd and 4th centuries): "written words, you may not (אי אתה רשאי) say them orally; oral words, you may not (אי אתה רשאי) say them in writing." Homily (b) is a *barraita* reported by someone from the school of R. Ishmael. By focusing on the deictic pronoun "[write for thee] these (אלה) words" (*Ex* 34:27), as if God were actually pointing at the Scroll of the Tora, homily (b) proposes that these, i.e., the words of the Tora, and only these, may be put in writing, "but you may not write *halakhot*" (as to the specific meaning of *halakhot* see below). Homily (c) by R. Johanan is directed against Christians who appropriated the Scripture, but discarded the oral tradition of Israel; see Section IV n. 120. The Talmud does not indicate the context of R. Judah b. Naḥmani's homily (on the original context, see below). From *Midrash Tanḥuma*, *Vayyera*, VI, vol. 1, pp. 87–88, we learn that this rule was applied to the *Targum* (Aramaic translation of the Tora). Specifically, that "… oral words," i.e., the *Targum* (which has the status of 'Oral,' see Appendix 61), should not be recited from a written copy. (R. Joseph, who was blind and could not read the Tora, was renowned for his expertise on the *Targum*, a text that had to be recited orally, see *Baba Qamma* 3b; (the comments by Rashi and *Tosafot ad loc.* s.v. *ki-dmetargem* are unintelligible to me). Conversely, "written words," i.e., the text of the Tora, "should not be recited by heart" (see editor's notes ibid.). Connected with this homily is a case mentioned in *Yerushalmi Megilla* IV, 1, 74d (cited by R. Isaac Alfasi, *Halakhot*, *Megilla* 14a), concerning "a scribe that was *copying* the *Targum* from a book" (the standard interpretation that the scribe was *reciting* the translation from a book, is wrong; cf. *Iyye ha-Yam*, 114b–115a). The scribe intended to produce a copy of the *Targum* to be used at the services. Since this contravened R. Judah b. Naḥmani's rule, the scribe was reprimanded. In this connection, we should point out that R. Isaac ibn Ghayyat and Maimonides expanded this principle to include the *qere* and *ketib* versions of Scripture, where some words are 'written' (הכתיב) one way but are to be 'recited' (והקרי) in another way. Therefore they ruled that in such cases, "written words," i.e., the 'כתיב' should not be said instead of the oral version 'הקרי'; and conversely, the oral version 'הקרי' should not be written in the scroll in place of the standard 'כתיב'; see *Golden Doves*, pp. 101–102.

The second source citing R. Judah b. Naḥmani's rule is *Temura* 14a-b. It concern a passage dealing with what appeared to be two contradictory sources, as to whether or not libations and other sacramental paraphernalia (מנחת נסכים) could be offered at sunset. Unable to resolve the contradiction, R. Joseph, head of the *Yeshiba*, instructed: "erase מנחת נסכים" from one of the sources. (It should be noted that the verb 'erase' (סמי) used in this conjunction indicates that the text was indeed written; cf. *IShG*, p. 56). On a visit to the Holy Land one of the participants in the discussion learned of another source according to which the emendation would be unnecessary. He said: "If I had an epistle (at hand) I would have mailed it to R. Joseph, saying: you don't (need to) erase מנחת נסכים." The Talmud then asks a question based on a string of three statements (see *Iyye ha-Yam*, 78b–79a), concerning the permissibility of writing an epistle notifying about an oral text. The first, in the name of R. Johanan, stipulates that those "writing *halakhot* are as if they burn the Tora, and whoever learns from them will have no reward." To further corroborate this point, homilies (a) and (b) mentioned above are cited. The answer is revealing: "A new matter, is different." In support for this distinction the rabbis called attention to the fact that both R. Johanan and Resh Laqqish, "were in the habit of perusing from a scroll of *aggada* on the Sabbath."

The reply was right on target. R. Johanan's criticism was directed against scribes writing *halakhot* for students who preferred to learn this material from codices, rather than from certified transmitters (*mashne, tanna*). The rationale for this criticism is evident once we realize that *halakhot* is synonymous with 'Mishna.' (On the identity *halakhot*/Mishna, see Section IV, n. 132. The Chapters of the Mishna are divided into *halakhot*; see standard editions of *Yerushalmi*, *Perush ha-Mishnayot,* etc. The current division of the Mishna into 'Mishna' (*sic*) is another index of the high acumen of the legendary masters of Talmudic lore). As mentioned earlier, the Mishna, in quality of *oral publication* required that the text be (i) conveyed orally by official transmitters, and (ii) thereafter by their certified students who, in turn, have learned the lesson by heart; see Chapter 33. What R. Judah b. Naḥmani was saying is that just as the text of Scripture can only be conveyed and corroborated from an authorized codex (*taj*), the text of the Mishna, too, must be conveyed and corroborated from authorized transmitters (*tanna*, *mashne*) and their students. Put in precise formulation, this rule states:

"Written words," i.e., the text of Scripture, "you may not say them," in the sense of authorized transmission, "by heart" but only from authorized codices. Conversely, "Oral words," that is the Mishna (and later on the Talmud), "you may not say them in writing." The reason is obvious. Prior to the destruction of the Temple, a work could be published by depositing (*manḥa*) an authorized copy in the National Archives; like *Megillat Ta'anit* that was "deposited" (*manḥa*) for all to read, to copy and cite; see *'Erubin* 60b, *Iyye ha-Yam*, 80a and *Golden Doves*, p. 102. Post-Temple Jewry did not have such archives. Through a strategic decision, having enormous impact on the intellectual and political development of Israel, the publication of the Mishna instituted a new class of National Archives: the memory of the Jewish people. Hence R. Johanan's censure of scribes that produced codices designed to help students wishing to circumvent the official transmission of the *mashne* and *tanna* and learn the Mishna 'on their own.'

The concern was imminent in the light of Christian appropriation of Scripture and their subsequent claim to be *Verus Israel*; see above Chapter 31. If the Mishna could be corroborated by a 'book,' in no time it would be appropriated by Israel's foes, who would then claim it as their own. R. Abin (3rd and 4th centuries), a distinguished disciple of R. Johanan, showed what could happen if the memory of Israel were canonized in a written text. In *Yerushalmi Pe'a* II, 6, 17a we read:

> If I (God) would have written most of my laws (= the Mishna), then you (Israel) could not be distinguished from impostors. 'What would the difference between you and the nations' be? These (the Jews) would put forward their Scroll (of the Tora) and these (the nations) would put forward their Scroll (of the Tora)! These (the Jews) would put forward their written notes [for the Mishna], and these (the nations) would put forward their written notes [for the Mishna]!

This passage should be read in conjunction with the passage from *Midrash Tanḥuma* cited in Section IV n. 120.

R. Johanan's criticism was balanced. He only rebuffed the conveyance and study of *halakhot* (= Mishna) from written codices, but not of other material. Evidence of this is the fact that he and Resh Laqqish would read from a scroll of *aggada* on the Sabbath. This was also the legal basis for mailing an epistle to R. Joseph about 'מנחת נסכים': R. Johanan had only censured the transmission of a *halakha*! However, since the epistle was about "a new matter," not a *halakha*, "it is different" and not included in R. Johanan's censure; see *Iyye ha-Yam*, 81a. Accordingly, there were scholars who regularly used written material for *aggada*, see *Yerushalmi Kil'ayim*

IX, 3, 32b. And yet, R. Johanan and Resh Laqqish felt the need to excuse themselves for using a scroll of *aggada*, by quoting *Ps* (119:126). Why?

The need to find some justification lies in the fact that at their time there were scholars, like R. Joshua b. Levi (2nd and 3rd centuries), who opposed, totally and unequivocally, the teaching and study of *aggada* from a written text. In *Yerushalmi Shabbat* XVI, 1 fol. 15c, we read:

> R. Joshua b. Levi said: Whoever writes an *aggada* has no portion in the world to come. Whoever comments upon it [the written text], will churn [in Hell, another version: מתברך 'is to be excommunicated']. Whoever hears it will receive no reward. R. Joshua b. Levi said: Except for once, I never looked at a book of *aggada*. I looked at it and found it written and learned... And yet, I am frightened at night. R. Ḥiyya b. Abba saw a book of *aggada*, and said: 'If what is written is correct, let the hand that wrote it be cut off!' Someone [in the audience] told him: 'It was the father of that man [himself] who wrote it [and nothing happened to him!]' He replied: 'So, I said: Let the hand that wrote it be cut off! And so it came to pass [that that individual lost his hand], just "like an error which proceeded from a ruler" (*Ec* 10:5).

The opposition was not against the study of *aggada* per se, but against the study of *aggada* from a written text. Evidence of this is the fact that R. Joshua b. Levi is depicted as a master of *aggada*; see *Baba Qamma* 55a. The reason, again, was motivated by the threat posed by the rise of heresy and ideologies bent on destroying Judaism. A 'book,' among the analphabetic and semi-literate, is a mighty amulet with magical—not literary—power. Thus, the opposition to *books* of *aggada*, containing esoteric material that could be manipulated by unscrupulous ideologues. The following story in *Yerushalmi Pesaḥim* V, 3, 32a illustrates our point:

> R. Simlai came to R. Jonathan. He asked him: 'Teach me *aggada.*' He answered him: 'I have a family tradition not to teach *aggada* to either a Babylonian or to a Southerner, because they are arrogant and have little knowledge of Tora. And you are from Nehar De'a, and live in the South.

Finally, some sages believed that the study of *aggada* in general was a waste of time. In *Yerushalmi Ma'aserot* III, 10, 51a, we read:

> Once, R. Ze'ira, R. Abba b. Kahana and R. Levi were seated (studying Tora). R. Ze'ira was teasing those [who were studying] *aggada*, and shouted at them: 'Books of Witchcraft!' R. Abba bar Kahana asked him: 'Why are you teasing them? Ask [them anything] and they will answer you [adequately]!'

R. Ze'ira asked a question to one of the students and a discussion ensued. At the end of the discussion, R. Ze'ira said to him:

—'Your explanation has spun over and over and it will keep on spinning,' i.e., 'there is nothing conclusive that one can learn from it [*aggada*]!'

Turning to his son, he told him:

—'Jeremiah, my son, keep on studying (the rule) about 'Two figs on one stick' [a halakhic question that was being discussed at the *Yeshiba*]—which is more valuable than anything else!'

By reading *aggada* from a *scroll*, R. Johanan and Resh Laqqish were defying their colleagues. Hence the need to offer some justification for teaching this material, particularly on the Sabbath (i.e., in public). For the critical text and notes on this passage, see Yehuda Felix, *Tractate Ma'aserot* (Heb.) (Ramat-Gan: Bar-Ilan University Press, 2005), pp. 173–174, and ibid, p. 7 n. 4.

In the area of contracts, rabbinic law distinguishes between two kinds of documentation, one intended 'to be written' (ניתנה להכתב), and a second 'not (intended) to be written' (לא ניתנה להכתב). There are some important differences between them. For our purposes, the principal difference is in the latitude of interpretation given to the court. A contract intended 'to be written' can be the object of wide interpretation, whereas if it was 'not (intended) to be written' is to be strictly interpreted. [On the basis of this the theory, Maimonides distinguishes between certain declarations of the testator made orally, which must be strictly interpreted, and a written will that could be interpreted differently than the testator's intentions; see *MT Naḥalot* 6:2; cf. *MT Zekhiya* 6:2]. The status of these documents is not affected by whether the contract was in fact put down in writing or not. Putting in writing a document that belongs to the 'not to be written' class will not affect its status, and vice versa; see *Golden Doves*, pp. 102–105. The same principle applies to the 'written' and 'oral' texts of Israel. Thus, we read in *The Mishnah of Rabbi Eliezer* (Heb.), VI, p. 122:

ומפני מה נתנה התורה ממשלה לחכמים כל זאת? לפי שדברי נבואה נתנו להכתב ודברי חכמים לא נתני להכתב, אלא חכמים מורין אותן לתלמידיהן ולתלימידי תלמידיהן הלכה למעשה

How is it that the Tora vested the sages with (interpetetive) authority?—Because the words of Prophecy [i.e. Scripture] are given to be written (ניתנו להכתב), whereas the words of the sages were not given to be written (לא ניתנו להכתב).

With this understanding in mind, R. Judah Almadari (13th–14th centuries) explained an enigmatic passage in *Sanhedrin* 99a, condemning someone who is "not attentive" (משגיח)—in the sense of not being sufficiently respectful—"of the Mishna." According to R. Almadari this passage addresses people "who belittle it (the Mishna), as if it would not be fundamental, since it was given orally and was not given to be written (לא ניתנה להכתב), while in fact it is the Word of God," *Sanhadre Gedola*, vol. 2 (Jerusalem: Makhon Harry Fischel, 5729/1969), p. 273; cf. *Shiṭṭa Mequbbeṣet* on *Temura* 14b n. 3.

Given that the Mishna and Talmud were not published 'to be written,' they retain their status of a non-book even when they were put in writing. In a *responsum* (*Teshubot* #92, 13a) addressing the status of written copies of the Talmud, R. Joseph ibn Megas wrote:

> ...the Talmud is the explication and interpretation of the Tora—not the true [i.e., pristine, original] Tora. Can't you see that it (the parchment where the Talmud is written) does not have traced lines [the earmark of a 'book' in Jewish tradition] as the true Tora has? From this (fact) you can learn that its sanctity (of the text of the Talmud) does not compare to the sanctity of the Tora itself, or even to the sanctity of the other books of Scripture. Therefore, considering the facts that (such a volume) does not render the hands of those who touch it impure [see above Appendix 5]; and furthermore, it does not require traced lines, [we may conclude] that one may not deposit it either on top of (a volume containing) the Hagiography, or on top of the Prophets, and of course not on top of the Tora.

Cf. R. David b. Abi Zimra, *Teshubot Radbaz,* 2 vols. (Warsaw, 5642/1882), vol. 1, Part II, #771; and Section IV, n. 161.

Concerning the status of portions of the Scripture that were not written in accordance with canon rules, matters are a little more complicated. There were Talmudic sages who regarded a scroll containing the *Haftaroth* (the portions of the Prophets to be read on the Sabbath), as a non-book. In their view, such a scroll cannot be used on the Sabbath, since "it was not given to be written" (לא ניתן להכתב). The final decision, however, was to uphold the dissenting opinion, and permit the usage of such a scroll (*Giṭṭin* 60a). This was not due to a special 'dispensation' (as per Catholic Canon law, see below Appendix 46). Rather, this decision was in line with the ruling concering the status of small parchment containing a portion of Scripture, such as the "*Hallel* or *Shema'* written for a child to study, (that) although not permitted (אינו רשאי), nonetheless they defile the hands," i.e., they have the status of a canonically valid text; *Tosefta Yadayim* 2:11, p. 683; cf. *MT She'ar Abot* 10:9. I would like to point out that ancient inscriptions and documents from rabbinic times are not germane to the questions of whether the Mishna and Talmud were regarded as 'written.' The issue is a matter of *legal status*, not of historical fact.

In conclusion, the Mishna and later on the Talmud belong to the class of documents that were 'not given to be written.' This means, first and foremost, that unlike the text of Scripture that is to be conveyed and authenticated from certified copies (*taj*), the text of the Mishna and Talmud can be conveyed only from official oral transmitters (*mashne, tanna*); cf. Section IV, n. 159. This understanding can help us appreciate R. Johanan's strong words against those "writing *halakhot*," i.e., the Mishna. Since such students would be relying on written copies, these scribes were in essence "burning the Tora." The sense of R. Johanan's charge is clear upon realizing that the whole strategy against the Christian challenge rested on the principle that *Verus Israel* is to be identified through her National Memory—not through books. The scribes facilitating written copies of the Mishna were in fact thwarting rabbinic strategy. Students availing themselves of such codices were undermining the very basis upon which the Mishna rests: the link *halakha*→*qabbala* 'authoritative conveyance,' which is to be effected by a frontal, direct reception from teacher to student; in the same manner as when God 'kissed' Israel at Sinai and gave them the Oral Law (see above Appendices 32, 35). Thus, R. Johanan added: "whoever learns from them [Mishna codices] will not receive reward." The rabbinic system of education was scrupulously maintained in the Geonic *Yeshibot*. In *IShG*, pp. 71–72 we read: "The Talmud and Mishna were not written," i.e., were not published to be transmitted in writing. Therefore, "the rabbis are careful to learn the *girsa* [of the Mishna and Talmud], by heart," that is, from certified transmitters, "not from written," i.e., pseudo-authoritative codices. In support of this tradition, R. Sherira Gaon cited the Talmud in *Temura* quoted above. This tradition was standard throughout the Near East, and it was followed in the *Yeshiba* established by R. Moses and his son R. Ḥanokh in Cordoba, see Chapters 49, 51. In Sepharad, the text of the Talmud had been originally delivered by R. Naṭruna'e Nasi "by heart, not from writing"; see Section V, nn. 12–13. This tradition reflects the principle that the text of the Talmud ought to be conveyed by heart, from an authoritative transmitter, rather than from codices copied without the authority of the *Yeshibot*. That was the case in Sepharad, at least until the triumph of the anti-Maimonidean revolution when the sense of *qabbala* was vacated to make room for 'Kabalah' (see Chapter 57). The change was only a first step in a process designed to transform the Tora into an amulet of super-magical power (see Section V). A few consequences resulting from this swap were noted by Maimonides in the *Guide* (see quotation in Section IV n. 173). We should call attention to the ancient institution of *Mishmara*, conducted every Sabbath afternoon, when the faithful gather to read a portion of the 24 books of the Hebrew Scripture and the Mishna. In this fashion, the text of the entire Hebrew Scripture and the Mishna is properly registered and transmitted to the community every single year. It is still scrupulously observed by some communities throughout the Middle East. The text of the *Mishmara*, and the sections to be read each Sabbath, have been recently edited in a work under the title, *Ḥoq le-Ya'aqob*, 2 vols. Jerusalem, 5755/1995.

46. Was there a 'Dispensation' to write the Oral Law?

A consequence of the notion that it is forbidden to write the Oral Law is the view that a special dispensation was issued to sanction the writing of the Mishna, Talmud and similar texts. This pivotal point was proposed by Rashi (*Giṭṭin* 60b s.v. *wu-dbarim*): "that it is not permitted to write the Talmud, but for the fact that otherwise the Tora would be forgotten." Obviously, Judaism, as all legal systems, recognizes that under special circumstances the authorities may issue exemptions or release someone from a legal obligation. Such exemptions, however, must be issued by either the political (*MT Roṣeaḥ* 2:4; *Sanhedrin* 18:6) or judicial (*MT Roṣeaḥ* 2:4) authorities—they cannot be inferred by an interested party! Moreover they must be temporary (*MT Sanhedrin* 24:4. For a survey of the principal sources and views on the subject, see *Encyclopedia Talmudit*, vol. 8, s.v. *hora'at sha'a*). Otherwise, they would be regarded as an 'abrogation' of the Law, and contravene one of the fundaments of the *berit* Sinai-Moab (see *MT Mamrim* 2:4; and *Studies in the Mishne Tora*, p. 16). What is especially disturbing about such a claim, from the point of view of traditional *halakha*, is that such a 'dispensation' is not explicit anywhere in rabbinic sources. One would expect that license to break the law, particularly in such an exact system as rabbinic *halakha*, would warrant a clear statement on the subject, either by the Talmud or Geonic authorities. The justification advanced by Rashi (*Temura* 14b *s.v. 'et*), based on his interpretation of *Ps* 119:126, that "when they do the thing for the sake of the sanctity of His Name, it would be worthy to annul Thy Tora, and it is better that it should be uprooted," sounds antinomian: through and through. In spirit, if not in fact, the notion that extenuating circumstances due to assumed mental and spiritual decay with the passing of time suffices, *ipso facto*, to abolish a law, seems to be modelled on the idea of 'dispensation' as per Church law, rather than anything remotely *halakhic*.

We shall now proceed to examine the alleged authorization to write the Oral Law. It is justified on the basis of *Ps* 119:126: "It is time to act for God, (because) they have voided Thy Law." According to Rashi *ad loc* this means: "that they transgress the words of the Tora in order to make a fence and boundary to Israel." See also R. Menaḥem Me'iri, *Perush Tehillim*, p. 247, etc., and subsequently Rashi on *Giṭṭin* 60a *s.v. 'et*; *Tosafot* on *Shabbat* 115a s.v. *lo*; R. Zeraḥya ha-Levi, *Ha-Ma'or ha- Qaṭan*, ibid, *s.v. itmar*; etc. In his Introduction to *Megillat Ester* (Venice, 5352/1592), R. Isaac de Leon reiterated the often repeated litany that R. Judah the Prince "expounded" (דרש) the above-mentioned verse, to justify "writing the Mishna." Such a *derasha* is an invention of commentators found nowhere in the Talmud. Similar 'justifications' to transgress a law for 'a good cause' was extended to other cases; see pseudo-Rashi on *Keritot* 8a s.v. *Nikhnas*; Rabad on *MT Mamrim* 2:9; Riṭba on *Yoma* 69a, s.v. *wb-medina*, and on *Baba Meṣi'a* 29b s.v. *tanu*; etc., etc. So convinced were later commentators of the soundness of this doctrine, that they did not hesitate to apply it, as a matter of fact, to 'explain' some 'difficult' passages in Maimonides; see *Kesef Mishne* on *MT Talmud Tora* 3:10; *Maggid Mishne* on *MT Shabbat* 23:26; and *Leḥem Mishne* on *MT Meḥussare Kappara* 1:10.

Respectfully, I submit that the above interpretation is unacceptable on two grounds. First, as pointed out above, it is fundamentally antinomian. The idea (Rashi, *Berakhot* 54a *s.v. 'et*) "that occasionally they abrogated (מבטלים) the words of the Tora to act on God's behalf" (cf. Rashi ibid. 63a s.v. *'et*, and *Giṭṭin* 60a s.v. *'et*), would make it possible to disrupt any legal system under the claim that one was acting for the "sake of Heaven," or for the "Sanctification of the Name of God," or to "safeguard" the Tora (see Rashi on *Temura* 14b quoted above). Who, exactly, is authorized to make such a claim, is—to say the least—problematic. Second, this interpretation of *Ps* 119:126 runs contrary to both its traditional interpretation as well as the literal sense of the verse; see *Targum ad loc*; *Midrash Tehillim* CXIX, 57, p. 501; as well as R. Se'adya Gaon and R. Abraham ibn 'Ezra *ad loc*. For a concise summary of the various interpretations, see Radaq on *Psalms*, pp. 276–277. With all due respect, we will see that not only is the above interpretation not justified by rabbinic sources, but it actually runs contrary to what the Talmud explicitly taught about the subject.

The above verse was first cited in Mishna *Berakhot* 9:7 to justify why, at a time that Israel was in one of the bleakest periods of her history, almost to the point of extinction, the rabbis instituted a rule urging the use of God's name when greeting a friend. To justify this enactment, the rabbis cited the above verse to teach that precisely at a moment of crisis, when God seemed to have abandoned Israel, we should show courage and trust in Him; see *Introductory Remarks*, Section IV. Thus we should mention His name repeatedly in our daily greetings. The Mishna reads as follow:

> ... They (further) instituted that one should greet a friend with the Name (of God). As it is written: "and Boaz arrived from Beth Leḥem, and said to the harvesters: 'May God be with you" (*Ruth* 2:4)... In addition it was said: "Do not feel embarrassed because your mother has aged" (*Pr* 23:22). It is also written: "It is time to act for God; they have made Thy Law void" (*Ps* 119:126). R. Nathan said: '(Have) they have made Thy Law void? (Then) it is time for God to act!'

Commenting on the Mishna and the addition brought in the name of R. Nathan, Raba, *Berakhot* 63a, remarked that this verse may be interpreted in either direction. "From beginning to end," as interpreted by the Mishna; in which case it means: "It is time to act for God—right now! Why?—Because they have voided Thy Law!" Or "from end to beginning," as interpreted by R. Nathan, in which case it means: "They," [we shall give details later] "have voided Thy Law"; i.e., have declared Thine Law null and void. Therefore, "It is time for God to act," that is: He shall punish them. See *Midrash Tehillim* CXIX, 57, p. 501 and Radaq on *Psalms*, pp. 276–277.

To clarify the context of Raba's remarks we should note that the previous paragraph in the Mishna reports a rule instituted by the rabbis to contravene the *minim* 'heretics.' Our rule, too, was instituted with the same purpose in mind. According to a tradition transmitted by R. Hayye Gaon, these *minim* were antinomian heretics who regarded the Tora as null and void. R. Hayye Gaon knew the details. To make public their view, the *minim* were in the habit of publicly invoking the Holy Trinity in their daily greetings. In response to this challenge, the rabbis instituted that we should mention *God's* Name in our greetings.

> When the heretics (*ha-minim*) faltered, they (the rabbis) instituted that one should greet his friend with the Name (of God). The reason for (having instituted such a rule) is the sorry situation (confronting the Jews, to be specified in what follows). Accordingly, the rabbis wanted that God's name should always be on the lips of the people. [The rule was instituted] because in their greeting, the heretics (*ha-minim*) would say: 'May you be blessed by the Father, the Son, and the Holy Ghost!' (ברוך מר! לאבא, וברא, ורוחא דקודשא!). In response, the rabbis instituted that we should say: 'May God bless you!' (יברכך יוי!)—thus distinguishing our [mode of greeting] '*shalom*' [from that of the *minim*].

Quoted by R. Zekharya Agamati, *Sefer ha-Ner* on *Berakhot* (British Museum, ms. 11361), fol. 50b. The attribution to R. Hayye Gaon is found ibid. fol. 51a.

Maimonides, *Perush ha-Mishnayot*, *Berakhot* 9:7, vol. 1, p. 91, further elucidated the purpose of citing *Pr* 23:22.

> It comes to teach that one should not disregard the rules instituted by the sages, although a (particular) rule may be old and dated. To illustrate this point, they cited Solomon's proverb ("Do not feel embarrassed because your mother has aged," i.e., don't be disrespectful to the ancient Law of Israel simply because it is 'old'!)

This point addresses the claim that the 'Old' Testament is voided by a 'New' one simply because one is 'old' and the other is 'new.' Concerning the interpretation of *Ps* 119:126 in *Giṭṭin* and *Temura*, see Appendix 45.

47. Hebrew *ḥibber* and Arabic *tadwin*

For psychological, rather than intellectual reasons, Professor Abramson, *R. Nissim Gaon*, p. 29 n. 2, failed to grasp the passage in *Sefer ha-Mafteaḥ*, 3b. There is no ambivalence or contradiction in the above, once we remember that Arabic speaking Jews used the Hebrew KTB not only in the general sense of 'writing,' but also as the semantic equivalent of the Arabic *tadwin*, 'to redact, to compile, to officially register.' See, for example, *Perush ha-Mishnayot*, *Megilla* 1:1, vol. 2, p. 344: *tadwin al-talmud*; cf. *Bekhorot* 4:4, vol. 5, p. 249. [In this sense this term was used by R. Se'adya Gaon, in *Perush Mishle*, p. 194 (the Hebrew translation is faulty)]. Similarly, according to a tradition recorded in *Sefer ha-'Ittim*, pp. 255–256, an illustrious sage, Prince R. Neṭruna'e b. Ḥakhina'e, who came to Spain from Babel around the year 770), "wrote (כתב) for the children of Sepharad the [text of the entire] Talmud by heart, not from a written [codex]." Here, the sense of the Hebrew 'writing' (כתב) is *tadwin* 'official compilation'. By emphasizing that it was transmitted "by heart, not from a written [codex]," the author was signaling that the conveyance of the text was done according to the proper procedure, and its authority derived from an authorized sage—not from a written codex! A more accurate translation of *tadwin* would be the Hebrew *ḥibber*; see *MT* "Introduction," ll. 54–55, where Maimonides states that R. Judah the Prince "compiled [*ḥibber* = *tadwin*] ... the book of the Mishna." Obviously, *ḥibber* here means 'redacted, officially registered' since, as we have seen in Section IV n. 161, Maimonides disallowed for such a [written] codex. Concerning the sage coming to Spain mentioned above, see Mordecai Margalioth, *Hilkhot Hannagid* (Heb.) (Jerusalem: The American Academy for Jewish Research, 1962), pp. 1–3.

48. *Gemara* and *Talmud*

The rabbis (*Baba Batra* 130b; *Nidda* 7b) established the following principle:

> One cannot learn a *halakha* either from the Mishna or from the Talmud or from a judicial act (מעשה) unless one had been instructed: 'implement (מעשה) [this]!' [Cf. *Eliahu Zoṭa* XVI, *Tana Debe Eliyahu*, part II (Lublin, 5657/1897), p. 132.

This doctrine was codified by R. Isaac Alfasi (*Halakhot*, *Yebamot* 17a; cf. ibid. '*Erubin* 11b; *Baba Batra* 58b), who stipulated that this principle is valid even when the Mishna has explicitly declared that the *halakha* is like a particular opinion. The same view had been expressed earlier by *Halakhot Gedolot*, ed. R. E. Hildesheimer, vol. 2. (Jerusalem: Mekize Nirdamim, 1980), p. 56; vol. 3, p. 352. It was subsequently accepted by other authorities, see *Perush R. Ḥanan'el la-Talmud*, p. 319; Maimonides, *Perush ha-Mishnayot*, *Shebi'it* 9:5, vol. 1, p. 259; R. Joseph b. 'Aqnin, *Mebo ha-Talmud* (Jerusalem: 5727/1967), p. 5; cf. *Studies in the Mishne Tora*, p. 39 n. 46. A good example of this principle is *Menaḥot* 37b, where R. Judah transmits the *halakha* in the name of Samuel, and it is rejected without the citation of a single authority (ולית הלכתא כותיה)! Notably, it was dismissed by Saboraitic, i.e., post-Talmudic, authority. (For further analysis of this source, see Appendix 53).

There is, however, a responsum by the saintly R. Solomon b. Adrete, vol. 1, #335 explaining that the rabbis meant only to limit the authority of the Mishna when it contradicts a rule

> ... stipulated by the *Gemara* (= Talmud); e.g. if they [i.e., the Mishna would have] said: 'the law is like the minority opinion,' or 'the law is like R. Eleazar *v.* R. Joshua.' However, when it does not contradict an accepted rule, why should we not learn [the *halakha*] from it [i.e., the Mishna]?

That sort of explanation does not provide useful guidance. R. Me'ir Abul'afia, in his *Yad Rama* on *Baba Batra* 130b, had called attention to the judicial principle that a judgment that "overlooks a matter in the Mishna, is reversible" (*Sanhedrin* 6a), implying thereby, that the Mishna is indeed authoritative. With reference to this, I would like to point out to an important passage in *Sifra*, *Emor* VII, 9:3, 93b (cited by Rashi on *Lev* 22:31; cf. ibid. *Aḥare Mot* VI, 12:10,74b; and *Sifre* #59, p. 125), on the verse "And you shall guard my *miṣvot*, and implement them" (*Lev* 22:31). It runs as follows:

> *And you shall guard* (ושמרת)—these are the Mishna; *and implement them*—these are the implementation (of the *miṣvot*): Whatever is not in the Mishna is not (subject to) implementation.

The sense of this passage is that the execution of *miṣvot* requires adequate knowledge of the specific rules and regulations (see Appendix 4), and that these rules are contained in the Mishna. Therefore, "Whatever is not in the Mishna is not (subject to) implementation." Thus establishing the fact that the Mishna is the most authoritative source of *halakha*! Incidentally, as it is often the case in Hebrew, *you shall guard* (ושמרת) is here interpreted 'to remember'—alluding to the fact that we must *guard* (ושמרת) the text of the Mishna by constant rehearsal and memorization.

One would like to know if there is substance—beyond R. Adrete's invocation—to the proposition that a later rabbinic rule could supersede the authority of a document published by the Supreme Court of Israel. The question is particularly poignant in view of the fact that the rabbis themselves taught that rules concerning the resolution of conflicts are not categorical; see *'Erubin* 29a; *Qiddushin* 34a; and *Yad Mal'akhi* ##23–24. (Concerning the difference of opinion between Maimonides and Rabad on this matter, see *MT 'Arakhin* 1:6 and *Kesef Mishne ad loc*). Finally, R. Adrete failed to address the rest of the passage stating that one may neither learn *halakha* from the Talmud!

To resolve the quandary posed by the principle "One cannot learn a *halakha* either from the Mishna or from the Talmud ... " some erased the 'ת' from *תלמוד*, rendering it למוד 'study'; see the commentaries of Rashbam, *ad loc* s.v. *wu-mor sabar*; R. Zachariah Aghamati, *Tractates Baba Kamma ...* (London: British Museum, 1961), 293a; and *Yad Rama*, ibid. To make this amendment consistent, other texts were also doctored; see *Halakhot Gedolot*, ed. R. E. Hildesheimer, vol. 3 (Jerusalem: Mekize Nirdamim, 1988), p. 352, and editor's note on *Halakhot Gedolot*, vol. 2, p. 56 n. 5. This permitted the commentators to establish such differences as 'before' and 'after' the Talmud was "written" (*sic*), etc. The doctored version, however, is not corroborated by early manuscripts; see Ch. Albeck, *Mabo la-Talmudim* (Tel-Aviv: Dvir, 1969), pp. 599–601. Rashi on *Nidda* 7b *s.v. ha*, proposed that "Talmud" in the above passage alluded to tannaitic material, and did not refer to *our* Talmud; cf. *IShG*, pp. 48–50. This view was accepted by other commentators; see Riṭba on *Baba Batra* 130b; etc.

R. Joseph ibn Megas (in his *Commentary* to *Baba Batra* 130b) proposed that "Talmud" in the preceding quotation alluded to the "Talmud" *before* it was edited by R. Ashe and his Court.

> Our Talmud constitutes a legislative pronouncement (הלכה למעשה). In view of the fact that it was edited after close reading and analysis, and [after] several redactions [see Appendix 53], is as if they would have said: 'it is a legislative pronouncement' (הלכה למעשה)—given that it was edited to be implemented!

This view was adopted by R. Zachariah Aghamati, on *Baba Batra*, *ibid*, 293a; R. Joseph b. 'Aqnin, *Mebo ha-Talmud*, p. 5; *Yad Rama*, *ibid*, etc.

To bring out the concrete meaning of this statement, it would be helpful to bear in mind that in the "Introduction" to the *MT* (ll. 111–112), Maimonides wrote that R. Ashe not only "edited" (חיבר) the Talmud but also "concluded it" (גמרו, root GMR). In Jewish law, *GeMaR ha-din* stands for the [i] 'deliberation process' when the evidence and arguments are weighed (*MT Sanhedrin* 22:9); [ii] followed by the voting of the judges (*MT Sanhedrin* Chapters 8–10; cf. 12:3); [iii] and concluding with the pronouncement of the verdict (*MT Sanhedrin* 21:3; 22:9; see *Kesef Mishne* on *Sanhedrin* 3:3; and ibid. 7:2, 11:8). After enumerating the different classes of law and judicial traditions edited in the Talmud (ll. 93–103), Maimonides emphasized (ll. 103–104) that R. Ashe edited the judicial determinations and traditions,

> which were adjudicated in the Court of that time, in accordance with the hermeneutical rules by which the Tora is explicated, and were decided by the elders [= members of the court], and concluded (גמרו) that the law is thus, all (of the preceding material)—from the days of Moses until his day—were edited (חיבר, see Appendix 47) by R. Ashe in the Talmud.

See "Introduction," *Perush ha-Mishnayot*, vol. 1, pp. 34–35, cited below. Maimonides' view stems from the tradition concerning the two revisions of the entire Talmud, conducted in the general assembly; see Chapter 37 and below Appendix 53. (The same applies to R. Joseph ibn Megas' statement quoted above, concerning the "several redactions" of the Talmud.)

The key term in the above quotation is 'גמרו,' root GMR. From the Aramaic translation of *Jb* 22:22, we learn that 'גמר' stands for a 'lesson learned orally from an authorized instructor.' The verse reads: "Receive, I pray thee, the Tora from His (God's) mouth (קח-נא תורה מפיו)." The *Targum* rendered the first three words (קח-נא תורה), as "*Gemar* thus the Law" (גמר כדון אוריתא). It would appear that a more literal translation would have been *qabbel* (קבל)—as it has been preserved in the more ancient *Targum to Job from Qumran Cave XI*, ed. Michael Sokoloff (Ramat-Gan: Bar-Ilan University, 1974), p. 40. [For a very valuable overview of the traditional *Targum* to *Job*, see Pinkhos Churgin, *The Targum to Hagiographa* (New York: Horeb, 1945), pp. 87–116]. I believe that the choice of *gemar* was intended to convey a fundamental aspect of 'oral transmission.' Namely, *gemar* does not merely refer to 'instruction,' but, specifically: 'instruction of the Law by the highest authority.' In this manner, the end of the verse, "and lay up His words in your heart," can be taken as exemplary of the classical rabbinic classroom, where the student was expected to memorize the lesson by heart. There is another aspect to this root. We had the opportunity to learn that "גמיר" in *Ezra* 7:12 parallels "עד תמם" in *Dt* 31:24. For that reason, it also conveys the sense of being 'complete' and 'thoroughly redacted'; see Section II, n. 6. We can now appreciate the rabbinic expression "learned the lesson from the mouth" of an authorized teacher (גמר שמעתתא מפומיה דרביה כרחבה דפומבדיתא), *Pesaḥim* 52b, to indicate that the sage in question had been the recipient of 'an authoritative and thoroughly redacted lesson'; cf. *Pesaḥim* 104b; *Beṣa* 27a; *Mo'ed Qaṭan* 22a; *Ḥagiga* 15b; *Ḥolin* 50a, 124a; *Nidda* 48a. Finally, some sages associated *gemara* in the Talmud with the above-mentioned *gemir* in *Ezra* 7:12; see *Midrash 'Ezra*, p. 128. In effect, in the Talmud, *gemara* stands for [i] a thoroughly edited lesson, which was [ii] formally approved by the *Yeshiba*. Its authority derives from the fact that thereafter it was [iii] 'instituted' (קבעו) in the official program of study, and therefore was known by academic tradition. Consequently, it was important to ascertain whether or not a lesson had been 'instituted in the *gemara*' (קבעיתו בגמרא, *'Erubin* 32b). See *'Erubin* 19a, 38b; *Pesaḥim* 115a; *Yebamot* 86a; *Qiddushin* 53a; *Shebu'ot* 12a; *Makkot* 23b; cf. *Berakhot* 12b. For further background, see *IShG*, pp. 41, 62–64; Rashi on *Yoma* 33a *s.v. Abayye*; *Perush ha-Mishnayot*, *Nazir* 1:2, vol. 3, p. 165; cf. p. 166.

Given that the authority of *gemara* stems from the fact that it was incorporated into the official curriculum of the *Yeshiba*, a view which had been originally derived from Biblical exegesis, even when the exegesis was originally intended as a mnemonic device (אסמכתא), acquires *ipso facto* the status of *gemara* by virtue of having been incorporated in the *gemara*-lesson. Accordingly, said exegesis is to be treated as substantive; cf. quotation of R. Ḥanan'el, in Shraga Abrahamson, *Perush R. Ḥanan'el la-Talmud*, p. 66; cf. *Yoma* 71b, *Ta'aniyot* 17b. The same applies to a view originating in *sebara* or of judicial reasoning. Once it had been incorporated in the *gemara*-lesson, it should be regarded, [as if it were] "*halakha le-Moshe mi-Sinai*"; see R. Ḥanan'el on *Sanhedrin* 53a. Cf. the note of R. Moses Zacuto, *Qol ha-Remez* (Amsterdam, 5479/1719), 133d: "גמרא... והיינו דתנן נמסרו"; [the new edition, Jerusalem 5754/1994, p. 389, has an *erratum*]; *IShG*, pp. 22 and 23; and Appendix 33). Therefore, although a *gemara*—lesson may have originally been derived from 'judicial analogy' (Ar. *qi'as*, see *Perush ha-Mishnayot*, vol. 2, p. 10), its authority is higher than 'legal opinion' (סברא). To illustrate, if one were to contest a 'legal opinion' (סברא) on the basis of an authoritative text, the dissenting party would surely retract it. However, "if he [the dissenting party] had received it as *gemara*-lesson he would not retract it" (*Nazir* 38b–39a, see *Tosafot s.v. Amar Rab Papa*; and cf. *Baba Qamma* 61a, *Ta'aniyot* 2b, *Ḥolin* 44b, *Nidda* 2b; and the story with R. Isaac b. Judah and Rame b. Ḥama, *Zebaḥim* 76b). Accordingly, R. Ḥanan'el (*'Erubin* 60a); R. Isaac Alfasi, (*Halakhot 'Erubin* 18a); and Maimonides (*MT 'Erubin* 5:20) codified the view of the *gemara*-lesson. On the authority of *gemara* over *sebara*, see *IShG*, pp. 43–46, and ibid. Appendix 7, pp. vi–vii; cf. Rama on *Yore De'a* #242:31; and José Faur, "On Martyrdom in Jewish Law," *Annual of Bar-Ilan University*, 30–31 (2006), pp. 401–403. The preceding will explain why Abayye (*'Erubin* 60a) inquired whether a legal view was a 'legal opinion' (סברא) or a *gemara*-lesson. When asked what difference that would make, he replied: "one that has become proficient in a *gemara*-lesson—should he be treated as if he were chanting a song?" (Concerning 'singing a song,' see *Ta'aniyot* 32a, and *Kelale Shemu'el* 8a). Consequently, he demanded from his teacher to be thorough when delivering to him a *gemara*-lesson; see *Shabbat* 106b and parallels. (On Abayye's predilection for the *gemara*-lesson, see *Yoma* 14b, 33a.) The description of Abayye's lessons as "chewing bones" in comparison to Raba's "juicy meat," in *Baba Batra* 22a may have been due to the fact that Abayye preferred to organize the teaching material as a *gemara*-lesson, while Raba preferred to develop his class on the basis of 'legal opinion' (סברא); cf. *'Erubin* 53a. The comparison of Abayye's lesson to "chewing bones" is an interplay of גמר—lesson/גרם-bone.

The study of *gemara* demanded arduous work; see *Baba Batra* 145b, cf. ibid. 121a; *Berakhot* 38b; *Nedarim* 41a; and Abayye's statement in *'Erubin* 53a. It also required a special method of instruction; cf. *IShG*, pp. 26–27. Some schools were renowned for the instruction of *gemara* and others for *sebara*. To take advantage of the situation, R. Me'ir learned *gemara* in the school of R. Ishmael and *sebara* in the school of R. 'Aqiba (*'Erubin* 13a). (This is why R. Sherira Gaon, *IShG*, pp. 26–27 found it necessary to clarify that the method used by R. Me'ir in redacting the Mishna— a method emulated later by R. Judah the Prince—was not the product of "his own mind (מלבו)," i.e., *sebara*, "but according to the *gemara*-method that he learned from his teachers." There were teachers in Talmudic times that managed to include both methods of study. Thus, after R. Ḥisda's lesson, some students "would first run through the *gemara* together" to commit it to memory, "and then examine the *sebara*" (*Sukka* 29a). Given that *gemara* is grounded on academic tradition, it can be neither construed from nor inferred on the basis of judicial reasoning; see *Giṭṭin* 6b. Furthermore, since *gemara* is a thoroughly redacted lesson, a student is not authorized to expand it; see *'Erubin* 38b; *Ḥolin* 103b. For the same reason, neither is he required to defend it; see *Rosh ha-Shana* 4a. Knowing a text at the *gemara* level presupposed a solid knowledge of the subject. (The term *gemara* in the standard version *'Erubin* 78a is not found in R. Ḥanan'el, Riṭba and other sages; cf. *Diqduqe Soferim ad loc*). Therefore, although one may not begin to learn chanting (= *girsa*) the *Book of Esther* on the Sabbath, if he had already mastered (*gamir*-knowledge) the text, he may study its *girsa* on the Sabbath; see R. Yehudai Gaon, *Halakhot Pesuqot*, ed. R. S. Sassoon (Jerusalem: Mekize Nirdamim, 1950), p. 38 (ll. 2–4); and the Hebrew version, in *Hilkhot Re'u*, (Versailles: Cerf et fils, 1886), p. 11.

The "masters of *gemara*" occupied a special position, second only to the "masters of Mishna" (*Baba Batra* 8a), and were compared to "flourishing pomegranates" of *Songs* 7:13; see *'Erubin* 21b. R. Sherira Gaon, *IShG*, pp. 43–44 explained that the high esteem enjoyed by sages with wide *gamir* knowledge was due to the fact there were revealed "to them the *ṭa'ame* of the Tora." Elsewhere, (*Tosefta Qiddushin* 5:21, p. 299) we are advised that at the end of the Patriarch Abraham's life, there were revealed to him "the *ṭa'ame* of the Tora"; cf. *IShG*, pp. 22 and 23. On the merits of a sage "teaching *ṭa'ame* of the Tora in public," see *Midrash Tanḥuma*, (Warsaw), *Teṣavve*, IX, 9, p. 86. The importance of this type of knowledge will be evident upon recalling that knowing the *ṭa'ame* of a law is an absolute requirement for qualifying to express an opinion on the subject; see above Appendix 19. Hence those who have mastered *gemara* are duly compared to "flourishing pomegranates"—ready to yield fruit.

A consequence of the preceding is that someone who is *gamir* but not *sabir* is better qualified than someone who is only *sabir*. R. Sherira Gaon, *IShG*, p. 44 explained:

> Given that one who is *gamir* can issue an authoritative instruction (הוראה) about those topics which he has learned, and issue a legislative pronouncement (הלכה למעשה). However, one who (only) knows a legal theory (סביר) cannot. What is the reason?—Because, how could someone having no *gemara* develop (his views) from a theory (סברא)?! However, someone knowing the *gemara* (about the law), the ruling would conform to what he has transmitted, and his judgment cannot be rejected on the basis of a theory (סברא)!

In line with R. Sherira Gaon, R. Joseph ibn Megas and Maimonides maintained that the editing of the Talmud, as finally redacted by R. Ashe's Court through two *mahdorot* (see Appendix 53), awarded it the status of *gemara*. It is pertinent to note that in Geonic and oriental tradition, the Babylonian Talmud was commonly referred to as '*gemara*.' (In the Maimonidean school [as well as in other regions of Spain] and in some oriental communities, the Talmud was known as *gemar* 'conclusion.'

Karraites, too, referred to the 'Talmud' as *gemar*; cf. the quotation in *Cairo Geniza*, p. 81. Since the text of the Talmud was conclusively edited (*gemar, gemara*), "we may neither add nor subtract from it"; "Introduction," *Perush ha-Mishnayot*, vol. 1, p. 46; see *Studies in the Mishne Tora*, p. 41. Together with the Mishna, the *gemar/gemara,* stands for "the formulated tradition" (Ar. *al-manqul al-manṣuṣ*) of Israel, *Perush ha-Mishnayot, Bekhorot* 4:4, vol. 5, p. 242. It would be of interest to note that according to the Geonim, *Sha'are Teshuba*, #61, etc., and R. Isaac Alfasi, on *Berakhot* 34a, etc., some early commentators and Maimonides twice, once in *Shemona Peraqim* IV, *Perush ha-Mishnayot*, vol. 4, 385 and another in *Bekhorot* 4:4, vol. 5, p. 242, the Talmud *Yerushalmi* is referred to as "גמרא דבני מערבא."

Talmud (Hebrew root LMD) is not synonymous with *limmud* 'study.' Its grammatical form is rare, and it had been examined by R. Solomon Finzi, *Mafteaḥ ha-Gemara*, IV, 93c. In my view, this grammatical form, like *t̲arbut* (*Nu* 32:14, see *Targum* and R. Se'adya *ad loc*), implies 'continuity, resolution,' as well as 'constancy,' and 'perseverance,' like with a devoted *t̲almid* (1*Ch* 25:8) 'disciple.' The same applies to the analogous structure *t̲agmul* (see *tagmulohi, Ps* 116:12) in the sense of 'constant and stable' reward. The same also applies to rabbinic idioms such as *t̲aḥrut*, *t̲anḥum*, etc. In this vein, *t̲almud* stands for a 'lesson,' either taught or learned, demanding 'constancy, unrelenting learning, and further inquiry.' It involves critical methodology; see Rashi cited by R. Isaac Abarbanel, *Naḥalat Abot* on *Abot* 4:16; cf. *IShG* p. 51 and *MT Talmud Tora* 1:11–12. In this context it is important to note that the rabbis associated *talmud* with the weights of a scale; see *Midrash Shemu'el*, p. 82. This supports the view that originally *talmud* stood for a *method*, rather than a particular subject or text; cf. *Berakhot* 11b, and Albeck, *Mabo la-Talmudim*, pp. 102–103. Probably that is the sense in which it appears in *Sefer ha-'Ittim*, p. 289.

Talmud stands for a session of intense study, when matters are critically analyzed and debated; see *'Arukh*, s.v. *mad* (1) and *MT Talmud Tora* 1:11–12, cited above, Appendix 31. The conclusions are tentative, and do not equal 'legal instruction' (הוראה), cf. *Kesef Mishne* on *Issure Bi'a* 10:10, and *Ma'aser* 4:8. Therefore, although someone who has drunk an alcoholic beverage during the Sabbath and Holidays is forbidden to impart legal instruction (הוראה), he nonetheless could teach *Talmud*; see *Keritot* 13b. [The printed text had been doctored; see however, *Babylonian Talmud, Codex Florence* (Jerusalem: Makor, 1972), vol. 1, p. 271; *Sifra* (Codex Assemani LXVI, New York: Jewish Theological Seminary, 1956), p. 200 where *Talmud* is excluded from 'legal instruction' (הוראה)]. In the final account, whether a lesson is הוראה or *Talmud* would depend on the instructor's intention, not on the text. This point has been made abundantly clear by R. Gereshom, in his *Perush* on *Keritot* 13b (= 15a). If the instructor used a text, whether of Scripture, Mishna or Talmud, as a medium to impart a legal instruction, the lesson would be regarded as הוראה, and he would be forbidden to teach it in case he had drunk an alcoholic beverage, such as on the Sabbath or Holidays. There is one exception. If the instructor regularly uses his lectures to impart הוראה, he should not teach at all after drinking, since the students would assume that he was imparting a legal instruction, rather than an academic lecture; see R. Gereshom, *ibid* and *MT Bi'at ha-Miqdash* 1:4.

Finally, the sages differentiated between Talmud and 'a (thoroughly) edited Talmudic lesson' (תלמוד ערוך); see *Shebu'ot* 40b; *Zebaḥim* 19a; *Menaḥot* 66b; *Me'ila* 17a. Such material is somehow analogous (but since it was not instituted in the official curriculum, not identical) to *gemara*. According to Maimonides, "תלמוד ערוך" stands "for an authentic tradition, which he [the author/transmitter] does not validate with exegesis and it does not originate from judicial analogy (Ar. קיאס)," *Perush ha-Mishnayot*, *Menaḥot* 2:2, vol. 5, p. 109; cf. Rashi, *Menaḥot* 14b s.v. *she'en*. This is the basis for the halakhic principle: "one should not discard it (תלמוד ערוך) because of a legal opinion (סברא)"; see R. Isaac Alfasi, *Halakhot, Yebamot* 29b; cf. ibid, *Ketubot* 63b; *Teshubot ha-Rambam* #345, vol. 2, p. 618; *Iggerot ha-Rambam*, vol. 2, p. 507, and cf. ibid, p. 443.

According to Maimonides, "Introduction," *Perush ha-Mishnayot*, vol. 1, pp. 34–35, the final redaction of the Talmud included four objectives:

> [1] To authenticate and explain the various and conflicting views around the Mishna.
> [2] To adjudicate conflicts concerning: (a) the text of the Mishna, (b) its legal definition, (c) and the principles deduced from it on the basis of judicial analysis. (Similarly in his *Iggerot*, vol. 2, p. 442, Maimonides wrote: "The Talmud has adjudicated each *halakha*, either specifically, or in general by [establishing] rules according to which the *halakhot* could be decided." Cf. *Studies in the Mishne Tora*, p. 39).
> [3] To record new laws and rulings by the sages, as well as newly enacted statutes. (Cf. "Introduction," *MT* ll.93–104).
> [4] To transmit, register, and set down hermeneutic and esoteric material concerning matters of faith and spirituality.

We have mentioned before that although a lesson may have been derived from exegesis, once it was given the status of *gemara* it could no longer be challenged either by faulting the exegesis or by offering an alternative explanation. The same applies to a lesson originally derived from a legal opinion (סברא). Once it had been awarded the status of *gemara*, it must be regarded [as if it were] "*halakha le-Moshe mi-Sinai*"; see R. Ḥanan'el on *Sanhedrin* 53a. In his *Perush* on *Baba Meṣi'a* 33a (Jerusalem: Mossad Harav Kook, 1988), p. 73, R. Ḥanan'el wrote:

> However, someone who scrutinizes the Talmud, instructing and explaining the *miṣvot* correctly, imparting legislative pronouncement (הלכה למעשה)—there is no measure higher than that (i.e., the Talmud)! Given that in the Talmud is to be found the interpretation of the Mishna and the Precept(s) known through tradition, as *halakha le-Moshe mi-Sinai*.

Accordingly, ignoring a Talmudic source constitutes "committing an error in a matter (exposed) in the Mishna," i.e., an authoritative text. That is the reason why if a judge or a scholar issued a legal decision, and "forgot said text, or [in the printed Arabic text and translation there is an *erratum*, read: *'o* (או) instead of *'an* (אן)] did not know it—then he had actually 'overlooked a matter in the Mishna'" (and the judgment is reversible); *Perush ha-Mishnayot, Bekhorot* 4:4, vol. 5, p. 242; see *Sanhedrin* 6a. The same applies to a *barraita*; see *Baba Qamma* 117a. Here the term 'Mishna' stands for 'authoritative text.' Conversely, a faulty or unreliable text is a 'non-Mishna' (אינו משנה); see, for example, *Berakhot* 36b; *Beṣa* 12b; *Yebamot* 43a; *Ketubot* 81b; *Ḥolin* 82a, etc.

We can now proceed to examine the statement, "One cannot learn a *halakha* either from the Mishna or from the Talmud or from adjudication (מעשה), unless he had been instructed: 'implement [this]'!" What the rabbis were saying is that rabbinic texts, including the Mishna, Talmud, etc., are not codes of law that would permit a student or an incompetent judge to declare what the *halakha* is because he 'had learned' thus from an authorized text. As a matter of fact, after citing the source proscribing "learning *halakha*" from the Talmud etc., three substantive notes were appended.

First, the exclusion is categorical only in the case of a 'sick' animal unfit for ritual slaughtering. In other cases, legal matters and authoritative texts could be generally cited to help gain knowledge of the matter at hand, as is customary in juridical studies.

Second, even when a court renders a decision, it could not be used as a legal precedent unless the court had explicitly instructed: implement [this]! Cf. *Horayot* 2b.

Third, Raba, head of the *Yeshiba*, instructed two of his disciples that had been appointed to the bench not to rely on his decisions if they did not know the טעמא, but, rather, they should follow what their eyes showed them; *Baba Batra* 130b–131a, quoted in Section V n. 321. The court's decisions were regularly signed by the judges; see *Yebamot* 22a; *Giṭṭin* 19b; *Yerushalmi Qiddushin* III, 12, 64d. Nonetheless, a *halakha* cannot be determined merely by quoting an 'authority' even as important as Raba, unless the judge is a competent sage *concurring* with the decision; cf. Appendix 69. The same ruling is applicable to a tannaitic source. A judicial decision rendered without knowledge of an authoritative source (or the general practice of the courts) could be reversed; see *Baba Qamma* 117a, and cf. *Sanhedrin* 6a. It is clear now why even a sage of the rank of R. Papa had to first consult with Raba before basing a legal decision on a rabbinic text unbeknown to him, which had been brought to his attention; see *Nidda* 12a-b. However, as pointed out by R. Mane, an authority who is *sebar*, i.e., a sage (see *Targum* to *Lev* 19:32) may derive the *halakha* from the Mishna, etc.; see *Yerushalmi Pe'a* II, 6, 17a.

Granted that the study of Talmud represents the highest form of legal studies (see *Baba Meṣi'a* 33a-b; *Yerushalmi Shabbat* XVI, 1, 15c; *Horayot* III, 5, 48c), nonetheless, neither the Mishna nor the Talmud are 'codes of law' authorizing a student or an incompetent judge to impart *halakha*. Only someone competent, preferably in both "the final conclusions (*gamir*, from *gemara*) and in the legal theory (*sabir*, from *sebara*) of the entire Tora," or at least competent in "the final conclusions (*gamir*) of the entire Tora," is authorized to declare what the *halakha* is; see *Horayot* 2b; cf. *Sanhedrin* 5b, 7b; and *Perush ha-Mishnayot, Bekhorot* 4:4, vol. 5, p. 244. Rather than codes of law, the Mishna and Talmud contain authentic legal traditions that point to "the path of the law" (דרך המשפט), which includes both judicial procedure and substantive law; see *MT* "Introduction," ll. 116, 123, 124; cf. *Iggerot*, vol. 2, p. 438. Maimonides used the same expression to translate the rule prohibiting the appointment to the bench of someone who "is not *gamir*"; see *Sanhedrin* 7b, and R. David ibn Abi Zimra, on *MT Sanhedrin* 3:8. In two places in the *MT*, in the section containing the 'Classification of the *Miṣvot*' according to subject matter, *Sefer Shofeṭim*, *Sanhedrin*, (*MT* "Introduction," l. 495, #2), and in the 'Register of the *Miṣvot*' #2, at the head of *Sanhedrin*, Maimonides reiterated the prohibition to appoint a judge that does not know "the path of the law" (דרך המשפט). In *Sefer ha-Miṣvot* (written in Arabic), negative precept #284, p. 313, Maimonides defined this prohibition as appointing to the bench someone who is not "fluent in the knowledge of Tora" (*shari'a*). [For both Muslims and Jews, this term stands for knowledge of the *legal apparatus of the 'Law'* (*'ilm shar'i*); cf. "Introduction," *Sefer ha-Miṣvot*, p. 2]. Since such an individual does not qualify as an "expert" (מומחה), his appointment to the bench is invalid; see *Perush ha-Mishnayot, Bekhorot* 4:4, vol. 5, pp. 242–243, and *MT Sanhedrin* 4:15. The qualification to be appointed to the bench varies. Maimonides, *Perush ha-Mishnayot, Bekhorot* 4:4, vol. 5, p. 244, referred to Tractate *Horayot* (most probably 2b) as the source for the rule stipulating that a judge must be "*gamir* in the entire Tora." This level of expertise, however, is not required for all judicial appointments; see ibid. pp. 244–245.

The concept of "the path of the law" (דרך המשפט) was basic to the intellectual background of the area. It was taken for granted, that to qualify to adjudicate a *halakhic* case, one would need not just fluency in rabbinic sources, but also in the "the path of the law" (דרך המשפט). That is why one is not authorized to derive *halakha* from the Talmud, unless one is fluent "... in the principles according to which it is correct to adjudicate the *halakha* from the Talmud," *Perush ha-Mishnayot, Soṭa* 2:4, vol. 3, p. 253. Therefore, in addition to mastery of "the *Babli*, *Yerushalmi, Sifra, Sifre* and *Tosefta*," to conclude the *halakha*, a sage should have

> ... an extensive mind, a judicious spirit, and lengthy time. Only then can it be known from them [the above-mentioned sources] the proper method concerning matters that are forbidden and that are permitted, and what the rest of the laws of the Tora are. ("Introduction," *MT* ll. 151–154.)

(About the four sources—*Babli* and *Yerushalmi* count as one, see *Golden Doves*, p. 96, and n. 83, pp. 185–186).

I would like to call attention to two questions submitted to Maimonides (probably appealing to the decision of a local judge), where it was specified that they were seeking to know the "the path of the law" (דרך המשפט) of the case in question; see *She'elot ha-Rambam*, #7, vol. 1, p. 10; and #66, p. 106. A similar term "the path of the *halakha*" (דרך ההלכה) was used by his son R. Abraham Maimonides, *Milḥamot ha-Shem*, pp. 50, 60, 67. Finally, I would like to point out that Justice Holmes delivered a lectured entitled, "The Path of The Law," see Section V, n. 303.

The Talmud represents settled law (see Appendix 68) as practiced in the various courts (= Ar. *al-'amal*) of Israel; see *Perush ha-Mishnayot, Bekhorot* 4:4, vol. 5, p. 242 (cf. *Perush ha-Mishnayot*, "Introduction," vol. 1, pp. 22, 48; *Ketubot* 9:2, vol. 3, p. 94; *Soṭa* 2:4, vol. 3, p. 254; *'Eduyot* 7:6, vol. 4, p. 329; etc.). Its authority rests on a single fact: the people accepted it as the supreme judicial authority. On the meaning of *'amal* in Islamic Jurisprudence, see Joseph Shacht, *Introduction to Islamic Law* (Oxford: Oxford University Press, 1964), pp. 61–62. See Section V n. 317.

There is a learned discussion by W. Bacher, "Gemara," *Hebrew Union College Annual* (1904), pp. 26–36, but in a completly different direction.

49. *Emora*

Generally, *emora* (pl. *emora'im*) serves to designate a Talmudic sage from after the period of the Mishna (2nd half of 3rd century) until the redaction of the Talmud by R. Ashe and his Court (2nd half of 5th century). The name derives from 'AMR, 'to say,' 'to make public'; see R. Eliahu Baḥur, *Meturgeman* (Izna, 5301/1541), *s.v. emora'a*, 6b. In rabbinic literature it stands for a 'sage skilled in the art of elocution and persuasion.' There were exercises specially designed to train the student in dialectics, where the teacher would assign one group to argue on behalf of one view, and another group to argue on behalf of the contrary view. These arguments would be [i] anonymous and [ii] prefaced with the expression 'אמר לך' usually mistranslated 'he said/ maintained,' but actually meaning 'he *could* have argued.' Accordingly, they cannot serve as evidence about the merits of the case, or the actual position of those arguing on its behalf; see *Kesef Mishne*, *MT Ma'ase ha-Qorbanot* 15:7. That it is why they are generally disregarded by the classical jurists, such as R. Isaac Alfasi and Maimonides. However, when the party proposing 'אמר לך' is named, it can serve as evidence that the party in question actually concurred with the position he was proposing; see *Kesef Mishne*, *MT Shebu'ot* 3:8. This point had been overlooked by *Yad Mal'akhi* #35. There are many expressions peculiar to rhetorical discourse, and was incumbent upon teacher and student to distinguish between a rhetorical and a strictly legal discourse; see for example, R. Menaḥem Me'iri, on *'Erubin*, pp. 244b; 245a, b; 246b, etc.

Semantically, *emora* is connected to the verse "Today you have declared (*he-'emarta*, root 'AMR) that the Lord is your God" (*Dt* 26:17). The *Targum* rendered *he-'emarta* as '*ḥaṭabat*.' As in Arabic, this Aramaic voice stands for 'persuasive and eloquent speech'; (see *Targum* to *Ps* 73:7 where *ḥoṭabehon* stands for 'articulation,' 'wording'; cf. *Midrash Tehillim* LXXIII, 3, p. 335; the note of R. Se'adya Gaon *ad loc.*, and R. Radaq *Perush*, p. 169. This is how the rabbis interpreted this verse, *Mekhilta*, *Shira* III, p. 126. Israel says:

> —(God) made me into a verse (*'imra*), and I, too, made Him into a verse (*'imra*).
> —He made me into a verse, as it is written: "And God declared unto you (*he-'emirekha*)" (*Dt* 26:18). I too made him into a verse, as it is written: "Today you have declared (*he-'emarta*) that the Lord is your God" (*Dt* 26:17).
> —But don't the nations of the world, too, offer their praises to God?
> —Yes, but mine are sweeter and more pleasant to Him!

See *Tosefta Soṭa* 7:10, p. 194.

The relation *he-'emarta*→*'imra*→*ḥaṭiba* is evident upon realizing that the Aramaic *ḥaṭiba* (which has nothing to do with the Hebrew homonym) means the same as its Arabic cognate *khaṭaba*, 'to deliver a public speech, to address someone.' In Judeo-Arabic this term is used exclusively for a 'formal proposal of matrimony' (it passed onto the Judeo-Spanish *apalabrar* 'to give your word in solemn promise of matrimony,' 'to be engaged'). Expanding on the *Targum* the rabbis (*Berakhot* 6a) taught:

> Said God to Israel: You have made me into a single *ḥaṭiba* in this world, i.e., you have declared My Uniqueness, as it is written 'Hear, O Israel, the Lord our God, the Lord is One' (*Dt* 6:4). I, too, shall make you into a single *ḥaṭiba* in this world, as it is written, 'Who is like Thine people Israel, one people in the world' (2*Sam* 7:23).

As it were, God and Israel exchanged vows of mutual love and commitment, as a groom and a bride. (This is precisely what R. Judah ha-Levi, cryptically quoted by R. Abraham ibn 'Ezra on *Dt* 26:17 had in mind; cf. *Kuzari* 2:55–56). Similarly, the expression "ומחטבי ברכות" from a Geniza fragment, in *Ba-Merkazim*, p. 166 stands for "the *formulators* or *reciters* of blessings."

Hebrew commentators overlooked the fact that the term *ḥaṭiba* in the above Talmudic passage comes from the *Targum*. Instead, it was assumed that it was a Hebrew word, failing consequently to grasp the sense of the sentence; see *Tosefta Ki-Fshuṭah, Soṭa,* p. 680. With all due respect, the term 'חטבות' in *Pr* 7:16 has nothing to do with the Targum '*ḥaṭiba*'; see ed. Frank Talmage, *The Commentaries on Proverbs of the Kimhi Family* (Heb.) (Jerusalem: Magness Press, 1990), pp. 36, 192, 365. Rather, the correct meaning is found in R. Se'adya Gaon's translation, that rendered 'חטבות' by the Aramaic 'ארוכא'—as per Rabbinic Hebrew 'ארוכות המטה' (Mishna *Sukka* 1:8, *Kelim* 19:6), that is "bedsteads' or two long boards resting on the four corners of the bed; see *Perush ha-Mishnayot, Kelim* 19:6, vol. 6, pp. 177–178. 'חטבות' are the corners (cf. *Ps* 142:12) where the two boards rest on top of the legs of the bed (cf. *Perush ha-Mishnayot, 'Eduyot* 7:7, vol. 4, pp. 329–330). There was a special quilt that "affluent people made (around) their bed strides" for decorative purposes; see *Perush ha-Ge'onim le-Seder Ṭaharot*, p. 52. According to R. Se'adya Gaon, the verb "adorned" (רבדתי) in the first part of the verse, also applies to the second part. So, that it reads, "I have adorned (רבדתי) my bed with tapestry; the bedstrides (resting) at the corners (חטבות) (I covered up, 'רבדתי' with quilt) stuffed (with padding) from Egypt"; see Arabic text, p. 69; the Hebrew translation is not exact. In a similar sense, 'חטבות' was used by the celebrated Talmudist R. Elḥanan (d. 1026), in an epistle, expressing the hope that God would "attire" the recipients as if they were "חטבות" or bed-posts, i.e., with 'stuffed tapestry' as prosperous men used to be dressed in. The letter was published by Prof. Abramson, *Bamerkazim wu-Batfuṣot*, p. 176 (l. 11).

Intimately connected with the preceding is the fact that according to the rabbis 'AMR (in contradistinction to *dibber*) denotes 'placid, temperate speech'; see *Mekhilta de-R. Yishma'el, Yitro, Beḥodesh*, II, p. 207; and *Midrash Tanḥuma, Vayyggash* 7, vol. 1, p. 206—a point that passed to the *Vulgate*; cf. Cyrus H. Gordon, "Rabbinic Exegesis in the Vulgate and Proverbs," *Jourrnal of Biblical Literature* 49 (1930), p. 391. The *emora*, too, like the Arabic *khaṭib*, was an 'orator' skilled in the art of eloquence and persuasion. His specific function had to do with the *Yeshiba* method of instruction. At the *Yeshiba*, the teacher conceptualized his lesson into a highly dense formula, and did not fully expound the lesson directly to the students. The task to expose and develop the lesson was left to the *emora*. His duty was twofold: to further explain, expand and develop the subject-matter, and to serve as a kind of loudspeaker, enunciating the material, clearly and loudly, to the students. The teacher remained seated and the *emora* would stand, bending down to hear *directly* from the mouth of the master the kernel of the lesson (see *Mo'ed Qaṭan* 21a, and the comic incident reported in *Sanhedrin* 7b). Generally, the classroom consisted of eight rows of students (see *Menaḥot* 29b; probably comprising eight students each. Thus the rule, *Soṭa* 5a, that an advanced student should only have "one eighth of one eighth" of self-pride; i.e., that he should bear the level of self-esteem tolerated of a novice). Depending on the row where the students were seated they would discuss the material with the *emora* and between themselves. Those seated in the front row would finally engage the teacher in an in-depth discussion of the lesson, witnessed by the entire student body; see *Ḥolin* 137b. The number of *emora'im* required for a given lesson would therefore depend on the number of students attending the class; see *Ketubot* 106a. Many distinguished sages, among them Rab, acted occasionally as the *emora* of another sage, see *Yoma* 20b.

A similar practice was adopted in the public *derasha*. The teacher or lecturer sat and the *emora* would stand and transmit the lecture; see *'Erubin* 16b, 104a; *Ta'aniyot* 8a; *Giṭṭin* 43a; *Baba Batra* 127a; *Sanhedrin* 44a; *Zebaḥim* 18a, 94b; *Ḥolin* 100a; *Keritot* 13b; *Nidda* 68a. The rabbis relate the *emora* institution to Moses and Aaron. According to *Midrash Tanḥuma, Va'era*, 10, vol. 2, p. 24, when Moses said to God that he could not possibly speak before Pharaoh, because he "was not a man of words" (*Ex* 4:10), God assured him that Aaron would assist him, "In the same manner that one who is delivering a public homily, the *emora* says before him"—the teacher, and then proceeds to expand and clearly enunciate the homily to the audience. "You (Moses) too, speak whatever I prescribe to you, and your brother Aaron will say it to Pharaoh."

The post-Mishna sage is designated *emora* because, as it were, he was expanding and enunciating the voice of the ancient masters to the classroom. There is a substantial reason for that. As we are reminded by R. Sherira Gaon, *IShG*, p. 36, the Mishna contains mainly "root-principles" redacted "in a concise style" (Aramaic *qeyaṭa* = Heb. *qeṣara*), as well as cryptic expressions (*remez*, see Appendix 31; and Section IV, notes 180, 181. The task of the Talmudic *emora'im* is to expose these matters to the future generations of students. Their authority was supreme. To wit, on the basis of their teachings, the sages would choose to depart from standard canons and rule in favor of the minority opinion; see *IShG*, p. 55; and *Teshubot ha-Geonim,* Harkavi, #439, p. 232. Hence, the rule of Rashbam on *Pesaḥim* 101b s.v. *leqib'e*, "that the [Talmudic] *emora* routinely expands"; cf. *Tosafot Beṣa* 25a, s.v. *kan*. Obviously, it was intended only as a *general*—not a categorical—rule; this meets the objections raised by *Yad Mal'akhi* #53.

In my view, the post-Talmudic *emora*, too, was also in charge of *expanding* the lesson taught at school, regardless of subject; as per *Targum* on *Job* 3:18: "the schoolchildren would no longer hear the voice of the *emora'a*."

50. National Publication for Use in Constitutional Interpretation: the Jewish and the US Systems

In the Jewish legal system the Tora is both the Constitution of Israel and its primary legal code (see above Chapters 6, 10 and Appendix 10). In Rabbinic times, to be quoted in the legal interpretation of the Tora or Constitution of Israel, a source or view had to be formally published, e.g., either as the Mishna, published by R. Judah the Prince (see Chapters 43–44), or the Talmud, published by the last National Court of Israel (see above Appendix 48). Sources and opinions that were not published by a national institution, such as *Sifra, Sifre* and various collections of *barraitot*, although proceeding from respected source, needed to be certified by the *Yeshiba* or *Bet Midrash* to qualify as a source of constitutional interpretation (see Chapters 45, 57). The Jewish Supreme Court deals directly with constitutional interpretation, in contrast to only analyzing prior judicial decisions or authorized statements of the Law as being correct or 'constitutional,' as is often the case in modern Western jurisprudence.

The USA legal system does not have a mechanism by which the national documentation and sources that could serve as authoritative material for constitutional interpretation are published. The values and collective mind frame (or *Mental Law*) that produced the US Constitution have not been officially recorded in a *national* volume. While US statutes and appellate opinions are in fact published, they are never officially conveyed (*nimsar*) to the general public. Even the US Constitution is not conveyed (*nimsar*) to the people, and thus there can never be a *hora'ath ta'uṭ*, or Constitutional reading that is objectively wrong"; see José Faur, "Law and Hermeneutics in Rabbinic Tradition." *Cardozo Law Review* 14 (1993), pp. 1657–1679. Thus 'publication' does not confer the same rights on US citizens that official publication confers on Israelites. A point in case is *The Federalist Papers* whose value as source of constitutional exegesis continue to be vigorously debated among constitutional scholars; for a critical and highly informative overview, see Dan T. Coenen, "A Rhetoric for Ratification: the Argument of *The Federalist* and its Impact on Constitutional Interpretation," *Duke Law Journal* 56 (2006), pp. 469–543. In this respect, the American legal system lacks an identifiable 'Mental Law' or National Memory. Rather, statutes seem to be self-executing and no publication is required for them to be effective. Once the governor or president, as appropriate, signs the law, it is effective.

In brief, our modern legal systems have neither a national depository of the legal decisions and opinions, parallel to the Mishna and Talmud; nor an equivalent to the *miṣva* to write a *Sefer* of the US Constituton, to be read and cherish; see below Appendix 62; nor a public forum 'to proclaim the Constitution,' as per the weakly reading of the Tora; see quotation from Josephus, in Section III, n. 343. In fact, modern civic education does not provide to the general student the necessary learning to properly understand and appreciate the Law of the land. And yet, as the ancient jurists taught: *Ignorantia non excusat lex.*

51. *Tanya Kevatteh* (תניא כוותיה)

It means there is 'a *tanya* that corroborates *his* view' (תניא כוותיה). It is used in the Babylonian Talmud when in the course of examining a thesis developed by a sage in the Holy Land, it was discovered that there was some tannaitic material supporting up that thesis. The terms appears in connection with lessons develped by R. Johanan, see: *Rosh ha-Shana* 3a; *Soṭa* 46b; *Giṭṭin* 87a; *'Aboda Zara* 53b; etc.; by R. Ḥiyya bar Abba, see: *Baba Batra* 82b; and by R. Amme, see: *Nedarim* 75a. Sometimes, however, a tannaitic source is mentioned not to corroborate, but to insinuate that the *emora* may be plagiarizing; see *Yebamot* 91a; *Ketubot* 19a; *Baba Batra* 133a. Our point meets the objection raised by Rashbam on *Pesaḥim* 101b s. v. *hakhi garsennan*. Quite often, this expression is used also to support a dissenting *emora* by quoting a *tanya* (תניא כוותיה); cf. *Sanhedrin* 21b as cited in *Midrash Daniel and Ezra*, p. 127 and editor's n. 11.

52. Leaning Towards the Majority

From its incipient moment, the Jewish legal systems recognized areas requiring judicial discretion and interpretation—the whole area of *Dinim Mufla'im* (see above Chapter 8)—or legislative action, to be resolved by a majority vote. (In Judaism both the legislature and judiciary are the prerogative of the *Sanhedrin* or Supreme Court). The justification for this procedure is *Ex* 23:2. This verse comprises three segments. First, it prohibits "following the majority to do iniquity (לרעות)." As per the *Targum* (לאבאשה), Hebrew 'לרעות' is a transitive verb. It addresses a judge convinced that the majority is erroneous. In such a case, the judge holding a minority opinion should not say, 'since anyhow the majority view will prevail, I might as well vote with them, so that the verdict of the court will be unanimous.' Thus the Tora instructs the judge: "Do not follow the majority opinion, to do [what in your view is] an inequity." The second segment reads: "and do not argue (תענה) in a litigation, to sway (לנטות)." Hebrew לנטות, is also a transitive verb; see R. Se'adya's translation. It applies to a judge either arguing just for the sake of departing from the established procedure; cf. *Dt* 27:19, and the *Targum*'s and R. Se'adya's translation; as well as to a judge deliberately *refraining* from raising an issue that could have pointed out to the court another aspect of the case; see *Targum ad loc*. The third segment instructs a judge holding a minority opinion to accept the verdict of the court, although in his view it is erroneous. Later (*Ex* 23:6–7) the Tora addresses a judge who is convinced that the accused, who appears "innocent and righteous" is actually guilty. The judge is instructed not to twist, either the law or the facts, for the sake of 'fairness.' Concerning a criminal who had either manipulated the judicial process or was unfairly exonerated by the court, God promises: "I will not regard as righteous, someone who is guilty"; i.e., his punishment is to be taken by God, not men. In case a judge is convinced that one of the witnesses is fraudulent, or that one of the plaintiffs is fooling the court, he should excuse himself (*MT Sanhedrin* 24:3), but should not twist either the law or the facts.

New cases without legal precedent were debated and decided by a majority vote; see Mishna *Yadayim* 3:5; 4:1, 3; cf. *Tosefta Sanhedrin* 7:1, p. 425; *Sanhedrin* 88b; "Introduction," *Perush ha-Mishnayot*, vol. 1, p. 4. The same applies to judicial uncertainties, where the law is not explicit or sufficiently clear; see *MT Ishut* 12:18; 18:19; *Zekhiyya* 3:8, 6:14; *Shekhenim* 12:1; *She'ela wu-Fiqqadon* 4:4; *Malve ve-Love* 14:3, 25:14; *Ṭo'en ve-Niṭ'an* 3:14, 5:10, 9:5.

The Jewish legal system excludes lawyers. The justices must fully conceptualize both sides of the case and simultaneously play the role of attorney and of judge. Therefore, is not sufficient for a member of the court to show that his view conforms to the law, but he has to show that he had also taken into account the contrary opinion. This attitude helps create an environment in which both sides of the case express "the words of the Living God." The final vote is the result of persuasion, not mere formal correctness. The rabbis acknowledged that members of the School of Shammai were sharper in their legal reasoning (*Yebamot* 14a). Nonetheless, the *halakha* was decided in favor of the School of Hillel because they were more courteous and understanding; taking into account the opposite view (*'Erubin* 13b). In this fashion the *halakha* is established on the basis of consensus and practical reasoning, rather than rigorous formalism.

Legal argumentation and rhetorical discourse presuppose a common foundation accepted by all parties. For the Hebrews, this is the Scripture, serving as the common ground, with a *sensus communis* or meaning of the text shared by the entire nation: sage and ordinary, traditional or sectarian (see *Sanhedrin* 33b and *Horayot* 4a, b). Therefore, it was incumbent on jurists and judges to express their views through Scripture and appeal to the *sensus communis* of the public, more or less, as we expect the decisions of our judges today to reflect public reasoning. There is an important aspect to be considered. Argumentation and modes of interpretation are not in themselves sources of authority, but only means to *persuade* the public by appealing to their cultural setting. Concerning the homilies (דרשות) of the rabbis, Maimonides explained that the methodology "is understood among those who comprehend their (the sages) words." Namely, "that for them (the sages) this is a form of poetic license (Ar. *nawadir al-sha'riya*), not the actual meaning of the text" (*Guide* III, 43, p. 419, ll. 24–26; cf. *Perush ha-Mishnayot, Sheqalim* 1:4, vol. 2, p. 207; there is an error in the Arabic text and it should read: *al-nawadir*). Erroneously, some Jewish scholars "imagine that [the *derashot*] intend to convey the actual meaning of that verse" (ibid. ll. 26–28). Consequently,

> ... they struggled to demonstrate and defend what they imagined to have been the correctness of the *derashot*. Since they believed that it was the actual meaning of the text, and that *derashot* were equal in rank to the legal tradition [that they conveyed]; failing to grasp the dissimilarity between them (legal tradition) with what (merely) was poetic license. In those days that (peculiar) methodology was popular and commonly used by everyone, as poetry is used nowdays by poets. (Ibid. p. 420, ll. 1–6)

Cf. "Introduction," *Perush ha-Mishnayot*, vol. 1, pp. 35–41. On 'poetic license,' see *Homo Mysticus*, p. 111.

A good model for *dinim mufla'im* is Quantum Mechanics, where a particle has many possible coordinates simultaneously (as provided by Schroedinger Equations). However, once you actually look at the particle via experiment/observation, the multiple possibilities coalesce into one—and only one—set of co-ordinates. In this fashion, the 'multivalent potentiality' of a particle becomes confined to one state, post-observation. Similarly, the various possibilities to execute a *miṣva* coalesce into one and only one, post-*perush* of *dinim mufla'im*, via the thirteen rules of rabbinic hermeneutics; see quotation in Section II, n. 104.

By way of conclusion let me point out the following three principles, intimately bound to the above. First, the perennial ambiguity intrinsic to *dinim mufla'im*. Simply put, there are aspects in the Law that escape a final, permanent and unexceptional definition. The Law cannot be executed by applying a certain code, as per classical mechanics. Rather, the court is charged to "lean" (להטות) in the direction pointed to by the majority, but it does not have the authority to restructure the Law, eradicate all vagueness, and render the text univocal, for all time to come. Second (and as a consequence of the preceding), although a superior court should not overrule a statute that was enacted by a previous court, unless it regards itself more knowledgeable and competent, if said statute was promulgated on the basis of a homily, the Geonim, Maimonides, as well as other rabbinic authorities, maintain that a later court may overrule it; see *Studies in the Mishne Tora*, pp. 31–32, 49. Finally, the authority of the court is to be expressed through rhetorical discourse, based on the foundations of Scripture, as rooted in the collective consciousness of the people. Thus, it would be incumbent upon the court to appeal to these values, rather than invoke violence or the threat of violence, celestial or otherwise.

For some insights on this subject, see R. Ḥayyim Alfandari, *Esh Dat*, 23d–25d; and *Justice, Law and Argument*, Chapter 14.

53. *Mahdora*

In Scripture and rabbinic literature the root HDR stands for 'splendor,' 'glory'; see *Dan* 4:15. Hence the sense of *meHaDdeRin* or praising God's 'splendor and glory' in the liturgy; see *Mekhilta de-R. Shim'on b. Yoḥai*, XIV, 14, p. 56; Mishna *Pesaḥim* 10:5; and cf. *Dan* 4:34. In a similar vein we find 'beautifying (*HiDduR*) a *miṣva*'; see *Baba Qamma* 9b and *Shabbat* 21b; and cf. *Shabbat* 133b and *Sukka* 11b. [The use of *mehadderin* to indicate a 'higher' standard of *prohibited* food is another illustration of the caliber of Tora-knowledge and intellectual honesty of those involved in the packaging and marketing of Judaism]. There is a homonym, from the root DWR 'circle' and 'serpentine,' as in a winding road; see *Is* 45:2 and R. Se'adya Gaon, *Tafsir*, p. 100; R. Judah ibn Bala'am, *Perush Yesha'yahu*, p. 189; R. Jonah ibn Jannaḥ, *Sefer ha-Shorashim, s.v.* HDR p. 117. Radaq, *Sefer ha-Shorashim, s.v.* HDR pointed to *Ḥolin* 113a where this root appears in the sense of 'serpentine,' as in 'coiled intestine' (*HaDRa*). In rabbinics, this root is also used in the sense of 'reverting' (your opinion, i.e., 'changin your mind'!), e.g., *HaDuR bakh*, in *Baba Meṣi'a* 49a, 51a, etc. or: *aHDaR bakh*, *Baba Batra* 111a, etc. The Aramaic expression *le-'ahdure* in *Qiddushin* 22a stands for the Hebrew "go around [begging] from door to door"; see Mishna *Ketubot* 13:3, *Baba Batra* 9:1; *Shabbat* 151b; cf. Rashi on *Qiddushin* 22a *s.v. le-'ahdure* in *Qiddushin* 22a; and R. Solomon Farḥon, *Maḥberet he-'Arukh*, ed. S. Gottlieb Stern (Presburg 5604/1844), 16b, *s.v.* HDR.

In our case the term *maHDoRa* stands for the thirty-year program 'cycle,' encompassing the entire Talmud. It is semantically close to the Latin *curriculum*, 'running course'; *curro* 'to move quickly,' and finally a 'program of study.' R. Jonah ibn Jannaḥ, *Sefer ha-Shorashim*, s.v. HDR, p. 117, registers a rabbinic expression (which I was unable to locate) *HoDRana di-qarta*, 'the path encircling a city' (could it be an *erratum* for: הדורה דכנתא, at *Ḥolin* 113a?)—somehow akin to *mahdora* encircling the entire study program. In Talmudic Aramaic *medorta* [= *mehdorta*] means 'to reach and catch someone'; see *Teshubot ha-Ge'onim* (Harkavi), #330, p. 158.

The fact that there were two such cycles explains why a view presented as conclusive (סתם) in the first *Mahdora* is rejected in the second *Mahdora*, on the basis of new evidence; see Section IV, n. 257. (This is why Maimonides decides in favor of the authority mentioned *afeterwards*, since it represents the second and final *Mahdora*; cf. "*Lebi'ur ha-Munnaḥ Qore be-Iggeret*," p. 27 n. 39). A good example of this procedure is found in *Menaḥot* 37b, where R. Judah transmits in the name of Samuel that the *halakha* is like R. Ishmael. Yet, without citing a contrary opinion, the Talmud rejects it!

The contrary opinion is never formulated. Rather, it may be *inferred* from an incident with Rabina and Mor b. Rab Ashe, mentioned ibid. To my mind, this indicates that the incident was brought to the attention of the *Kalla* sages at a later point, and there was not sufficient time to redact it.

Generally, the expression *HaDRakh 'alan ve-HaDRan 'alakh*, found at the end of the Talmudic tractates, is explained as 'return': "You shall *return* to us and we shall *return* [or 'we have came back'] to you." I am not certain, but I think that the late Professor Lieberman explained it in the sense of 'beauty,' as when bidding farewell to a friend, or as when bidding farewell to the altar, see Mishna *Sukka* 4:5 and *Hellenism in Jewish Palestine*, p. 11 n. 46. In the same manner, when completing a tractate, we bid farewell to it: 'Let your *beauty* be upon us and our *beauty* be upon thee!' These parting words, said when completing an entire tractate, intend to convey that we shall remember only thy beauty, rather than the toil we encountered when learning that tractate. At the same time, we beg the tractate to overlook our errors and faulty interpretations and remember our good will, etc. [There is either a scribal error or a misprint in the text of R. Judah ibn Bala'am, *Perush Yesha'yahu*, p. 189 cited above. From the Arabic text, it is evident that he intended to explain the rabbinic expression *HaDuR bakh* ('revert'!)—not, as per the Hebrew: *hadran 'alakh*!]. I would like to suggest another explanation. Occasionally, as a form of poetic license (cf. above Appendix 52), the senses of these roots are applied to each other; see *Sukka* 31b, 35a; and *Shir ha-Shirim Rabba* VII, 1, [9], p. 75. Accordingly, the parting words: *HaDRakh 'alan ve-HaDRan 'alakh*, stand for: 'Thy *splendor* is upon us and we shall *return* to Thee!'

For a detailed study of the root HDR in rabbinics; see *'Aruk ha-Shalem*, s.v. *hadar* (3) and s.v. *hadura*.

54. "Little Foxes"

Poorly trained rabbinic students and bogus rabbis were a disrupting factor in Jewish life throughout the ages; see Chapter 63. Because Israel was never organized hierarchically as the Catholic Church, with the power to regiment and impose its will on the clergy, it was relatively easier for unqualified rabbis and students to fool the faithful. Even outstanding rabbinic figures had to cope with the "little foxes" sowing havoc and discord in their respective communities; see R. Eliahu Mizraḥi, *She'elot wu-Tshubot Re'em* (Jerusalem, 5698/1938), #15, 33a; #66, 215a; R. Moses al-Ashqar, *She'elot*, #112, pp. 180–182; R. Levi b. Ḥabib, *She'elot* (Venice, 5325/1565) #31;

R. Samuel de Medina, *Teshubot Meharashdam, Eben ha-'Ezer* (Saloniki, 5358/1598), #43, 37a; etc, etc. This problem was further exacerbated by the 'rabbinic ordination' (סמיכה) awarded in the Ashkenazic rabbinate; see R. Isaac bar Sheshet, *Teshubot She'elot* (New York, 5714/1954), ##270–271, 74b–76c. As in all systems, 'ordination' was occasionally awarded to unworthy pupils; see R. Moses Iserlin, *Teshubot ha-Rama*, #55, 34a. For an overview of the problem, see Professor Meir Benayahu, 'Introduction,' R. David ha-Kohen, *Teshubot She'elot* (Jerusalem: Yad ha-Rab Nissim, 5748/1988), pp. 33–36. It goes without saying that in such circumstances the 'ordination' is worthless; see *MT Sanhedrin* 4:15 and below Appendix 69. In this context, it is worth noting that the Sephardic rabbinate did not award ordination at all; see R. Isaac Abarbanel, *Naḥalat Abot*, on *Abot* 6:1, p. 376; R. Jacob Castro, *'Erekh Leḥem* (Constantinople, 5478/1718), *Yore De'a*, CCXLII, 6, 47d–48a. On the Ashkenazic Ordination, see M. Broyer, "The Ashkenazi Semikha," (Heb) *Zion* 33 (1968), pp. 15–46. On the ordination and the rise of the professional Rabbi, see Irving A. Agus, *Responsa of the Tosaphist's* (Heb), (New York: Talpioth, Yeshiva University, 1954), pp. 18–28. Cf. below Appendix 67.

55. *Minim* and *Minut*

The rabbis classified *minim* (sin. *min*) as "those that have rejected (one) of the principles" (כופר בעקר) of the Jewish faith; see R. Ḥanan'el and Rashi, on *Shabbat* 75a; *'Arukh s.v.* GDF; and cf. Rashi on *Dt* 1:12. Similarly, Maimonides, *Teshubot ha-Rambam*, #263, vol. 2, p. 499, defined *min* "as someone that rejects one of the principles of the Tora; e.g., someone postulating that the Tora is not from Heaven"; see ibid., #449, p. 730; *Perush ha-Mishnayot*, *Berakhot* 9:7, vol. 1, p. 90; cf. *Sanhedrin* 10:1, vol. 4, pp. 209, 217; *Guide* II, 19, p. 215, l. 12; III, 17, 335, ll. 8–16. According to Maimonides there are five such principles; see above Chapter 25. In the rabbinic mind, a *min* is the most shameful type of 'heretic'—more wretched and evil than even the infamous epicurean (the *apiqoros* of rabbinic literature). What makes the *minim* particularly odious is their methodology of deception. They are perfidious: they use Scripture not to teach but to mislead the naive. They beguile the gullible, exposing a single aspect of their doctrines in order to block the prey's judgment, thus driving him/her to do things that he/she will lament for the rest of his/her life. Their manifest reliance on the Tora and their use of Jewish terms and sources are gimmicks intended to take in the dull-witted. In spite of their pretentious religiosity, they are cynics who believe in no religion. In brief, for them the end justifies the means; see quotation from Jung at Section III, n. 225. This is how Maimonides, in his *Iggeret ha-Shmad*, *Iggerot ha-Rambam*, vol. 1, p. 37, described them:

> ... *Minut* is more heinous than idolatry, because the *minim*—may God cut them off!—poke fun at (all) religions, and say: 'Those who propose them are wicked. Those who study them are crazy.' In fact, they deny prophecy altogether.

Cf. *Perush ha-Mishnayot*, *Ḥolin* 1:2, vol. 5, p. 175; *Yadayim* 4:6, vol. 7, p. 717, and Section III n. 209.

Through a peculiar type of 'hermeneutics' a metamorphosis takes place whereby the Tora is not only 'dead' but also 'deadly.' On this point, see José Faur, "Don Quixote—Talmudist and *mucho más*," *Review of Rabbinic Judaism* 4 (2001), pp. 143–144. Appropriately, the rabbis compared *minut* to "toxic waters," which appear crystalline and placid, but are fatal to any and all who would drink from them; see *Abot* 1:11 and *Perush ha-Mishnayot*, vol. 4, p. 414; cf. *Perush ha-Mishnayot*, *Nedarim* 10:8, vol. 3, p. 153. *Minimim* are perfidious through and through because they use the Tora as a ploy to dupe the innocent. Therefore, a Scroll of Tora written by a *min* ought to be incinerated together with the names of God that it contains; see *MT Yesode ha-Tora* 6:8 [the standard version 'אפיקורס' is wrong, instead read: 'מין ישראל']. The underlying theory is that even the Tetragrammaton, representing the holy of holiest, is contaminated with their idolatrous schemes. Addressing this rule, the rabbis, *Shabbat* 116a, cited the verse: "and behind the entrance at the door-post (*mezuza*) you (i. e. the *minim*) have placed your remembrance" (*Is* 57:8)—that is, your idolatrous fabrications. Meaning: you use the *mezuza*—a sacred Jewish object—as a ploy to ensnare the innocent! See the note of R. Jacob ibn Forna, cited by R. Ḥayyim Algazi, *Ba'e Ḥayye* (Orta-Kivvae, 5479/1719), 64a; cf. *Keli Faz*, 217d–218a. In Judaism, context is of the essence. Thus, the texts of the Tora that were not written with the proper sanctity (קדושה) have no standing. Similarly, to study Tora and reflect about it have no merits in an environment which is not clean; see R. Jacob Ḥajez, *Halakhot Qeṭannot*, Part 1, #15, 3d. For the same reason it is not appropriate to teach Tora to an unethical student; see *MT Talmud Tora* 4:1

The motivation behind the *min* and *minut* pertains to the morbid and pathological; 'theology' is but a cover to camouflage their abnormal impulse to pervert the innocent. (Accordingly, this type of immorality is referred to in Judeo-Spanish as "*pecado de padre*"). The rabbis associate *minut* with sexual aberrations and political collaboration with the *enemies* of Israel; see *'Aboda Zara* 17a-b, *Homo Mysticus*, pp. 37–38, and the corresponding note on p. 203. They are sick, "and beyond healing"; see Maimonides, *Perush ha-Mishnayot*, *Abot* 2:17, vol. 4, p. 429. Let us note, in passing, that the sex of *minut* has nothing to do with the "dynamic call" discussed by D. H. Lawrence, or the "erotic" excitement involved in the "unveiling of the truth," by Roland Barthes; see *Golden Doves*, p. 115. Rather, it is the gruesome, sinister sex, described by D. M. Thomas, *The White Hotel* (New York: Viking Press, 1981). The purpose of this type of 'sex' is to agonize the victim, like the Spanish *Conquistador* raping Native American wives while having the husband tied under the bed; see "Jews, *Conversos* and Native Americans: The Iberian Experience," p. 106. On the pathological aspects of the *min*-mentality, see my "De-authorization of the Law: Paul and the Oedipal Model," *Journal of Psychiatry and the Humanities* 11 (1989), pp. 222–243.

Consequently, whereas all types of sinners may be accepted back into the fold after 'repenting' (תשובה), see *MT Teshuba* 3:7, 14, "Jewish *minim* are not Jews in any matter whatsoever, and can never be accepted as repentant," *MT 'Aboda Zara* 2:5. Maimonides, *Teshubot ha-Rambam*, vol. 2, pp. 501–502 explained that if their contrition is sincere, God would surely forgive them, just as He forgives every penitent. However, since *minut* is grounded on make-believe and deception, only God can know whether a *min* had actually repented. Plain humans, however, can never be sure that "the piety that they show is not because of fear or to take in the people." The Geonic decision, *Sha'are Ṣedeq*, III, vi, 11, p. 56, accepting an inveterate offender back into the fold after undergoing proper repentance, concerns an entrenched sinner—not an ideological *min*.

The status of *min* applies to someone who practices *minut* because of his own personal ideology, see *MT 'Edut* 11:10; however, someone who denies a principle of Jewish faith because he was raised in a community disparaging some of the fundamental principles of Israel is not a *min*; see *MT Mamrim* 3:3. This distinction was widely accepted by other legal authorities; see *Besamim Rosh* #240, cf. *ibid.* #251; *Teshubot Radbaz*, IV, #187 (= 1255); and R. Joseph Albo, *Sefer ha-'Iqqarim* I, 2.

In later rabbinic parlance *min*, *minut* were used to designate a Jew or group of Jews that because of personal ideology and/ or behavior caused rift in Israel. That is why R. Samuel ha-Nagid classified bogus-Talmudists as *minim*; see Section V, n. 34. The same designation was applied to communities that did not observe the standard norms of Israel; see *Sha'are Ṣedeq*, III, vi, 7, pp. 54–55; ibid. 10, p. 55. Cf. the question presented to

Maimonides, *Teshubot ha-Rambam*, #263, vol. 2, pp. 495–498. It was on this basis alone that congregations that no longer recited the *Targum* at the Synagogue were described as having a "facet of *minut*" (צד מינות); see Section V, n. 35; or as R. Judah al-Bargeloni, *Perush Sefer Yeṣira*, p. 5 wrote that, they were "close to *minim*" since they were departing from accepted standards. The matter was graver when a community chose to depart from standard rabbinic practice and adapt a more 'stringent' position in compliance with Karraite custom; see *Teshubot ha-Rambam*, #320, vol. 2, pp. 588–589. One of the distinguishing features of *minim* was that they "fabricate" (בדו) their ideology "out of their hearts"; see *Teshubot ha-Rambam*, #449, vol. 2, p. 730; cf. ibid. #242, p. 437; and Section V, nn. 39–40. In this aspect, they emulated the ancient Zadokites that fabricated their laws "out of their own minds, not from tradition" (שמורים מהעולה על רוחם, לא מן הקבלה), *MT Para* 1:14. Maimonides classified departure from standard ritual in compliance with Karraite practice as *minut*; see *Teshubot ha-Rambam*, #242, vol. 2, p. 436: (מינות גמורה), (מנהג מינות) and (אמונת המינים); p. 437: (מינות), and (מעשה המינים); p. 439: (מינות גמורה); and (שמחזיקין במינות זו); p. 441: (דרכי המינים). Thus, the gravity of abrogating the *Targum*—a practice first initiated by the Karraite Synagogue; see Section V, n. 35 and below Appendix 61.

56. *Tukku* (תכו)

Tukku (תֻּכּוּ) is a homonym appearing twice in Scripture. First, the root NKH (נכ"ה), *Is* 1:5; and second, from the root TKhKh/TKK (תכ"כ) *Dt* 33:3. In Judeo-Arabic, 'תכא' [*dagesh ḥazaq*] stands for a 'cushion' used for reclining on the floor; e.g., the small pillow that the faithful bring to the Synagogue to rest on; see A. S. Yahuda, "A Contribution to *Qur'an* and *Hadith* Interpretation," *Ignance Goldziher*, part I, pp. 293–295; hence the verb 'יתכא,' see *Perush Mishnayot*, *Berakhot* 8:4, vol. 1, p. 84. Among Jews from Syria it is used metaphorically in the sense of 'reclining' and 'resting' (אנ-תכא) on a sofa or divan; cf. *Perush Mishnayot*, *Berakhot* 1:6, 7, vol. 1, p. 72. This may be the gist of Raba's statement, *Berakhot* 63b, playing on the term 'הסכת' (*Dt* 27:9); as if it were written 'כת' + 'הס,' he expounded: "At all times, one should learn Tora (= 'הס') and then 'reflect' (כת = 'יהגה' or ככת, reclining on a sofa). I was informed that Moroccan Jews use 'תכא' [no *dagesh*] for a 'small table' or 'tray' put before the guest. In this sense it mostly appears in the Talmud; see *Berakhot* 46b; *Pesaḥim* 100b, 110b, 115b; *Giṭṭin* 67b, etc.

People were in the habit of reclining on the 'תכא.' Hence the expression, *Berakhot* 42a: "I am reclining on the 'תכא' of the Exilarch," to explain that although the attendants have removed the tray from before the guests, the meal was not formally over until the 'תכא' was removed from before the host. Having many 'תכא' [no *dagesh*] in one's home to accommodate guests and friends—be they 'cushions' or 'trays'—was a sign of wealth and influence. Accordingly, we read in *Pr* 29:13: "A poor man and a man having (many) pillows/trays (תככים) met, the Lord enlightens the eyes of both of them," i.e., God cares about the wealthy and the poor equally.

In sum, whether in the sense of 'cushion' or 'tray,' the root TKhKh/TKK indicates an object serving as the 'seat,' 'base,' or 'venue' whereon something rests or stands. In this precise sense, R. Se'adya Gaon interpreted "תֻּכּוּ" *Dt* 33:3, cf. *Targum*, Rashi and R. Abraham ibn 'Ezra. Accordingly, the English rendition of this verse should be, "(Although) He loves the people," that is humanity in general, "all His holy ones"—a reference to Israel—"are in Your hand," that is, they enjoy special providence. The second half of the verse explains why Israel merits such privilege: "And," which in Semitic languages has the gist of 'since,' "they are the recipients (תֻּכּוּ) of your footsteps, the transmitters of your instructions." In the style of homilies made 'in the manner of poetic license,' see Section V, n. 48, R. Joseph (*Baba Batra* 8a) interpreted our "תֻּכּוּ" here, root TKhKh/TKK (תכ"כ), in light of the homonym in *Is* 1:5, root NKH (נכ"ה), and lectured: "These"—the recipients (תֻּכּוּ, root תכ"כ) of your footsteps, the transmitters of your instructions—"are the disciples of sages, hurting (תֻּכּוּ, root נכ"ה) their feet, traveling from town to town and from city to city to learn Tora"— a reference to the end of the verse—to be tutored by the transmitters of your instructions.

57. About "Strict Talmudists"

According to R. Adrete, the view proposed by R. Qaṭina that after the year 6000 the world shall be 'destroyed' (two versions: חרוב, and another: חריב; see below) for one thousand years (*Rosh ha-Shana* 31a and parallels), is a cardinal principle of Judaism. It ought to be accepted *verbatim*, since "we find no one in the Talmud disagreeing" with it (*Teshubot ha-Rishba*, vol. 1 #9, 5a, cited in Section V, n. 146). Before proceeding with an analysis of the text, let us point out that this is the most important rabbinic source in the anti-Maimonidean arsenal. It provided a strategic argument: if this view had indeed been accepted by *all* the Talmudic sages, it could then be argued that the Maimonidean and Geonic view about the stability of the physical world and the laws of nature is untruthful and heretical. It could also be argued, as maintained by Ramban and other anti-Maimonidean mystics, that "No one could believe in the Tora and in the validity of nature, at all" (cited above Section V, n. 169). It would then follow that to confine the interpretation of the *aggadot* to the restraints of nature and common sense, as per Geonic and Maimonidean scholarship, is a denial of Jewish faith.

A close reading of *Rosh ha-Shana* 31a, however, makes it abundantly clear that the anti-Maimonidean interpretation is untenable, and that it was construed for argumentative purposes, not for instruction. The Talmudic passage centers on the rationale for each of the seven *psalms* recited by the Levites at the Temple, one on each of the corresponding days of the week (see Mishna *Tamid* 6:7). R. 'Aqiba explained that the first six *psalms* celebrate the Six Days of Creation, while the seventh *psalm* celebrates the future Sabbath, "a day which (will be) thoroughly Sabbath" (ליום שכולו שבת), i.e., the Sabbath which God will institute at the end of days. Let us point out that the text before R. Ḥanan'el read: "ליום שעתיד להיות כולו שבת." R. Ḥanan'el explained:

> On the Seventh Day (the Levites sang), "A Song for the Sabbath Day" (*Ps* 92:1)—to a Day that in the future shall be thoroughly Sabbath. That is 'one-thousand years,' which is 'God's Day' [cf. *Sanhedrin* 97a], and it will be followed by the Resurrection of the Dead.

Two major points emerge from the above. The world *will not* be destroyed, and after the year 6000 there shall be a millennium of bliss, symbolized by the Sabbath. This is a reference to the Hebrew concept of palingenesis which will occur at the end of days; see *Introductory Remarks*, Section III and *Kesef Mishne* on *Teshuba* 8:2, 8. On the connection between Resurrection and the future Sabbath, see below.

The explanation reported in the name of R. 'Aqiba was contested by R. Neḥamya (2nd century). In his view, just as the first six *psalms* celebrate the Days of Creation, the seventh *psalm*, too, comes to celebrate the Sabbath of Creation, when God "ceased" from creating (see R. Ḥanan'el *ad loc.* and *Golden Doves*, pp. 51–52). At this point, the Talmud introduces R. Qaṭina's view, with an important remark: "And the preceding controversy (between R. 'Aqiba and R. Neḥamya) concerns R. Qaṭina's view (וקמיפלגי בדרב קטינא), that the world will last for six-thousand years, and (for) one will be destroyed." The remark "and the preceding controversy concerns the view of…" (וקמיפלגי בדרב…) is a technical term, common in Talmudic literature. It proposes that a view expressed by *one* of the contesting parties mentioned earlier, in our case R. 'Aqiba, is conceptually linked to a view independently proposed by another sage, in our case R. Qaṭina. It would follow, then, that R. Qaṭina *does not* concur with R. Neḥamya, who ascribes the seventh *psalm* to the Sabbath of Creation and not to the future Sabbath at the end of times. Patently, this seems to rebut the claim that, "we find no one in the Talmud disagreeing with him," (*Teshubot ha-Rishba*, vol. 1, #9, 5a, cited Section V, n. 146). Support to R. Adrete's view may be found in Rashi *ad loc. s.v. ve-qa*, stating that *both*, R. 'Aqiba and R. Neḥamya concur that the *psalm* of the Seventh Day refers to the Sabbath at the end of time. (I would like to point out that Rashi's style is awkward. Also, at least one line is missing from the corresponding passage in R. Ḥanan'el. Could it be that pious hands doctored the text so as not to offend an overly zealous public?). R. Adrete proposed that both R. 'Aqiba and R. Neḥamya were alluding to the future Sabbath at the end of the year 6000, and they only disagree on the length of the future Sabbath: R. 'Aqiba maintained that it will last for one thousand years, whereas R. Neḥamya maintained that it will last for two thousand years. According to this line of thought, R. Neḥamya held a view later introduced in the name of Abayye, namely, that the future Sabbath will last two thousand years (אמר אביי: תרי חרוב).

There are two technical difficulties with this explanation, both of which concern the rules of citation. When the Talmud wishes to connect two independent controversies with one another, it *first* cites both controversies, and *then* it stipulates that the second controversy is somehow related to the first. In our case, after introducing the controversy between R. 'Aqiba and R. Neḥamya, the Talmud should have cited the alleged controversy between R. Qaṭina and Abayye, and *then* it should have stipulated that these two controversies are somehow related (וקמיפלגי בפלוגתא דרבי עקיבא ורבי נחמיה, ר' קטינא כרבי עקיבא ואביי כרבי נחמיה); see, for example, *Ketubot* 88b; *Qiddushin* 69b; *Sanhedrin* 9a; *Bekhorot* 25b, etc. In our case, however, the Talmud states: וקמיפלגי בדרב קטינא "and the preceding controversy is relevant to the view of R. Qaṭina" alone—not to R. Qaṭina <u>and</u> Abayye! Furthermore, when citing two authorities, if the second authority *does not* oppose the first, the Talmudic formula is "אמר" and then the name of the authority. However, if the second authority *opposes* the preceding authority, first it cites the name of the authority, and then "אמר." Thus, if Abayye would have opposed R. Qaṭina, the Talmud should have said: "אביי אמר." (Concerning this rule, see "On Martyrdom in Jewish Law," p. 398). However, ancient editions and mss read: "אמר אביי"—not "אביי אמר"!

There is a more substantial problem. The term "חריב/חרוב" in connection with R. Qaṭina's millennium *does not* mean 'annihilated'—as assumed by R. Adrete—but to 'lie in waste.' E.g., as with the Temple "that is חריב,"

that is, 'in ruins'; see *Sanhedrin* 96b; cf. *Giṭṭin* 57a; etc. The same applies with the form 'חרוב.' It means 'devastated by war'; see *Megilla* 4a; *Giṭṭin* 55b; *'Aboda Zara* 50a; *'Arakhin* 12a, b; etc. For example, the *Targum* on *Hos* 4:3 rendered "Therefore doth the land <u>mourn,</u>" as: <u>תחרוב</u> ארעא. Accordingly, the sense of R. Qaṭina is that this "world" (עלמא), standing for pagan dominion and civilization, would last for a period of six-thousand years. This period would be followed by a millennium of bliss, during which pagan civilization and dominion would collapse (חריב/חרוב). (On this type of celebration, see *Berakhot* 57b and *Yebamot* 17a). This millennium alludes to the Messianic Age (see Mishna *Berakhot* 1:5), preceding the Resurrection of the Dead and the recognition of the Kingdom of God by the entire world. In keeping with this line of thought, the Talmud cites the view of Abayye that the world will "lie in waste for two (thousand years)." In support, Abayye quotes *Hos* 6:2: "After <u>two days</u>, He will revive us on the third day. He will raise us up, that we may live in His presence" (as cited in full by R. Ḥanan'el). The *Targum* interpreted this verse as a prayer: "May (God) revive us in the Days of Solace, which will come in the future, on the Day of the Resurrection of the Dead. He will raise us up, and we shall live in His presence." Having the *Targum* in mind, Abayye proposed that the Messianic Age would be followed by the Resurrection of the Dead. Thus, Resurrection will be the link bridging the collapse of pagan civilization, forecasted by R. Qaṭina, and the future Sabbath of R. 'Aqiba that will come to pass at the end of time. Hence, the 'two-millennia' of Abayye: one for the collapse of paganism and the other for Resurrection.

In short, the interpretation offered by R. Adrete suffers from serious shortcomings. Conceptually, it is somehow problematic to see how the Talmud could have linked R. Qaṭina's view, that the world will be destroyed, with R. 'Aqiba's Sabbath suggesting heavenly bliss (cf. *AdRN*, *Hosafa* II, p. 152, s.v. *bayyom*). Of course, we can always point in his defense to Rashi. But, what about those who follow the text of the Talmud and the explanation offered by R. Ḥanan'el? Are we to dismiss them as heretics? Can we perhaps reconsider the plea submitted by R. Saportas to the anti-Maimonideans? It seems eminently sensible:

> I am very astonished at you, O superior scholars, for you have cast these matters behind your back! What is most amazing about that is that you damned anyone who does not explain the words of our rabbis and their *aggadot* according to Rashi. (Quoted in Section V, nn. 178–179).

The idea that rabbinic scholarship and punctilious adherence to the Talmud were the decisive sources underlying anti-Maimonidean zeal needs to be carefully examined. See Section V, n. 115.

The preceding may help one understand why the anti-Maimonideans were determined to prevent sages of the rank of R. David Qimḥi from presenting a defense of Maimonides in Toledo; see Section V nn. 106, 298.

58. Semantic Assimilation

We had the opportunity to notice that in the intellectual tradition of Israel a semiotic relationship prevails between the text of Scripture and the Mental Law, whereby the Mental Law functions in the capacity of interpretor and the Scripture as the interpreted system. This relationship cannot be inverted; functioning as the interpretor system the Mental Law cannot be interpreted by another system, just as we cannot interpret mathematics in terms of chemical phenomena or language in terms of the Morse code (see Chapter 6). A major consequence of the bogus-Talmudists' unawareness of Scripture (see Chapter 51) was that the Mental Law could no longer function as the *interpretor* system of Scripture. Rather, the Talmud and the entire corpus of rabbinic literature comprising the Mental Law became the *interpreted* system! The *interpetor* system was the analphabetic environment that bogus-Talmudists shared with their less sophisticated neighbors. Thus the twaddle and gabble peculiar to their 'dissertations': they hardly make sense!

The rabbis were sensitive to the dangers of semantic assimilation. A word severed from the 'signified', e.g., as in incomprehensible liturgical pieces, is void of meaning; see Section V, n. 61. In such a situation the 'signifier' could be attached to whatever 'poets' and unscrupulous leaders wish to connect it; see Chapter 4 and above Appendix 7. Worse than this, the text of Scripture could be used as the *signifier* to a *signified* absorbed from antagonistic cultures and value-systems alien to Judaism. We have previously observed that in Judaism context is of the essence, and that the Tora and even the Tetragrammaton have no standing in a tainted environment, see Appendix 56. The same applies to the Semantics of the Law. Since the meaning of an expression and its syntactical combinations are conditioned by, and interpreted within, the linguistic context of the community, without semantic autonomy, the traditional texts of Israel, Talmud included, can be reduced to a string of incoherent cacophonies, as with the 'Talmudists' in "The Day of the Willow" (see above Chapter 51). At the worst, the sacred texts could be used as tools to undermine the Tora and promote discord in Israel, as with 'Heroic Virtue,' see Chapter 52.

Jews preserved semantic autonomy through the study of the text and language of Scripture. Therefore, the rabbis prescribed that as soon as a child "can speak, his father must teach him the language of the Tora"; see *Yerushalmi Sukka* III, 12, 54a; cf. *Tosefta Ḥagiga* 1:2, p. 375; *Sifre* #46, p. 104; *Sukka* 42a; and *Tosefta Ki-Fshuṭah, Mo'ed*, p. 1269. This foundational duty is registered in the major codes of law; see *MT Talmud Tora* 1:6; *Shulḥan 'Arukh, Yore De'a* CCXLV, 5. It consists of mastering the *Hebrew* text of Scripture. In this respect, translations—including the official Aramaic *Targum*—do not equal 'Scripture'; see *Nedarim* 36b. Someone reading a translation of the Bible has not discharged this foundational responsibility; see *MT Shabbat* 23:26 and below Appendix 60. Biblical commentaries, too, do not equal 'Scripture'; see *MT Talmud Tora* 1:12. Therefore, the parental responsibility consists in having their children master the proper "reading of the entire Scripture"; see *MT Talmud Tora* 1:7; *Shulḥan 'Arukh, Yore De'a* CCXLV, 6; cf. *Qiddushin* 30a, *Bait Ḥadash* on *Ṭur Yore De'a* CCXLV, *s.v. haya*; and *Be'ur Hagra* on *Shulḥan 'Arukh, ibid.* #14. Often, to justify Biblical illiteracy, bogus-Talmudists cite R. Tam's view, *Tosafot Qiddushin* 30a *s.v. lo*. This 'proof' illustrates the level of appraisal and the reading evaluation peculiar to Scriptural-illiterate 'Talmudists.' R. Tam, himself an accomplished poet and Hebrew grammarian, was not referring to the foundational duty of mastering the text of the Hebrew Scripture, incumbent upon every Jew. Rather, he was referring to the daily requirement to study Tora incumbent upon everyone, including accomplished scholars. Obviously, when R. Tam said that "*we* (אנו) rely on ... " the study of the Babylonian Talmud alone, he was including in the first person plural, seasoned scholars like himself—not illiterate students unfamiliar with the rudiments of Scripture. Incidentally, R. Tam's view was shared by Maimonides, *MT Talmud Tora* 1:12. (Respectfully, I don't agree with the interpretation of *Leḥem Mishne*, *ad loc*).

Hebrew 'reading' comprises not only correct diction, but also mastery of Hebrew prosody (*ṭe'amim*); see *Nedarim* 36b and "Concerning the term *qore be-iggeret*" (Heb.), p. 23. Their importance can be seen in the fact that the rabbis associated the prosody (*ṭe'amim*) with King Solomon; see *'Erubin* 21b. On the supreme importance of mastering the vocalization *and* prosody of the Scripture, see *Kuzari* II, 72–73; III, 30–31.

Given that Jews lived in a hostile cultural environment, 'studying Tora' could amount to little if the hallowed texts and values are processed according to the linguistic and logical syntax of pagan society. The rabbis (*'Erubin* 53a-b) reported that unlike Galileans, Judeans did not assimilate because they were "punctilious" (הקפידו) about their language. To ensure this, they appended [vocalization] signs (ומתנחי להו סימני). R. Jonah ibn Jannaḥ, *Kitab al-Luma'*, p. 2 ll. 11–13, translated this expression to mean: "וצ'ע אלאעראב ואלתדקיק ואלתעליל." In Judeo-Arabic, 'אלאעראב,' stands not for 'grammatical inflection,' etc., as in classical Arabic, but for the punctuation appended to the text to signal the vocalization of the Hebrew wording. The term "וצ'ע" is an exact translation of "מתנחי," 'to place,' cf. *Baba Batra* 14b. Accordingly, "וצ'ע אלאעראב" are the vocalization marks *placed* on the text, designed to ensure the correct pronunciation of a word. The second term "תדקיק" stands for 'precision.' In Arabic, *mudaqqdiq*, as per its Hebrew cognate, is someone who pronounces (see Mishna *Berakhot* 2:3) or acts (see *Yerushalmi Berakhot* II, 1, 4b) with 'precision.' In our context, it probably refers to the accurate enunciation of the word, as per tonic and atonic syllables, *dagesh*, etc., as well as the rules of prosody. The third term means 'to know or to examine the operative causes' of something. Since the topic is grammar, R. Jonah ibn Jannaḥ probably had in mind the morphologies of the language. Finally, on the basis of parallels from rabbinic texts, he explained the verb 'הקפידו' as to be 'conscientious,' 'scrupulous,' and 'demanding.' According to this explanation, the rabbis said that because "Judeans were punctilious about their language," they developed a system by which to transmit its proper vocalization and linguistic nuances. Therefore, "their Tora stood firmly in their hands." Let us note, that the three-fold division proposed by R. Jonah ibn Jannaḥ ("וצ'ע אלאעראב/ ואלתדקיק/ ואלתעליל") is implicit in *Neh* 8:8; see *Megilla* 3a; *Yerushalmi Megilla* IV, 1, 74d; *Nedarim* 36b; and cf. *Midrash 'Ezra*, p. 150. In addition to correct speech, Judeans learned from a single teacher. This awarded them semantic consistency and standardization. Finally, they published the text of the tractate that they taught, thus, authorizing review and formal transmission of the material. In this fashion, they avoided long and contentious divisions. In contrast, the Galileans neglected all these; they failed to preserve their intellectual heritage (לא נתקיימא תורתן בידם), and ended up assimilating. Jewish sages in the Middle Ages, beginning with R. Se'adya Gaon (882–942), too, called attention to the dangers of linguistic neglect, taking place all the way from the late Biblical period; see his *Ha'egron*, ed. N. Allony (Jerusalem: The Academy of the Hebrew Language, 1969), pp. 158–160.

Throughout the Diaspora, the Scripture was Israel's virtual Temple. Upon opening the hallowed text, the faithful — no matter where and when — unlocked the Gates of Heaven and entered hallowed ground. Thus, the Jew could hear the voices of the Patriarchs and Moses and the Prophets; David's sweet songs, Job and his friends dissertations about the Ways of the Lord, and multitudes of men and women speaking to God and hearing His words. On occasion, she/he discovered that God was in fact talking to her/him at that very moment. This essential point was made by R. Isaac Profiaṭ Duran (died ca. 1414), *Ma'ase Efod*, p. 11.

> ...Just as the Temple was the ground of God's continuous presence (שכינה) in the bosom of Israel... so this Sacred Book (= the Hebrew Scripture) is the operational vehicle by which the Divine Providence is manifest within the Nation (of Israel): when intensely studying it with the proper attitude, and further penetrating its precious pronouncements. It (the Scripture) is the means by which (the Jewish) continuity is preserved, for the ability (of the Jewish people) to overcome (adversity) and gain success...

Scripture is also the means by which Israel will obtain atonement for her past follies and regain national redemption.

> Just as at the Temple, the Nation's sins... were atoned through the performance of the solemn sacramental rituals, studying this Sacred Book, with the appropriate attitude, keeping it always in mind, and retaining it in the hearts (of the people), will be the grounds for God's pardoning the Nation's sins and her failings...

To give coherence to his argument, R. Duran went on to show that both Scripture and Temple were structured into three parallel sections.

> This Sacred Book has properties similar to those of the Temple. It is (also) divided into three sections. [1] The Temple comprised the Holy of Holiest, where the Ark containing the Scroll of the Law was placed. [2] Then the Sanctuary, where the table, the menorah, and the golden altar stood. [3] And the Hall or Yard containing the altar of the holocaust... Similarly, this Sacred Book contains [three sections]. [First] the Divine Law, conveyed by God to Moses our Teacher, may he rest in peace, Lord of the Prophets, whose prophecy is categoric unlike that of any other prophets, God having spoken to him face to face. The second section consists of the *Prophets* that although proceeding from God were conveyed through angels... The third section contains the *Hagiography* which was pronounced by the Holy Spirit, a [prophetic] class lower than Prophecy.

Cf. Dov Rafel, "*Haqdamat Sefer 'Ma'ase Efod' le-Profiaṭ Duran*," *Sinai*, Jubilee Volume, 100 (1987), vol. 2, p. 756.

R. Raḥamim Menaḥem Miṭrani (d. 5627/1867), author of *Me'am Lo'ez*, on *Joshua*, put forward a similar thesis. The book was written in Judeo-Spanish, and translated into Hebrew by Samuel Yerushalmi (Jerusalem: Ḥ. Vagshal, 5732/1972). In the author's *Introduction*, p. 10, we read:

...The Twenty-four [books comprising the Hebrew Scripture] were called by our sages 'Sacred Books'—in analogy to God's Sanctuary [see above Section II, n. 70]. Given that presently we have no Sanctuary, the Sacred Books shielded us just as the Temple had previously shield Israel. It is thanks to these Twenty-four Sacred Books that we are able to survive this brutal Exile. Thus, in the same fashion that the sacramental sacrifices atoned for us (at the Temple), the Sacred Books, too, atone for us... Since the Twenty-four Sacred Books parallel the Temple. They are divided into three sections: the *Law*, *Prophets*, and *Hagiography*, similar to the Temple that contained three sections: the Holy of Holiest, the Sanctuary (*Hekhal*), and the Hall. For this reason they were called 'God's Sanctuary.' The Twenty-four Books [comprising the Hebrew Scripture] parallel the twenty-four Priestly Guards serving at the Temple.

When Israel went into Exile to Babylonia, they were eventually saved because they studied the *Law*, and sought to understand it. As it is written: "And they read the Scroll of God's Law, distinctly, and they gave the sense [of the text], and caused them to understand the reading" (*Neh* 8:8)—since they would read from the Scroll of the Law and explain the text with great acumen and rationale and understanding of what they studied. Because of this good habit they had the merits to have the Second Temple built in their own days. Later, after they went once more into Exile, they repented and again began to study the *Law*, *Prophets*, and *Hagiography*. And God gave us grace in the eyes of the nations, and evil decrees (against Jews) were called off. (The Jews of) France and Germany, however, were the exception, and many misfortunes befell them because they were lax and did not set daily classes to study the *Law*, *Prophets*, and *Hagiography*. The Expulsion from Sepharad, too, came about for the same reason: the people of Sepharad had neglected this [see above Chapter 66]. The people of Aragon, however, were the exception, and they were saved because they studied the *Law*, *Prophets*, and *Hagiography*. Among us in the Ottoman Empire, where the majority (of Jews) came from the Expulsion from Sepharad, they are still lax in their study of the *Prophets* and *Hagiography*. Even the few souls that study them, do not study their explanation properly. What are we to respond in the Celestial Court when they will ask us why we have neglected to study them?

Sigmund Freud, too, sensed something similar. When referring to the dispersion of Israel he wrote, *Moses and Monotheism*, tr. Katherine Jones (New York: Vintage Books, 1955), p. 147: "From now on, it was the Holy Book, and the study of it, that kept the scattered people together." We can now appreciate the feeling of disgust by men of the ilk of R. Samuel ha-Nagid and R. Jonah ibn Jannaḥ at the analphabetic reading of bogus-Talmudists. Indeed, if you believe that the Scripture *is* God's Sanctuary, reading the Tora with contempt to basic Masoretic rules is no less offensive than someone stepping all over the Holy of Holiest, trashing this under his feet and knocking that down, with rude indifference. See above Chapter 51.

The purpose of Maimonides' definition of key-Biblical terms in the first part of the *Guide* was to expose the semantic assimilation that these terms underwent as a consequence of analphabetic interpretation. On the propensity of the persecuted to absorb the mental norms of the persecutor, see *In the Shadow of History*, pp. 9–12; a good example of this phenomenon is the identification of *'aboda zara* with 'idolatry' (see Appendix 11). On the assimilation of 'theological' doctrines proposed by hostile religions, see *Homo Mysticus*, pp. 96–98. An important characteristic of semantic assimilation is the fact that the victim is never aware that the ideas and values which he had absorbed will end up devouring him from within; see *Homo Mysticus*, pp. 130–131 and above Chapters 56, 57. One of the most harmful forms of Jewish assimilation is the notion of monolingualism, according to which 'Hebrew' is the equivalent of some sort of superior language with magical power. It would be of some interest to note that Johann Gottlieb Fichte (1762–1814), whom Russell regarded as the spiritual father of Nazism, maintained that, "The purity of the German language makes the German alone capable of profundity." Therefore, "to have character and to be German undoubtedly means the same"; cited by Bertrand Russell, "The Ancestry of Fascism," (1935), in idem, *Let the People Think* (London: Watts & Co., 1941), pp. 68–69. See Fichte, *Addresses to the German Nation*, tr. R. F. Jones and G. H. Turnbull (Chicago: Open Court, 1922); and idem, "On the Linguistic Capacity and the Origin of Language," in tr. and ed. Jere Paul Surber, *Language and German Idealism: Fichte's Linguistic Philosophy* (Atlantic Highland, N.J.: Humanities Press, 1996). For further thoughts on the subject, see above Chapter 2.

59. Heroes and Heroism

'Heroism' and 'heroic action and behavior' are pagan concepts; see *The New Science*, ##610–611, p. 225–226; cf. ibid. ##637–641, pp. 239–242. The identification of 'martyrdom' (מסירות נפש) with 'heroism' is another instance of semantic assimilation. Judaism does not recognize heroism as a virtue—the highest form of personal endeavor—whereby an individual offers his life for the sake of a belief or ideal. What Scripture applauds is a high level of magnanimity and virtuous *behavior* towards fellow human beings; see C. Gancho, "Heroísmo Religioso," *Enciclopedia Bíblica*, vol. 3 (Barcelona: Ediciones Garriaga, 1964), cols. 1212–1213.

Maimonides was particularly sensitive to the dangers of mental assimilation affecting some Jewish scholars as well as the general public; see *Guide* II, 11, p. 192, ll. 17–29. In an important passage in *Shemona Peraqim* IV, *Perush ha-Mishnayot*, vol. 4, 384, where he criticized Jews that had adopted certain ascetic ideals, he wrote:

> ... Those members of our religion who mimic the nations have postulated—and I am addressing myself specifically to them—that (the reason) they inflict pain onto their bodies and repress their bodily pleasures (Ar. מן אשקא אג'סאמהם וקטע לד'תהם), is to prepare the bodily faculties (to worship God)... they are wrong, as I shall explain.

Cf. ibid, p. 383 n. 22. In *Shemona Peraqim* VI, *Perush ha-Mishnayot*, vol. 4, 392, Maimonides referred to "some of our later scholars that have contracted the sickness (Ar. מרצ'וא) of theologians (Ar. מתכלמין)." About these theologians, see *Homo Mysticus*, pp. 94–98. One of the symptoms "is a sickness which they find in their soul (Ar. מרץ' יג'דונה פי אנפסהם), and which they can neither articulate nor express." That is their belief that the precepts of the Tora have no rationale; see *Guide* III, 31, p. 382, ll. 23–24; cf. ibid. 32, p. 385, l. 19.

The association *qadosh*/hero is the effect of semantic assimilation. The notion that 'sanctity' (קדושה) can be obtained outside the fulfillment of a 'precept' (מצוה) contradicts the rabbinic doctrine stipulating that "holiness is acquired through [the fulfillment] of each one of the precepts" (קדושת כל המצות); see Appendix 4. For that reason, Maimonides classified heroism as wrongdoing, not a virtue. When discussing the 'golden rule' of balancing two extreme tendencies affecting the individual's behavior, *Shemona Peraqim* IV, *Perush ha-Mishnayot*, vol. 4, 381, he observed:

> Many people are in error about these actions, supposing that one of these extremes is 'good' and constitutes a 'moral virtue' of the soul. Sometimes, they suppose the former extreme to be 'good'—as when they suppose 'heroism' to be a moral quality, and call the heroes 'brave.' And when they see someone behaving with extreme daring and intrepidness, challenging danger and purposely putting himself in harm's way, and perchance he is saved, they praise him and say: 'this is a brave person!'

Cf. *Homo Mysticus*, p. 156. The *converso* writer, too, was anti-hero, for example, *Lazarillo de Tormes* and *Don Qixote*; see *In the Shadow of History*, pp. 62, 69–70. Let us note that no lesser a thinker than Luis Víves espoused what may be properly described as an anti-hero ideology; see ibid. p. 240 n. 75.

The preceding bears directly on the concept of 'martyrdom.' For Judaism, 'Sanctification of the Name [of God]' (קדוש השם) or 'martyrdom' is not a reworked version of Christian 'heroism'; see above Section V n. 75. As with all precepts, this, too, is regulated by precise legal definitions. Therefore, although martyrdom is commendable under the circumstances defined by the Law, it is sinful if done when not required by the Law. Rather, such an individual is responsible for his own death, and would have to render account for his folly before his Maker; see *MT Yesode ha-Tora* 5:1. For a detailed analysis of this precept in Jewish Law, see "On Martyrdom in Jewish Law: Maimonides and Nahmanides," pp. 373–407.

The place of 'religious fervor' in Judaism was the focus of a dispute between Maimonides and an anonymous rabbi urging North African Jews to martyrdom, rather than confess Muhammad's mission; see *Iggeret ha-Shmad* in *Iggerot ha-Rambam*, vol. 1, pp. 30–59. Maimonides' point was that only when a Jew is coerced to worship in a manner specifically defined by Jewish law as *'aboda zara* is martyrdom commendable. On the halakhic issues involved, see "Two Models of Jewish Spirituality," pp. 11–17. The real concern, however, pertained to assimilation. Inspired by Christian (and Muslim) religious fervor, the anonymous rabbi argued that since Christians would "rather die than confess his [Muhammad] mission," Jews, too, should choose martyrdom. To which Maimonides retorted, "Is it that there is no God in Israel that we have to learn about our faith from Moslems and Christians?" If one were to accept the notion that pious fervor is a true expression of religiosity, then, Maimonides reasoned, "we would have to burn ourselves and our children in the service of God," as heathens practiced in Biblical times. Maimonides concluded that the rabbi was espousing "the view of heretics (*minim*; cf. ibid. p. 37 and above Appendix 55) and Christians," *ibid* p. 33. Maimonides' argument coincides with the position of R. Judah ha-Levi, *Kuzari* III, 23, rejecting the role of 'religious fervor' from Judaism. Otherwise, we would have to adopt the practices of "believers in dualism, in the eternity of the world, in [the conjuration of] spirits, in the ways of hermits dwelling in seclusion in mountains, and those that burn their children in fire [as a religious service], given that they, too, are also striving (*mujtahidun*) to draw near God." See above Appendices 4 and 51.

Let us note, in conclusion, that the whole idea of 'heroism' involves the notion of 'triumph' and 'war' and 'violence.' Thomas Carlyle (1795–1881), who was a great admirer of Fichte, and was the author of *On Heroes and Hero Worship* (1841), believed that "There is no objective criterion of 'nobility' except success in war"; cited by Russell, *Let the People Think*, p. 70. See Jorge Luis Borges, "Dos Libros," in *Obras Completas* (Madrid: Ultramar, 1977), pp. 723–726.

60. *Ḥasid* and *Ḥasidut*

There is a concerted effort among modern historians, both 'religious' and 'secular' to discredit Maimonides and the Maimonidean tradition by claiming that, on the one hand, he was 'too' rationalist, and on other hand, that his son was 'too' mystical. Their primary intent is to validate current models of Judaism, of either a soulless, absurd rationalism, or a brainless piety. Both these models are the effect of semantic assimilation, see above Appendix 58, and have nothing to do with either the Hebrew Scripture or the Talmud. A principal consideration of my *Homo Mysticus* was the centrality of a genuine mystical experience in Maimonides' intellectual apparatus, and consequently, of the importance of exposing brainless *ḥasidut*. Thus the need to further develop and expose the meaning of *Jewish* piety, something about which our modern historians know nothing.

Let me point out to the extraordinary fact that Maimonides' descendants for six generations composed works on *ḥasidut*. His son, R. Abraham, wrote *The Ways of Perfection*, and thus did his children and children's children! The last descendant known to us—Maimonides' sixth generation—R. David Maimon, penned *Al-Mirshad*, ed. and tr. P. B. Fenton (Jerusalem: Mekize Nirdamim, 1987). Before embarking upon an exposition of this topic, let us make clear that the prevailing definition of *ḥasidut* as doing *more* than what the Tora requires, as per heroic-*qedoshim* virtue, is incorrect. If we are to come to grips with the Jewish concept of *ḥasidut* we must remember that although the fulfillment of a single *miṣva* suffices for salvation, see above Appendix 4, it is still incumbent upon everyone, if and whenever possible, to try and fulfill every single *miṣva*. In light of this doctrine it would be presumptuous for any individual to boast of having done *more* than what the Tora has required; that somehow he *never* missed an opportunity to do what was incumbent upon him and that in no way has he ever erred. There is a remarkable passage, in *The High Way of Perfection*, vol. 2, pp. 65–69, addressing this common fallacy:

> Now it is necessary that we call thy attention also to the fact that just as some of the scholars err by being conceited about their knowledge until they return to the correct point of view to the principles and general (outlines) to which we have called attention, thus some pious err by being conceited about their religiosity and their piety until they return to the correct point of view to the principles and general (outlines) to which we shall call attention. And that is that thou must know that we are commanded by Him, exalted be He, (nay) held accountable, for the performance of *all* "The commandments of the Torah," its (positive) commands as well as its prohibitions—and thou knowest the

> multitude of their numbers and what is specified for thee to perform of them, and no one in Israel may content himself with the performance of some of them to the exclusion of certain others that are specified for him. He said, exalted be He: "Oh that they had a heart like this always, to fear Me, to keep all My commandments always" (*Dt* 5:26). Mark (well) His statement "all my commandments" and "always." And such (statements) are numerous in the Bible—"In all the ways which the Lord your God hath commanded you, shall ye walk" (*Dt* 5:30). "And ye shall do all my commandments" (*Nu* 15:40)...
>
> If, then, we were to assume (the existence of) a person who obeys all that is incumbent upon him of the "positive commandments" not being remiss in anything that is incumbent upon him thereof, (and who at the same time) refrains from (transgressing) all "negative commands" not perpetrating anything thereof except one "commandment," that would be a defect in (his observance of) "he did not keep all His commandments," but overstepped or transgressed some of them; and even if we were to assume that he be safe from all that, always, for the (entire) length of his life except one time, as for example that he trespass in the (matter of the) "love of a neighbor" on some day or he transgress (the prohibition of) "keeping (a grudge)" for some time, that would be a defect in (his observance of) religion because "he did not keep (the commandments) always" as God, exalted be He, had commanded.
>
> ...And in accordance with this observation Solomon stated categorically and publicly saying: "For there is not a righteous man upon earth who doeth good and sinneth not" (*Ec* 7:20). How, then, is it conceivable that a human being should pride himself on religiosity?...
>
> Moreover is it necessary to remember the expressed statement of the Torah that cautions the adherent of the Law against thinking that he possesses complete piety and he is deserving of His salvation...
>
> If, now, thou beest of those that are externally religious, how, then, canst thou be vain thereof, when before thee is inward religiosity which is the aim of the external (type)? If, again, thou art of those who serve (God) with inward religiosity, how then, canst thou be vain thereof, when thou art held accountable for errors, as they (*Yebamot* 121b) have said: "The Holy One Blessed Be He deals with those around Him strictly, even to a hair's breadth?"

The following anecdote about Maimonides, *ibid.* p. 71, is an illuminating example of his opinion of those believing themselves to be faultless.

> It was said in his (Maimonides) presence that one of the religious said on the night of (the day) of "atonement": "I do not know what sin I should repent from." Said my father and teacher, the memory of the righteous is blessed, when he heard that: "Poor fellow! If he had (only) known what he ought to know, he would have repented from thinking within himself that he has no sin to repent. (Cf. *The High Way of Perfection*, vol. 1, p. 54)

We now return to *ḥasid* and *ḥasidut.* German *ḥasidut*, tells us Professor Marcus,

It is centered on the premise that God's will consists of more than what was explicitly revealed in the Torah and mediated by rabbinic law. Infinite in scope, the will of the Creator is required of the Pietist. Complementing that idea is the infinite obligation which the Pietist has of being "forever resourceful in fearing God," of engaging continuously in a search for the hidden will by striving to discover new prohibitions, make new safeguards, new ways of serving God by "fearing Him," by loving Him selflessly, sacrificially, totally. But the total process of this search requires that the Pietists experience divinely arranged trials expressed in the power of evil impulse in oneself and in society. Those trials are designed to provide opportunities for the Pietist to earn reward and to make it possible for a righteous person to appear. Finally, the soteriological basis for the Qalonides' [a distinguished rabbinic family flourishing in Ashkenaz] pietistic ideal is expressed as a reinterpretation of the maxim that "reward is proportional to pain." (Ivan G. Marcus, *Piety and Society,* Leiden: E. J. Brill, 1981, p. 35)

This view, however, has nothing to do with either the Hebrew Scripture or Talmud, but with the tendencies of submission and domination discussed in *Escape from Freedom*, Chapter 5. Concerning the term *ḥasid*, it should be noted that in *Jer* 3:12 God depicts Himself as *ḥasid*, a term which in *Ps* 145:17 is used to depict the exquisite and wondrous workings of the Lord; cf. *Guide* III, 53, p. 465, ll. 9–18. *Ḥasid* may also apply to individuals, see 2*Sam* 22:26, *Mi* 7:2, *Ps* 12:2; a well as to nations, *Ps* 43:1. The rabbis regarded *ḥasidut* and *middat ḥasidut*, 'norm of *ḥasidut*' as an exemplary conduct, not required by *halakha* but that one should try to do as a kind of *noblesse oblige*; see *Baba Meṣi'a* 52b, *Ḥolin* 130b, etc., in contradistinction to *middat din* 'legal norm'; see *Yerushalmi Shebi'it* X, 4, 39d, etc. In the Golden Age of Spain, *ḥasid* was used to depict an individual 'sensitive' to the exquisite providence exhibited by God. The title was given to gentiles; see *MT Teshuba* 3:5; cf. *Sefer Sha'ashu'im*, p. 7 n. 3 (cf. however, *Sefer ha-Kuzari* II, 49). In this respect, we should note that the rabbis extended this term metaphorically to indicate gracious habits among animals; see *Ḥolin* 63a, *Midrash Tehillim*, CIV, 14, p. 444; cf. *Abot de-R. Natan,* VIII, A, p. 38. In my opinion, Biblical *ḥesed*, too, indicates a behavior reflecting exquisite attention and care. (Occasionally it is used as a euphemism for 'shame,' 'abomination,' e.g. *Lev* 20:17). For a different understanding of this term, see Nelson Glueck, *Ḥesed in the Bible* (Cincinnati: Hebrew Union College, 1967).

Not everything exceeding the strict requirement of *halakha* qualifies as *ḥasidut*; see *Yerushalmi Berakhot* II, 9, 5d; *Perush ha-Mishnayot*, *Soṭa* 3:3, vol. 3, p. 256. There must be a rationale to 'devotion.' On one occasion, upon examining the merits of some 'devotional' act, the individual in question was censured for the nonsense he was doing, instead of being commended for it, see *Abot de-R. Natan,* XII, A, p. 56 and cf. *Tosefta Soṭa* 15:11–12, p. 243–244. An example of senseless *ḥasidut* would be someone becoming destitute as a result of squandering all of his assets for charity; see *MT 'Arakhin* 9:13. Similarly, Mishna *Soṭa* 3:3 denounces "a foolish *ḥasid.*"

A *ḥasid* is much more than a *ḥakham* ('sage'), as we will now demonstrate. The latter is someone who had acquired a measure of both intellectual and ethical qualities; see *Perush ha-Mishnayot, Abot* 5:6, vol. 4, p. 458, and *Guide* III, 54. A *ḥasid* is an individual that in addition to having developed his intellectual and ethical faculties (see *Perush ha-Mishnayot, Abot* 2:10, vol. 4, p. 425), is committed to a life-long process of spiritual edification and excellence. Given that the forces and impulses within an individual are not perfectly calibrated, see *MT De'ot* 1:1, a *ḥasid* is someone who in the process of harmonizing these forces within, tilts one of these impulses slightly in one direction in such a manner that results in spiritual development and enhancement; see *Perush ha-Mishnayot, Abot* 5:11–13, pp. 460–463; cf. ibid. 4:4, p. 440 and *Sefer ha-Kuzari* II, 50; III, 4. We should note in this context that in *Nedarim* 32b the "good tendency" in man (יצר הטוב) is likened to "a wise, but frail individual." Although having "wisdom," this individual needs to struggle to contravene the "bad tendency" (יצר הרע)—who is a "mighty king," implying cunning and physical power. In this manner, man's inner conflicts are liken to a struggle between wisdom and might. Maimonides dedicated the bulk of *Shemona Peraqim, Perush ha-Mishnayot,* vol. 4, pp. 372–407, as well as *MT De'ot* Chapter 1, to explain how to proceed with this type of intellectual and ethical calibration. Accordingly, *ḥasidut* involves a continuous process of introspection and evaluation; cf. *Mo'ed Qaṭan* 5a and *Baba Batra* 78b.

Before presenting an outline of Maimonides' general theory of *ḥasid* (Ar. פאצ'ל), it would be helpful to examine a few key Arabic terms that he used in developing this subject. These terms are well known from Sufist's literature. Nonetheless, to bring out their concrete meaning, a few notes would be helpful. The first term, 'אנקטאע,' conveys the general sense of 'dedication' and 'consecration,' and this is how it is rendered by Jewish translators. There is a fundamental aspect to this term that could be lost in translation. The root of 'אנקטאע' is 'קט"ע,' which means 'to excise,' 'to cut,' and 'break off.' In our case, it involves a *psychological process* by which the individual 'dissociates himself from his surroundings' by mentally 'excising himself' from the mundane and daily routine. E.g., Israel's "אנקטאע" from the worldly by journeying into the Desert, and putting her faith in God's providence; see *Ps* 78:52 and *Guide* III, 24, p. 362, l. 24; cf.

R. Abraham, *Perush*, p. 379. (Hence the term *ḥesed* in *Jer* 2:2; see *Homo Mysticus*, p. 163, and cf. ibid. pp. 156, 158). The second term, 'כ'לואת' root כ'ל"ו, is commonly found in Sufist literature in the sense of 'solitude.' Let us note in passing that this is one of the many Hebrew and Aramaic key theological and legal terms brought into the Muslim world by Arabic speaking Jews. It appears in *Jer* 32:2: "כלוא"; root 'כל"א,' cf. *Nu* 11:28: "כלאם," denoting 'imprisonment,' 'detention'; see *Targum* and R. Se'adya Gaon *ad loc*; and cf. *2K* 17:4; *Ps* 88:9, etc. The form 'כלא' (cf. *Jer* 37:4) is used in Modern Hebrew to designate 'jail' and the 'penitentiary' in general. In our context, it refers to the 'boundaries' that an individual resolves to set *upon* himself, to shelter himself from a specific lure lurking 'outside,' affecting one of his weak points; cf. *Ḥolin* 6a. Maimonides' son, R. Abraham, dedicated an entire Chapter to explain and analyze the niceties of this facet of *ḥasidut*; see *The High Ways of Perfection*, vol. 2, pp. 382–425; and cf. his *Perush*, p. 307. The third term, 'אנפראד,' root פר"ד, means 'to be alone in seclusion.' It also implies 'uniqueness' and 'singularity.' In our case, the individual seeks 'seclusion' to be 'alone in the Presence of God.' The fourth term, 'תסעי,' root סע"י, has the general meaning of 'to endeavor.' In our context, however, it stands for 'journeying' and 'marching' towards a given destination. The Hebrew cognate is used in the Scripture to describe Israel's journey through the Desert; see *Ex* 13:20; 14:15; *Nu* 30:28; *Ps* 78:52, etc; and *Homo Mysticus*, p. 245 n. 246. Maimonides used this term to describe the 'journey' ahead, challenging those who had the grit to cross onto the threshold of the Heavenly Palace; see *Guide* III, 51, p. 455, l. 4; p. 456, l. 26; p. 457, l. 8; p. 459, l. 27; p. 463, ll. 15–16.

The first three terms are found in a passage where Maimonides discussed the special "kind of worship" that comes "after" the individual "formed an intellectual conception" of God.

> It was thus explained that the object of [the intellectual] conception [of God] is to be able to excise oneself (אנקטאע) [from the mundane] for Him, and drive the intellect towards His love, always. This could best be accomplished in solitude (כ'לואת) and retreat (אנפראד). That is the reason why every *ḥasid* (Ar. פאצ'ל) favors retreat (אנפראד), and shuns human contact except for necessity. (*Guide* III, 51, p. 457, ll. 12–15.)

The fourth term appears in a passage proposing that the special type of worship is possible only after the individual has perceived God in rational terms.

> However, one ought to endeavor to proceed towards this class of worship only after having formed an intellectual conception [of God]. Then, when one is

> able to conceive God and His works according to what reason determines, one should proceed and endeavor to excise oneself (אנקטאע) [from the mundane] and advance in His direction (Ar. ותסעי, root סע"י) towards His nearness. Also, one should strengthen the link between oneself and God, which is the mind. (*Guide* III, 51, p. 456, ll. 24–27.)

I take the 'intellectual conception of God,' 'breaking off' with the mundane, and then 'journeying' towards the ultimate quest, as an inner dynamic process in which each step is predicated on the other. Cf. *MT Teshuba* 10:6: ליחד עצמו (= כ'לואת), להבין ולהשכיל בחכמות ותבונות (= אנקטאע) המודיעים לו את קונו כפי כח שיש באדם להבין ולהשיג (= אנפראד).

Maimonides alerted the reader that in his quest, the individual would have to "persist constantly" (Ar. אלחץ' אבדא) and conceptualize God mentally, "not on the basis of social convention or imagination"; *Guide* III, 51, p. 457, ll. 10–11. It is at this state of mind, that the faithful can attain what the rabbis designated

> ...worship of the heart (Heb. עבודה שבלב), which means to me to direct the mind towards the First Intelligence and to withdraw (Ar. אנפראד) according to his faculties. This is the reason why at his deathbed, David instructed Solomon and stressed these matters (to him). I mean, to journey (Ar. אלסעי) towards His perception, and advance (Ar. אלסעי) towards worshipping Him after (rational) discernment. (*Guide* III, 51, p. 457, ll. 5–9.)

The rabbinic source is Mishna *Berakhot* 5:1, where it is reported that before prayers (= עבודה שבלב), "the ancient *ḥasidim* would withdraw for one hour." Maimonides, *Perush ha-Mishnayot*, vol. 1, p. 74 explained that these men "would discontinue (Ar. יקטעון, root קט"ע) conversation and thought and then get ready to pray." Cf. *MT Tefilla* 4:16 and R. Abraham Maimonides, *Teshubot,* #62, pp. 62–65. For some insight and background, see *Homo Mysticus*, pp. 168–180. Thus, God's "praise" may be found only "in the community of *ḥasidim*" (*Ps* 149:1).

Although we should all strive to adopt some norms of *ḥasidut*, particularly acts of compassion towards others, see *MT 'Abadim* 9:5 and *Mattanot 'Aniyyim* 10:1–3, not everyone can actually be a *ḥasid*. In fact, the rabbis ranked *ḥasidut* as one of the highest degrees of human development; see Mishna *Soṭa* 9:5, *'Aboda Zara* 20a, *Yerushalmi Sheqalim*, III, 3, 47c, etc. Maimonides ranked *ḥasidut* to be only one step below prophecy; see 'Introduction,' *Shemona Peraqim, Perush ha-Mishnayot*, vol. 4, p. 372; cf. "Introduction," *Perush ha-Mishnayot*, vol. 1, pp. 42–43. In the course of time genuine *ḥasidut* became a rarity; see *Tosefta Soṭa* 15:5, p. 240 and *Yerushalmi Soṭa*, IX, 16, 24c.

Summing up our discussion so far, although an ignorant person could and should adopt some of the *norms* peculiar to *ḥasidut*, either as a matter of social habit or personal disposition, see *Perush ha-Mishnayot*, *Abot* 2:6, vol. 4, p. 424; 5:6, p. 457, he cannot possibly be a *ḥasid*. Having the bogus-*ḥasid* in mind, Maimonides wrote that to believe that "an illiterate person could be a *ḥasid* is not only a flat denial of what the rabbis have categorically rejected (see *Abot* 2:5), but also of reason" ('Introduction,' *Perush ha-Mishnayot*, vol. 1, p. 43). On the reasons moving some people to pretend being a *ḥasid*, see *Ḥobot ha-Lebabot*, IX, 3, pp. 391–393. Not only is it that an illiterate person (עם הארץ) could not be a *ḥasid*, but close contact with such people would hinder mental and spiritual edification. This is why, although the rabbis cautioned one not to be anti-social, see *Perush ha-Mishanyot, Soṭa* 3:3, vol. 3, p. 256, and urged all to be courteous to everyone, see *Abot* 4:1 and cf. Mishna *Berakhot* 2:2, nonetheless, one should not fraternize in the company of illiterate people (עמי הארץ); see *The High Way of Perfection*, vol. 2, p. 79. And least of all, one should not eat and consort with them, see *Pesaḥim* 49a. The reason is that this level of fraternization would hinder the kind of internal solitude essential for *ḥasidut*. For this reason the *ḥasid* "will avoid human contact except for necessity" (*Guide* III, 51, p. 457, ll. 10–15). Bearing this in mind, the Pharisees, Heb. 'פרושים'—a term that in Judeo-Arabic linguistic tradition is synonymous with 'asceticism' (Ar. *zuhd*)—avoided fraternizing with ill-bred and ignominious people; see *MT Ṭum'at Okhalin* 16:12. (As it was pointed out by A. S. Yahuda, *Ereb ve-'Arab*, p. 159 n. 8, 'Pharisees' have nothing to do with the '*Mu'tazila*').

The anti-Pharisee diatribe in *Matt* 23:1–39, etc. needs to be critically examined. Obviously, there were bogus-Pharisees, see Mishna *Soṭa* 3:3; *Soṭa* 22a; *Yerushalmi Berakhot* IX, 5, 14b; *Abot de-R. Natan* XXXVII, A, p. 109; XLV, B, p. 124 and the editor's notes *ad loc*; cf. *Guide* III, 33, p. 390, ll. 11–20, etc.—just as there were bogus-*ḥasidim*; see *Ḥobot ha-Lebabot*, IX, 3, pp. 391–393. Conceit and phony religiosity are not exclusive to Jews and Judaism (with the minor difference that Jews do their utmost to expose their own religious impostors, whereas in other systems they do their utmost to conceal them). Abominations of all kinds are not strange to the Christian clergy. Spanish speaking Sephardim used the expression *Pecado de padre* 'A sin of a Christian-priest,' to designate 'a repulsive outrage.' Rather, the Pharisees were maligned because they disclosed something highly sensitive about Jesus' background and life-style. Contrary to popular myth, Jesus did not belong to the 'unprivileged' class. In some circles, he gained a reputation as a lover of food and wine.

"The Son of Man came eating and drinking and they say, 'Look, a glutton and winebibber, a friend of tax-collectors and sinners!'" (*Matt* 11:19). This alone should suffice to dispel the myth about Jesus' poverty and frugal habits. His family tomb, recently discovered in Talpioth, between ancient Jerusalem and Beth Lehem, proves beyond the shadow of a doubt that the image of 'helpless-baby in the manger,' as portrayed in *Lk* 2:7, pertains to the Jesus of myth, not to the Jesus of history. Concerning his family's tomb, see Simcha Jacobovici and Charles Pellegrino, *Jesus Family Tomb* (San Francisco: Harper, 2007). I propose that the main rationale for the anti-Pharisee diatribe is because they dared censure Jesus for consorting with "tax-collectors and sinners"; see *Matt* 9:9–13; 10:3; cf. *Lk* 18:9–14, etc. The Pharisees did not censure Jesus' disciples, but, as per *Matt* 9:11, *only* Jesus himself. (The fact that this point went unnoticed by specialists on the subject is indicative of the level of intellectual integrity peculiar to those involved in explaining the Christian Scripture). The following is the translation of the passage in *Matt* 9:10–11, as rendered in *Pocket Interlinear New Testament*, Jay P. Green, Sr. Editor (Grand Rapids, Michigan: Baker Book House, 1982), p. 19:

> And it happened as he [Jesus] reclined in the house, Behold many tax-collectors and sinners coming, *they* were reclining with Jesus and his disciples. And seeing, the Pharisees said to his disciples, Why does your teacher eat with tax-collectors and sinners?

Let us pay close attention to two remarkable details casually overlooked by specialists. First, the expression "reclined in the house" reminds us of the triclinium, peculiar to Roman luxury homes, commonly used by the upper classes for reclining at the *coena* or dinner. This ties up with an important custom connected with the triclinium: the "washing of the feet"—but not the hands, see below—mentioned in connection to Jesus (*Jn* 12:2–4) and his disciples (*Jn* 13:2–4). As we learn from numerous paintings and brass-relief, people reclined barefooted for fear of soiling the triclinium. We can now understand the need for washing the feet before reclining. Usually, the washing was made by servants standing ready to minister to the guest. In the case of Jesus (*Jn* 12:2–4) and his disciples (*Jn* 13:3–16) it was made by someone important, as a sign of affection. The fact that Jesus did not seem to mind that Mary "anointed his feet" with costly oil (*Jn* 12:1–3), rather than as proposed by Judas (the prototype 'Jew') to distribute the money among the poor (cf. *Jn* 12:8), indicates that he was not a stranger to these types of amenities. From the fact that after washing the feet of his disciples, Jesus "reclined" (*Jn* 13:12, as accurately translated in the

Pocket Interlinear New Testament, p. 263: "reclining again"), we learn that the participants in the Last Supper were lying on a triclinium, as peculiar to Roman luxury dinners. Second, is the fact that "tax-collectors"—the *publicans* of the Vulgate—dined at a place frequented by Jesus and his disciples. Tax-collectors were men of great wealth, who paid large amounts of money to purchase from the Roman authorities the right to extort taxes from the people. They were greedy and predatory and evil. One does not need to be particularly perspicacious to realize that "tax-collectors and sinners" would not share their triclinium with penniless preachers and lily-white youths. A most telling detail is that *they* came to Jesus and *they* reclined with him, indicating that *they* cherished him. Why?

Jesus was the darling of tax-collectors—and for a good reason! His famous dictum: "Render unto Caesar the things which are Caesar's" (*Matt* 22:21), gave these thugs a mantle of respectability. This was consistent with his theory that in the mode of Roman tax-collectors it was permited to seize property on his behalf without due process; see *Matt* 21:2–3 and above Appendix 22. From the sumptuous tombs of the early Christians in the Talpioth area, it is obvious that these mausoleums belonged to very affluent families, who could not possibly have made their fortunes as shop-keepers, laborers, and artisans. Our point is supported by the uncensored version of the Talmud (mss original of *Sanhedrin* 43a, Yad ha-Rab Herzog; Firenzi, III, 7–9; etc.). Concerning Jesus' trial, it says: "the case of Jesus [trial] was idiosyncratic because he was close to the ruling circles" (שאני ישוע הנצרי שקרוב למלכות היה). How? We propose that these were the tax-collectors with whom he shared the triclinium. One such individual was Joseph of Arimathea, desribed as a "rich man," who was "a disciple of Jesus." In the idiom of the rabbis, he must have been quite 'close to the ruling circles.' Evidence to this is the fact that he had direct access to Pilate, and could walk straight into him and ask "for the body of Jesus." At once, Pilate complied, and "commanded the body [of Jesus] to be given to him." (People acquainted with the ways of 'the ruling circles'—then and now—know that tyrants and bully autocrats are extremely accommodating and pleasing with those who provide them with sustenance. In our case, tax collectors). It is highly symbolic that before being moved to his family mausoleum, Jesus was laid to rest in the "new tomb which he (Joseph of Arimathea) had hewn out of the rock" for himself (*Matt* 27:57–60); thus sharing with tax-collectors, something much more symbolic than the triclinium.

A point of some interest: We have mentioned that in deference to the habits of the wealthy and mighty, Jesus and his disciples would wash their feet before reclining at the triclinium. At the same time, they treated with contempt and derision the washing of the hands before eating, as prescribed by Jewish tradition. Because it was the habit of the well-to-do and haughty to poke fun at the poor for washing their hands, the rabbis taught that "whoever sneers at the washing of the hands, (המזלזל בנטילת ידים) will himself become destitute"; see *Shabbat* 62b. Such an individual, "will be pulled-up from the world" (נעקר מן העולם), i.e., violently; see *Soṭa* 4b. In fact, it was considered so grave an offense that such an individual merit excommunication; see *Berakhot* 19a. And yet, as we read in the Christian Scripture, Jesus defended such a conduct:

> Then the Pharisees and some of the srcibes came together to Him, having come from Jerusalem. Now when they saw some of His disciples eat bread with defiled, that is, with unwashed hands, they found fault. For the Pharisees and all the Jews do not eat unless they wash *their* hands in a special way, holding the tradition of the elders. *When they come* from the marketplace, they do not eat unless they wash. And there are many other things which they have received and hold, *like* the washing of the cups, pitchers, copper vessels, and couches. Then the Pharisees and scribes asked Him, "Why do Your disciples not walk according to the traditions of the elders, but eat bread with unwashed hands?" (*Matt* 7:1–5)

The question seems eminently sensible. It would certainly not be entirely irrelevant to ask why washing the feet with costly oil in the manner of the lavish and opulent is preferable to the washing of the hands as practiced by Israel? It should be noted that the Pharisees and scribes addressed Jesus respectfully. In response, Jesus allegedly retorted with a barrage of insults. (See *Matt* 7:6–23). (I personally don't believe that Jesus had actually uttered any of these insults. Note that when R. Eli'ezer, who had contact with Jesus' disciples was asked if "פלוני"—an obvious allusion to Jesus—"has a portion in the World-to-Come," he refused to answer; see *Yoma* 66b. If Jesus had actually acted as described in *Matt* and other similar passagesin the Christian Scripture, their question and his declining to answer would make little sense.)

Summing up all of the above: As per Judeo-Arabic tradition, the Pharisees represented true *ḥasidut*. Because they had succeeded in freeing themselves (אנקטאע) from 'the ruling circles,' they dared to confront those preaching spirituality to the poor, while sharing the triclinium with heartless tax-collectors and depraved sinners. Hence, the close, intimate relationship between *minut*, *minim* and the *rashut* or 'ruling circles'; see Chapter 26, and the texts cited in Section III, nn. 321–323; and cf. Appendix 55. Thus, the imperative of maligning the Pharisees, and all those daring to disturb the *coena* of the mighty: old and new.

61. The *Targum*

The term *Targum* has two distinct connotations. Generally, in rabbinic parlance it refers to the Aramaic versions of the Tora and Prophets, used in the liturgical services, see *Megilla* 3a and still practiced in the Yemenite Synagogue; see R. Raṣon 'Arusi, "*Qeri'at Tirgum ha-Tora veha-Hafṭara be-Ṣibbur*," *Sinai* 89 (5742/1982), pp. 219–238. For a reason that will become clear in what follows, these versions were not regarded as 'translations' but as a *perush* 'commentary.' (Hence, the wealth of exegetical material found in these 'translations'; e.g. *Targum Neophyti* 1). The sages associated these versions with *Neh* 8:8, where the term "explicit" (מפורש) is identified as *Targum*. Therefore, these translations are to be treated as *perush* 'explanations' of the Scripture; see *Nedarim* 37b, and are consequently classified as 'oral texts'; see *Yerushalmi Nedarim* IV, 3, 38c; *Sefer ha-'Ittim*, p. 244; *Studies in the Mishne Tora*, p.179 n. 28; *Golden Doves*, p. 54, and above Appendix 58. The sages in *Megilla* 3a described the publication of the Aramaic *Targum* to the Tora as recited "from the mouth (מפי) of R. Eli'ezer and R. Joshua." This expression is found in all Babylonian sources. In the parallel source in *Yerushalmi Megilla* I, 9, 71c, when referring to Aqila's Greek translation, it is said that it was recited "before (לפני) R. Eli'ezer and R. Joshua." There is no substantial difference between these expressions, and they stand for 'reciting under the supervision and authority,' or 'with the approval of.'

Targum is also used in the sense of 'literal rendering' of Scripture; see R. Ḥanna'el cited in *Tosafot Soṭa* 33a, s.v. *kol*. R. Judah al-Bargeloni, *An Eleventh Century Introduction to the Hebrew Bible,* p. 22, observed that there are three views on the status of these translations. First, is the early position, representing the majority view, "that all the books of Scripture may be written in all languages" (Mishna *Megilla* 1:8). This position is reflected in the Mishna *Shabbat* 16:1 establishing that "every sacred writing (i.e., Scripture) is to be rescued on the Sabbath in the case of fire ... Although written in any language, it still requires proper storage (*geniza*)." For some valuable notes and clarifications, see Professor Abraham Goldberg, *Commentary to the Mishna Shabbat* (Heb.) (Jerusalem: Jewish Theological Seminary, 1976), pp. 285–286. Second is the opinion reported in Mishna *Yadayim* 4:5, that all the books of Scripture must be "written in square [Hebrew] script, on a parchment and with ink." Third, is the view of Rabban Simeon b. Gamliel that "all the Books of Scripture can only be written in Hebrew; with the exception of the Tora (which may be written in Greek). When they gave permission to write the Scripture in Greek, they only permitted (the writing of) the Scroll of the Tora" (Mishna *Megilla* 1:8).

The basis for this exemption was the translation of the Septuagint; see *Megilla* 9a-b. An important precedent was the scroll of the *Targum* to Job, which was brought to the attention of Rabban Gamliel the elder (1st century), and he ordered that it should be "stored away" (*geniza*), i.e., to be removed from circulation. The details and context of that decision were contested (*Tosefta Shabbat* 13:2–3, p. 57). Eventually, as stipulated by the Mishna *Yadayim* 4:5, only Scriptural texts written in Hebrew, in the traditional square script, on a parchment and with ink, "defile the hands," i.e., they carry canonical status; see *MT Sefer Tora* 10:1[9]; cf. *Ma'ase Efod*, p. 10. Later Talmudic authorities, in *Shabbat* 115a debated whether or not such translations could be rescued on the Sabbath in case of fire. For the textual basis of this conflict, see *Golden Doves*, p. 184. R. Ḥisda argued that they should be rescued since to let them burn may be construed as a "disgrace of sacred writings." In the end, the view of R. Hunna prevailed that these translations have no canonical status; see *MT She'ar Abot* 9:6–7. Consequently, they may neither be rescued from fire on the Sabbath, nor should they be read even during weekdays; see *MT Shabbat* 23:26. Why?

Here again, we are dealing with the Christian appropriation of the Scripture. Principally, the *minut*-strategy of displacing the Hebrew Scripture with tendentious and fraudulent 'translations,' the purpose of which was to mislead the credulous, the analphabetic, and the semi-literate. R. Judah noted that a 'translation' might be tendentious and disingenuous even if verbally accurate. "Whoever translates a verse literally," he remarked, could occasionally be "a counterfeiter"; and conversely, "whoever adds to it [the text] may be a blasphemer," *Tosefta Megilla* 3:41, p. 364; see *Oṣar ha-Geonim, Qiddushin*, vol. 9, p. 129; and the note of R. Benjamin Musafia, *'Arukh* s.v. *Targum*. In *Sha'are Teshuba* #330, 29c we read: "The *Targum* to which the sages refer is that which is in our hands, but other translations do not carry the same sanctity as does the *Targum*." Thus, the distinction between "*our* Targum" (*Qiddushin* 49a), which is legitimate, and 'their' *Targum* which by implication is not; cf. *Tosefta Ki-Fshuṭah*, p. 1223.

We can now appreciate the wisdom of assigning to the official *Targum* the status of *perush* 'commentary.' Thus, not only it may not displace the original Scripture, but it is conditioned by it. By denying the *Targum/perush* the status of a 'written text' and classifying it as 'oral,' the rabbis were making sure that it could not be used to challenge the Scripture itself. Furthermore, not only did the rabbis prohibit the use of written copies of the *Targum* in the Synagogue services, but they further prohibited the reader of the Tora "to assist the translator, lest they should say that 'the Targum is written in the (scroll) of the Tora,'" *Megilla* 32a. See Appendix 45.

In sum, the *Targum* that the rabbis prohibited is a "written *Targum*" (כתובין תרגום) or "a Scroll containing the *Targum* of *Job*," as per *Tosefta Shabbat* 13:2, p. 57; i.e., translations intended to substitute and eventually displace the Scripture itself—not *our Targum* functioning as *perush*. To ensure that the public would know that such translations had nothing to do with the Jewish Scriptures, the rabbis instructed that one may not rescue them on the Sabbath. To further emphasize this point, Maimonides, *MT Shabbat* 23:26 declared that even "on weekdays it is prohibited to read them." The distinction between the common translations referred to by Maimonides, and "our *Targum*" was overlooked by his grandson, R. Joshua Maimonides, *Teshubot R. Joshua ha-Nagid*, ed. and tr. R. Y. Ratzabi (Jerusalem: Makhon le-Ḥeqer Mishnat ha-Rambam, 5749/1989), #25, pp. 73–74. A final point must be made here. Arabic-speaking Jews designate the translations made by R. Se'adya Gaon and others, *sharaḥ* 'analysis'—never *naqal* 'translation.' Likewise, Spanish-speaking Jews referred to the Judeo-Spanish rendition as *ladinar*, not as a *tradución*. To my knowledge, the first Spanish *tradución* made by Jews was for the specific use of *conversos* returning to Judaism. According to R. Menaḥem Me'iri, *Bet ha- Beḥira, Berakhot* (Jerusalem: Makhon ha-Talmud ha-Israeli, 5725/1965), p. 40, studying the Scripture in translation suffices to fulfill the *miṣva* of 'studying Tora.' See, however, *Halakhot Qeṭannot*, Part 1, #15, 3d. Both these sages overlooked *MT Shabbat* 23:26 mentioned above. We should also note that translations of Scripture would render the Jewish reader captive to the semantic nuances and developments of a foreign linguistic environment; see Appendix 58. That may be the reason why "the land of Israel trembled" when the Scripture was translated; see *Megilla* 3a.

The oral presentation of the *Targum* at the public reading of the Tora is an institution which according to the rabbis went all the way back to Ezra the Scribe; see *Megilla* 3a. The Karraites were the first ones to eliminate the recitation of the *Targum* from the Synagogue services; see Section V, n. 35. Others soon followed, and the recitation of the *Targum* was abrogated; see Chapters 53–54. Failing to take account of the ruling of R. Neṭruna'e Gaon on behalf of the recitation the *Targum*, registered in *Seder Rab 'Amram Gaon*, p. 77, R. Asher, *Hilkhot ha-Rosh, Megilla* III, 6, justified the abrogation of the *Targum* as follows:

> It seems that they would recite the *Targum* to explain it to this public, because this public spoke Aramaic. But to us, what advantage is there (מה תועלת יש) to the *Targum* since they don't understand it? One should not say, "Let us emulate them [i.e., the rabbis that endeavored to render a version of the Tora

in the language of the public], and consequently that [someone] should explain [the Tora portion] in a language that they understand." Since we can say, "The *Targum* is different because it was established by the Holy Spirit!"

The explanation is problematic. The *Targum* was not composed for "the illiterate people who did not know Hebrew," as proposed by R. Asher; see also his *Tosafot ha-Rosh*, on *Berakhot* 8a, *s.v. afi*, in *Berakha Meshulleshet* (Warsaw, 5623/1853), 6b; *Hilkhot ha-Rosh, Berakhot* I, 8. Rather, it was composed in the official literary Aramaic; see Paul Kahle, *The Cairo Geniza*, pp. 192–195. One does not need to be an expert in Semitic philology to realize that the language of the *Targum* was not the Aramaic spoken by Jews in Talmudic times, and yet, it continued to be recited and understood by the educated public. (Just as the King James Bible continues to be read and studied although its dialectic of English is no longer spoken). R. Joseph, an expert in the *Targum*, pointed to its usefulness even for seasoned scholars; see *Megilla* 3a, *Mo'ed Qaṭan* 28b, *Sanhedrin* 94b; and cf. *Tosafot* on *Baba Qama* 3b, *s.v. ki-dmetargem*. This point had been the focus of a highly persuasive and thoughtful study by Samuel David Luzzatto, *Philoxenus* (Heb.) (Cracow, 1895), see especially, pp. v–23. Thus, the argument that since "they don't understand" the *Targum*, it should be eliminated from the services does not cohere. The fact that the *Targum* of the Passover and *Shabu'ot Hafṭarot* continued to be recited in the Synagogue (see *Tosafot* on *Megilla* 24a *s.v. ve-im*), although "they" could not understand a word of it, undermines this argument. Let us consider, in passing, that according to the Talmud, *Shabbat* 12b, Aramaic was regarded to be particularly suitable for liturgical purposes, and therefore the *Qaddish* is recited in that language; see *Ṭur Oraḥ Ḥayyim* LVI. Then, should the *Qaddish* also be eliminated because "they" don't understand Aramaic? Were one to pursue this logic, it would be necessary to dismiss the entire Prayer Book, since "they"—the same folks that supposedly don't understand the *Targum*—would surely not understand the Hebrew prayers.

If one were to take seriously the alleged concern for the general public, it would be expected to recite in its place a translation of the weekly portion of the Tora in "a language that they understand" (cf. R. Neṭruna'e Gaon, in *Seder Rab 'Amram Gaon*, p. 77). Anticipating this point, R. Asher countered that no translation could parallel the *Targum*, since it "was established by the Holy Spirit"! (*Hilkhot ha-Rosh, Berakhot* I, 8; *Tosafot ha-Rosh s.v. afi'*, 6b; cf. *Tosafot R. Yehuda he-Ḥasid* on *Berakhot* 8a, *s.v shenayim*, in *Berakha Meshulleshet*, 1a; *Tosafot* on *Berakhot* 8a *s.v. shenayim*). The argument is unclear. To begin with, at no place did the rabbis state that the *Targum* "was established by the Holy Spirit." At the same time, it seems awkward to dismiss a liturgical piece supposedly "established by the Holy Spirit," simply because "they don't understand it"?! It should be of some interest to note that R. Asher, *Hilkhot ha-Rosh, Berakhot* I, 8; *Tosafot ha-Rosh s.v. afi',* 6b, maintained that "by reading a *perush* (commentary) to the Tora" at home, "one had fulfilled the duty of reading the *Targum*" together with the weekly portion of the Tora, "since it contains the explanation of every single word." R. Asher did not care to identify which *perush* (commentary), although it would be safe to assume that it *was not* the one penned by R. Abraham ibn 'Ezra; cf. *Bet Yosef, Oraḥ Ḥayyim* CCLXXXV, 2. Curiously, in the case of the *perush* (commentary), "the Holy Spirit" was no longer a factor. Moreover, if there were any substance to the concerns about the welfare of the general public, then some efforts should have been made to instruct the public that "don't understand it." Significantly, this argument has been made by R. Neṭruna'e Gaon, *Seder Rab 'Amram Gaon*, p. 77. Addressing those who wanted to eliminate the *Targum* from the services because they did not understand it, he replied: "let them learn the *Targum*!" Sadly, even rabbis of formidable reputation could no longer come to grips with relatively simple words; see R. Solomon b. Adrete, *Teshubot*, vol. 1, #164, and the note of R. Yayḥya Qoraḥ, *Marpe Lashon* on *Gn* 25:27. Hence the introduction of *pilpul*, ending with the total disarray of Talmudic studies; see Section V, nn. 93 and 371.

The other point advanced by R. Asher for the elimination of the *Targum*: "what advantage is there (מה תועלת יש) to the *Targum*?"—is mind-boggling! It had been introduced by Paul to denigratethe circumcision, Rom 3:1: "What advantage then hath the Jew? On what profit is there for circumcision?" To appreciate the catastrophic implications of this argument it would be important to consider the semantic connotations of "what advantage is there (מה תועלת יש)." It appears only once in the Talmud (*Pesaḥim* 108b), in connection to whether it would be better to give children nuts (and other such goodies) to eat, to celebrate the Passover Seder, or to serve them wine. According to the rabbis it would be better to give children special goodies for the holiday, rather than the ceremonial wine, since "what advantage is there in serving wine to infants?" (מה תועלת יש לתינוקות ביין). In this sense it was also used by R. Asher, *Hilkhot ha-Rosh, Baba Batra* I, 29. Medieval authors used this expression for a 'purposeless action'; see *Rashi* on *Ketubot* 69b *s.v. ve-khi*; *Baba Meṣi'a* 39b *s.v. amar*; *Tosafot*, *Shabbat* 78b, *s.v. tanna qamma*; and *Ketubot* 56a, *s.v. ke-sheshobartah*; *Hilkhot ha-Rosh, 'Erubin* IV, 3; *Mo'ed Qaṭan* III, 36 (= *Ketubot* I, 6); *Baba Batra* V, 4; *'Aboda Zara* V, 36; *Teshubot ha-Rosh*, XIII, 20; CVIII, 2; etc., etc. It was also used to indicate something that is spiritually meaningless. In a Medieval *Midrash*, ed. J. D. Eisenstein, *Ozar Midrashim*, 2 vols. (New York, 1915), vol. 1, p. 5, Abraham said to an old woman worshipping an idol: "it is of no benefit (אין בו תועלת) either for itself or for someone worshipping it." According to Rashi, *Yoma* 67b *s.v. ha-saṭan*, Satan attempted to persuade Israel, "that the Tora is not true, since what is the benefit in all these?" (שהתורה אינה אמת, כי מה תועלת בכל אלו). R. Tam, too, quoted by R. Asher, *Hilkhot ha-Rosh, Rosh ha-Shana*, I, 5, used this expression to denote something religiously meaningless. In this exact sense, R. Asher used this idiom in *Teshubot ha-Rosh*, IV, 22; XIII, 14, etc.

A subordinate, but significant issue is whether or not there is any rationale, other than bias, to insist on the recitation of impenetrable and inexplicable hymns (פיוטים), which *nobody* understands, in many cases penned by anonymous writers, and casually dismiss an institution established by Ezra (and "the Holy Spirit"!), because "what advantage is there?" (מה תועלת יש), and also since "they don't understand it?!" Cf. Chapter 53.

62. Writing a *Sefer Tora*

The proposal to substitute the precept to write the Tora was made by R. Asher, "*Hilkhot Sefer Tora,*" #1, *Halakhot Qeṭannot* (printed at the end of Talmud *Menaḥot*). The justification for this reform was the doctrine "what advantage is there" (מה תועלת יש); see *Teshubot ha-Rosh,* #13:14 and above Appendix 61. This is also the position of his son R. Jacob, in *Ṭur, Yore De'a* CCLXXX, at the beginning; see *Perisha ad loc., Shakh* n. #v; *ha-Gra* n. #iv; R. Aharon Kotler, *Mishnat Aharon*. Vol. 1 (Jerusalem: Makhon Yerushalayim, 5745/1985), #32, p. 152. It is pertinent to our discussion to recall that R. Arie Lieb, *Sha'agat Arye*, #36 had shown that the *miṣva* to write the Tora has nothing to do with the *miṣva* to study Tora. Because the hermeneutic theory underlying R. Asher's position was not fully understood, some insisted that R. Asher meant to say that in *addition* to writing a Scroll of the Tora one should also write the commentaries, etc; see Maran Joseph Caro, *Shulḥan 'Arukh, Yore De'a* CCLXXX, 2. For a summary discussion of this view, see R. Ḥayyim Palaggi, *Birkat Mo'adekha le- Ḥayyim*, vol. 1 (Izmir, 5628/1868), 50a ff. For some additional notes, see *Studies in the Mishne Tora*, p. 181 nn. 36 and 39. Recently, the view of R. Asher was brought to bear on the following question. In sickness, a lady made a vow to donate a Scroll of the Tora to a synagogue. Upon her recovery a formal question was submitted to the late R. Aharon Kotler as to whether she could renounce her vow and instead donate the sum to assist a rabbinic student to continue his studies. An important factor in the decision to permit her to do that was R. Asher's thesis; see *Mishnat Aharon,* vol. 1, pp. 152–159; and cf. *Teshubot ha-Rosh,* #13:14.

63. The Sorrowful Scholarship of Professor Baer

When I first met Professor Baer on a visit to Israel in 1961, I remember asking him if he could name a single Jewish Averroist who converted to Christianity; see *In the Shadow of History*, p. 235 n. 55. In earnest, I don't think the good professor read a line of Averroes in his life, and if he did, I doubt that he could understand a word. As in most of his research, he relied on secondary sources; in this case, on Ernst Rénan's classical work, *Averroès et l'Averroism* (Paris: Calman-Lévy, 1852). Baer's reasoning is impeccable, what Rénan said about Christians in Italy during the 15th and 16th centuries must surely apply to Jews in Spain in the 12th and 13th centuries. Any further investigation would only have hampered the methodology developed by this celebrated historian.

An example of his methodology may be found in his *Toledot Hayyehudim bi-Sfarad ha-Noṣrit* (Tel Aviv: Am Oved: 5719/1959), pp. 519–520 n. 71. Without a single insight into the legal issues between R. Judah and R. ha-Arukh examined above in Chapter 65, he disposed of the decision of the Court of Segovia simply by *imputing* to the members of Court the *views* assigned to them by R. Judah. Pointing a blaming finger at the Court of Seville (for siding with R. ha-Arukh) Baer intoned this grave sentence: "It means that they decided against clear-cut *halakha* and against the view of the preachers of the generation in Toledo," i.e., R. Judah. Incredibly, this remark was made by an individual who could not read a single *halakhic responsum* on his own!

An example of Baer's competence pertains to a remark made by R. ha-Arukh concerning an opinion held by R. Moses de Coucy. Apparently, there were some conflicting views conerning the status of one of the witnesses, in which case there would have been only a single witness testifying to the alleged wedding. De Coucy believed that a marriage performed in the presence of a single witness has some validity (חוששין לקדושיו). Since this view had been rejected by most authorities, including R. Judah's father, R. Asher (see *Hilkhot ha-Rosh, Qiddushin* III, 12), R. ha-Arukh, in accordance with standard halakhic practice in Sepharad (*Bet Yosef*, *Eben ha-'Ezer* XLII, s. v. *hameqaddesh*), dismissed that view. It is pertinent to add that in the case at hand, where the alleged bride denied having consented to the marriage, even those authorities upholding R. de Coucy's view considered the case without merits (see *Bet Yosef* and R. Moses Iserlich, *Darke Moshe* ibid., n. ii). Accordingly, R. ha-Arukh dismissed de Coucy's view with the remark "לית דחש לקימחיה" ('no one cares about his flour'), i.e., no one accepts his view; see *Zikhron Yehuda*, 37a. This is the *only* quotation of R. ha-Arukh made by R. Judah! Why? Since he could not find something substantive to assail him, he found a pretext to abuse him personally by alleging that this was an offensive remark. To this effect, he wrote: "In order that not even a single letter (of what R. ha-Arukh wrote) would be regarded as true, we have to be extensive and discredit him by citing his own words." R. Judah, who was an expert in diversionary tactics and name-calling, jumped at the opportunity to heave against the rabbi a series of invectives: "This alone suffices to excommunicate you, for you have spoken ill of the world luminaries and slurred them [in the plural]. [Scholars who are] greater than you and your teachers upheld and apply his decisions" (namely himself—not a single legal authority in Spain shared this view! His younger brother, R. Jacob, simply *mentions* this opinion, without declaring that the *halakha* is according to this view. How could he? Specially, since his father and mentor, decided against de Coucy!) There is nothing remotely offensive about the expression "לית דחש לקימחיה" ('no one cares about his flour'). It is found in the Talmud (*Sukka* 54a and parallels), and means 'heedlessness' (see Rashi *ad loc*., s. v. *dela*). In fact, Maran Joseph Caro used it to dismiss a view held by R. Jacob b. ha-Rosh; see *Ṭur* and *Bet Yosef, Yore De'a,* CCCXL, s. v. *ve-shi'ura* (*in fine*). A similar expression "*let de-ḥash lah*" is found in *Baba Meṣi'a* 110b, *Bekhorot* 3b, etc. In *Nedarim* 7b it was used to dismiss a view held by no lesser a figure than R. 'Aqiba! (לית דחש להא דר' עקיבא). Hoping for a rabbinically illiterate reader, R. Judah grabbed the opportunity to assail his opponent and create a diversionary tactic. On the basis of prejudice, and without having the foggiest idea of the meaning of these words, Baer repeats the same gibberish about "לית דחש לקימחיה"; see *ibid.* Cautioning against this type of historiography, scholars, from Graetz to Baron, warned about historians acting as theologians; in our case, of preaching rather than teaching. Incidentally, R. Isaac bar Sheshet, *Teshubot ha-Ribash* #230, *in fine*, addressed the son of our R. Ḥayyim, as "the wise and learned Rabbi, our teacher Menaḥem, may God guard him, the son of the honorable Rabbi, our teacher Ḥayyim, may he rest in peace, ha-Arukh." A similar formula is found at the end of #233.

For a detailed discussion of the halakhic issues of this particular case, see Y. Shiber, "The status and confirmation of witnesses at wedding ceremonies in Jewish law," Ph. D. Thesis presented at Bar Ilan University, Fall, 2002, pp. 126–129.

64. Medieval Jewish Prophets

On these superior men, see the magisterial essay by Abraham Heschel, "Inspiration in the Middle Ages," in *Alexander Marx Jubilee Volume*, Hebrew Section (New York: The Jewish Theological Seminary of America, 1950), pp.175–208. On the title *nabi*, see ibid. pp. 180–190. For a description of the method by which the "early *ḥasidim*" and "prophets" reached prophecy, see R. Adrete, in ed. R. Sh. M. Weinberger, *Ḥiddushe ha-Rishba 'al Aggadot ha-Shas* (Jerusalem, 5726/1966), pp. 81–82; *Zohar*, vol. 2, 144b. This has nothing to do with the expression "as I was shown from Heaven," etc., in Geonic literature, which is nothing more than 'I was inspired to say that'; in contemporary idiom: 'it is my considered opinion.' See "Inspiration in the Middle Ages," pp. 192–193. Access to the supernatural excuses faulty scholarship. When faced with a difficult query, all that a rabbi was required to do was to formulate the question in his dreams (*she'elat ḥalom*), and promptly and without delay would receive an authoritative reply from heavens. One such an individual was R. Jacob de Mervaise [or Marvege] (12th and 13th centuries). He published his questions and answers, *She'elot wu-Tshubot min ha-Shamayim* ('Queries and Replies from Heaven'), ed. R. Reuben Margoliot Jerusalem: Mossad Harav Kook, 1957. All these men were in possession of *Ruwaḥ ha-Qodesh* ('Holy Spirit') and were thus infallible. How else could one explain that every stroke of their pen contained such wondrous wisdom? See "Inspiration in the Middle Ages," pp. 193–195; and Israel Ta-Shma, "Tosafot Gornish," *Sinai* 68 (1971), pp. 85–86. It would not be surprising to discover that in this tradition, the occult is a fundamental dimension of 'rabbinic wisdom.' Hence, the function of conjurations, mystical lore, and the occult in general among these rabbis, cf. "Inspiration in the Middle Ages," pp. 190–208.

65. The Science of Necromancy

About the flight and cry of birds, the following story in Josephus, *Against Apion*, I, 192–194, *Josephus*, vol. 1, p. 241, may be instructive. It was witnessed by Hecataeus of Abderas (c. 300 BCE) in a campaign around the Red Sea. The soldiers were going back and forth, following the instructions given to them by a seer. When a Jewish soldier inquired for the strange behavior, the seer pointed out to a bird that he was watching.

> The Jew, without saying a word, drew his bow, shot and struck the bird, and killed it... taking the bird in his hands, continued, 'Pray, how could any sound information about our march be given by this creatures, which could not provide for its own safety? Had it been gifted with divination, it would not have come to this spot, for fear of being killed by an arrow of Mosolamus [משולם] the Jew.'

Concerning the rational basis of necromancy and its relationship to astrology, Ramban, *Perush ha-Tora* on *Dt* 18:9, vol. 2, p. 427, explained:

> And now learn and understand the subjects of witchcraft! The Creator blessed be He, when creating everything out of nothing, made that the higher should rule over the lower beneath it. He placed the power of the earth and all that is in it (the earth) under the stars and constellations, in accordance to their trajectory and their view of them [on the earth], as it is demonstrated in the science of astrology (בחכמת האיצטגנינות). He also appointed rulers, angels, and ministers over the stars and constellations, which are their soul. Behold, their rule, from the moment that they came to be and forever, must be according to the decree of the superior which (God) had appointed over them. However, it was part of His mighty wonders that He put into the potency of the superior rulers types of images and powers that could invert the ruling of what lies underneath them. That if in the sight of the stars ahead, facing earth, is good or bad to the earth, or to a nation, or to a person, those superior faces could be inverted by altering that very sight [i. e. through astrological images]. As they [Kabbalist astrologers] said: the inversion of *NeGa'* [נ-ג-ע plague] will turn into *'oNeG* [ע-נ-ג delight]. [Cf. R. 'Azriel, *Commentary on Talmudic Aggadoth*, p. 28.] He did so because He Himself, blessed be His Name, "Changes the seasons and the times" (*Dan* 2:21)... without changing the nature of the world, and that the stars and constellations would make their trajectory according to their order. The author of *Sefer ha-Lebana* ('The Book of the Moon')—who was an expert in necromancy—instructed that when the Moon, for example, which is called 'the sphere of the world' is at the head of Aries, and there is such and such a zodiac sign, to make an image of such and such material, engrave on it [the image], and [mark] the name of the [astrological] time and the angel appointed over it [the zodiac sign], according to the names mentioned in that book. And if one were to offer such and such incense, in such and such a manner, then it [the zodiac sign] would look upon it [the object] for evil, to uproot and to destroy, to demolish and to ravage. However, when the moon is in another constellation, [he prescribes to] make an image and (offer) incense in a different manner for all good, to build and to plant.

For magic and witchcraft among Jews in late Antiquity, see Mordecai Margalioth, *Sepher ha-Razim* (Heb.) (Jerusalem: The American Academy for Jewish research, 1966).

Concerning *Dt* 18:12, stating that all sorts of divination and magic are "abominations" (תועבות), Ramban, *Perush ha-Tora*, vol. 2, p. 427, argued:

> The Scripture said: "For all who do these (כל-עשה אלה) things are an abomination (תועבת) unto the Lord"—but it did not say, "Anyone that does any of these" (עושה כל-אלה)! Because the Scripture was [only] referring to most of these [witch works], since a soothsayer and enchanter are not an abomination (אינה תועבה).

Hebrew syntax does not allow for such a hermeneutical option. If the text would have said, "Who does all of these" (עשה כל-אלה), as suggested by Ramban, then it would have meant that only doing *all* of the above would constitute an 'abomination' (תועבה)! Another consideration, to make head or tail of this argument, the verse has to be read *kol, 'ose elle*. However, in the Masoretic text *kol* and *'ose* are joined by a *makkaf*: *kol-'ose*! More fundamental, such an interpretation would have to ignore the particle *ki* ('because,' 'since,' 'that'), the most powerful conjunction in the Hebrew language, joining vv. 9–12. Specifically, v. 9 begins with *ki*, introducing the prohibition of doing any of the "abominations" of the Canaanites; vv. 10–11, enumerate the magical practices of the Canaanites, including augury and astrology. These are followed by v. 12 beginning with *ki*, thus including all the terms first introduced by the same conjunction in v. 9. Let us point out that in the introductory v. 9, we have "abominations" (תועבות) in the plural; meaning: all of the following cases to be enumerated in vv. 10–11. However, in the concluding v. 12, we have "abomination" (תועבת)—in the singular; meaning: each of the above mentioned! Finally, the rabbis, *Sifre* #173, p. 220, taught:

> "For it is an abomination unto the Lord whosoever does any of these things."—Perhaps (you would say) that he is not guilty unless he would transgress all of them (abominations)? Therefore the Scripture taught: "whosoever does any of these"—even one of these!

Cf. *Makkot* 24a.

It seems that there were people prior to Ramban who explain "abominations" in a similar vein. To alert the public that such a view runs contrary to the rabbis, Rashi on *Dt* 18:12 quoted the above-mentioned *Sifre*.

66. The Mandate of the Jewish Court According to Ramban

Concerning the mandate of the Jewish Court, the Scripture states: "Throughout your generations, in all your dwellings" (*Nu* 35:29)—that is, even after the destruction of the Temple and throughout the Diaspora. Nonetheless, Ramban, *Perush ha-Tora*, vol. 2, p. 339, declared: "After the Destruction of the Temple it [the Jewish Court] has no mandate either in the Land of Israel or the Diaspora." (Contrary to Rashi on *Ḥolin* 52a s. v. *ella*). He further elaborated this thesis in *Hasagot ha-Ramban*, in *Sefer ha-Miṣvot le-ha-Rambam,* ed. Ch. Chavel (Jerusalem: Mossad Harav Kook, 1981), *Miṣvat 'Ase* #153, pp. 212–226; see *Studies in the Mishne Tora*, p. 43 n. 72. This means that the entire rabbinic apparatus and institutions, including the Mishna, Talmud, and Calendar establishing the Jewish Holidays, have no legal mandate. We should remind the reader that Ramban also rejected Maimonides' position that the authority of the rabbis (including the Mishna and Talmudic periods) to legislate new statutes is from the Tora; see his *Hasagot ha-Ramban*, *Sefer ha-Miṣvot le-ha-Rambam,* I, and *Studies in the Mishne Tora*, pp. 14–15, 19–25. Later on, this doctrine was exploited by Spinoza to argue that rabbinic authority was null and void.

67. The Ministry of Luminous Rabbis: Unerring and Inerrable

Ramban rejected the doctrine that the Tora awarded the rabbis authority to legislate and promulgate new ordinances, see above Appendix 66. At the same time, he maintained that rabbinic interpretations of the Tora equaled Tora; see Section V, n. 240. Thus presupposing a Cosmic Truth, reachable only to self-selecting elites, such as the heroic-*qedoshim-ḥasidim* (later displaced by the secular *europaischen Menschentums* in the realm of Jewish political and communal leadership), standing between the vulgar and the godly; see Section V, n. 333. A consequence of this view was the validation of a hierarchic system of governance and truth, stipulating that those standing above 'know best' and those below ought to obey by virtue of a truth that they are too stupid to understand, ever.

Essential to Ramban's doctrine described above, Appendix 66, is the belief that the rabbinic sages derived their authority, not from the national institutions of Israel (the Rabbinic Academies and the judiciary), but because, like the ancient prophets, they had access to the Holy Spirit;

cf. Appendix 64, and "Nahmanides, *Kabbalah, Halakha,* and Spiritual Leadership," pp. 69–70. There are no rabbinic sources to support this doctrine. In an unpublished paper, R. Josh Yuter, "Ramban," located this doctrine in Tertullian, *De Pudicita*, 21, tr. Henry Bettenson, *The Later Christian Fathers: A Selection from the Writings of the Fathers from St. Cyril of Jerusalem to St. Leo the Great* (Oxford: Oxford University Press 1977), p. 113:

> For the Church is properly and primarily the Spirit, in whom is the trinity of the one divinity, the Father, the Son, and the Holy Spirit. The Spirit makes the assembly of the Church, which the Lord established in three persons. And thus, the whole number of those who have leagued together in this faith is given the status of the Church by the Church's author and consecrator... For the right of judgment belongs to the Lord, not to the servant; to God himself, not to the priest.

In line with the foregoing, the author of *Sefer ha-Ḥinnukh*, ed. R. Ch. Chavel (Jerusalem: Mossad Harav Kook, 5729/1969), #492 (a member of Ramban's circle) proposed the radical view that the Biblical precept to submit to the decisions of the Supreme Court is now to be fulfilled by obeying "the great sages among us during our days." The submission must be total, whoever does not "... obey the counsel of the great Tora sages of the time *in everything that they command* is disregarding a positive precept and his penalty is very grave." He arrived at this view by surreptitiously introducing two revolutionary ideas. First, the authority of the Supreme Court includes the power to determine "what is the mystery of the Tora" (סוד התורה). Second, he redefined the term 'judge' (שופט) to mean 'sage.' Thus, when paraphrasing the Scriptural precept establishing the judicial authority of the Supreme Court (*Dt* 17:10), *Sefer ha-Ḥinnukh*, #508 [4], p. 627, he declared:

> Included in this precept is the obligation to obey and execute at all times, what was ordered by the judge, that is, *the greatest sage among us in our time*. As our rabbis of blessed memory taught, "Jephtah was in his time as Samuel was in his."

This idea was the result of combining Ramban's view, that after the destruction of the Temple the authority of rabbis was a consequence of their superior knowledge (and not of their judicial office), with Rashi's view *Ḥolin* 52a s. v. *ella*, that even in post-Talmudic times a judge (that is, a member of the community's *Bet Din*) had Scriptural mandate. Accordingly, the author of *Sefer ha-Ḥinnukh* reinterpreted the rabbinic principle, "Jephftah was in his time as Samuel was in his" (*Rosh ha-Shana* 25b), to mean that the *sages* of one generation [although not members of the *Bet Din*], were equivalent to Prophet Samuel and must be equally obeyed, regardless of how insignificant they appeared in the eyes of their contemporaries. This interpretation runs contrary to Scripture (1*Ch* 9:20) and the rabbis, who maintained that Pinehas, Aaron's grandson, was alive during Jephtah's time; see *Bereshit Rabba*, LX, 13, vol. 2, p. 643. And yet, the rabbis recognized the authority of Jephtah—the presiding Judge—and not of Pinehas! It follows that the interpretation of the Law rests in the hands of the judiciary, not the 'sages'! Rather, as taught by R. Se'adya Gaon and Maimonides, the principle "Jephftah was in his time as Samuel was in his," comes to establish *parity* between the Supreme Court at different historical periods, e.g., the Court Presided by Prophet Samuel and the Court Presided by Jephtah have equal rank and should be equally acknowledged; see *Studies in the Mishne Tora*, p. 36 n. 28.

There are several consequences to the above-mentioned view. First, given that the author failed to outline how it could be determined who in fact is "the greatest sage among us in our time," conflicting views, for all practical purposes, could only be resolved through strife and violence. Thus, the strategy of faultfinding, misinformation, and intimidation accepted as standard norms of 'rabbinic discourse' (past and present). Second, the 'sage' as personified by anti-Maimonidean ideology, was possessed by "the Holy Spirit" and therefore was unerring and inerrable; see Section V, nn. 333–336. God Himself acts through these judges, and He "is the real factor that decides and, accordingly, a court cannot fail to decide justly" ("Nahmanides, *Kabbalah, Halakhah,* and Spiritual Leadership," p. 71).

The best model and inspiration for this kind of ministry was the celebrated R. Abraham of Posquièrs, who, thanks to his being possessed by "the Holy Spirit" enjoyed total clairvoyance in matters earthly and divine—with the exception of plain geometry; see above Chapter 64. Some maintained that the same status should be extended to the local rabbi: he must be obeyed as if he were "the Supreme Court having authority over (the people) of their generation." He, too, was inerrant and his decisions could not be appealed:

> ...Although all the city's sages and notables may surpass the community rabbi in wisdom and expertise, they are irrelevant in regard to him. Since his authority was appointed over them, he has the legal status of royalty, ranking as the Supreme Court of Jerusalem, in regards to which all sages are irrelevant.

Quoted in *She'elot wu-Tshubot Re'em*, #57, p. 185.

Some rabbis in France believed that their authority should extend to other communities, including Spain. One such rabbi was Moses ha-Levi who on his own promulgated a decree which on account of his rank must be obeyed by other communities. To whom, R. Isaac bar Sheshet (1326–1408), *Teshubot ha-Ribash* #271, responded:

> Indeed, our teacher R. Moses ha-Levi is superb in wisdom and is superb in expertiece. However, he is not yet a Prince standing over the members of our Nation in place of our Teacher Moses, as the head of the Superior Court (סנהדרי גדולה), with the authority to promulgate decrees over all Israel, and prohibit that which is permitted. Furthermore, even a Prince could not pass decrees on his own but with the unanimous or majority consent of the Court (סנהדרין).

After extensive documentation on this point, R. Isaac bar Sheshet added: "No individual scholar, however, promulgated prohibitions upon all Israel, but only upon the residents of his city and precinct. Others, however, need not accept his prohibitions."

According to legal tradition, the new regulations promulgated by Joshua were made in conjunction with "his [Supreme] Court," *MT Nizqe Mamon* 5:3 (יהושע ובית דינו). The same applied to King David, see *MT Issure Bi'a* 22:1 (דוד ובית דינו); and his son Solomon, see *MT 'Erubin* 1:2; *She'ar Abot* 8:8 (שלמה ובית דינו); Ezra, see *MT Shema'* 1:7; 4:8; *Tefilla* 1:4; *Berakhot* 1:5 (עזרא ובית דינו); Rabban Gamli'el, see *MT Tefilla* 2:1 (רבן גמליאל ובית דינו); *et al.* In his own mind, however, the new rabbi felt that he was in fact *superior* to the Supreme Court of Israel at the Temple in Jerusalem. The latter is subject to error, in which case the Court must bring an expiatory sacrifice; see *Lev* 4:13, *Nu* 15:24, Mishna *Horayot*, *Tosefta* as well as Talmud *Bali* and *Yerushalmi* (two versions); see "Law and Hermeneutics," pp. 1670–1672; "One-Dimensional Jew," pp. 34–36. Talmudic sages, too, were prone to error and did not hesitate to announce their blunder publicly; see *'Erubin* 16b, 104a; *Zebaḥim* 94b; *Ḥolin* 56a; *Nidda* 68a. (The term *darash* found in these sources, except for *Nidda* 68a, stands for a *public* announcement; see R. Jonah ibn Jannaḥ, *Sefer ha-Shorashim*, p. 114. The reason that *darash* is absent from the passage in *Nidda* 68a is that the sage in question could not make his retraction personally and had to send his retraction through a messenger). Disagreement between jurists, as reflected in every line of the Talmud, is quite common, and neither party was necessarily 'wrong'; see above Chapter 45. Traditional rabbis, too, did not hesitate to admit error; Rashi confessed that he "did not know"; see his Commentary to *Gn* 28:5, 35:13. On the other hand, luminous rabbis, having gained their privileged position through some sort of revelatory experiences, could not possibly be 'wrong' or 'not know.' Since they were acting by and through the 'Holy Spirit,' to presume or infer that they could be in error would be nothing less than heresy. In the words of R. Josh Yuter, this allowed privileged rabbis to enjoy "a greater creativity in the domain of *Halakhah.*" R. Yuter also showed that the submission of *halakha* to luminous interpretation meant that there were no legal norms that could not be manipulated by theological considerations. In such a system 'Tora' is nothing more than a rhetorical tool designed to justify the rabbi's whims. As argued by R. Yuter: "This allows for almost limitless subjectivity regarding what is considered to be the Law." It meant that "rabbis cannot be held accountable to an objective source," simply because "there is no objective source which could not be manipulated to reach any desired conclusion." ("Nahmanides, *Kabbalah, Halakha,* and Spiritual Leadership," p. 71). The net result was unrestrained manipulation of *halakha* for either theological or political ideologies. For all practical purposes this equaled the abrogation of the whole institution of *halakha* and its substitution by a system to be justified by pointless casuistry and mystical noise. In contemporary circles this ideology is known as "*daas* Tora"; see "One-Dimensional Jew," p. 45; and *The World of the Yeshiva,* pp. 68–69. A more effective and less pompous expression, used in similar circles, is "the spirit of *halakha.*" This allows privileged rabbis halakhic clairvoyance without the need to know a single *iota* of Jewish law.

In sum, in Old Sepharad, rabbinic authority was centered on the judicial institutions established by the local communities. A principal objective of the anti-Maimonideans was to undermine their authority. Toward this end it was crucial to de-legitimize the *Mishne Tora* and to discredit the values of Israel formulated by the Geonim and the sages of the Golden Age. The anti-Maimonidean rabbis would fill the ensuing vacuum.

Not all *qedoshim*-rabbis claimed to be inerrant. Consider the *responsum* penned by R. Moses Sofer (1762–1839), *Ḥatam Sofer, Qobeṣ Teshubot* (Jerusalem: 5733/1973), #65, 76b. He was the spiritual leader of Hungarian Jewry, one of the most important communities at the time. His standing and reputation for sanctity, wisdom, and leadership was unique. See the learned study by Aaron M. Schreiber, "The Ḥatam Sofer's Nuanced Attitude Toward Secular Learning, Maskilim, and Reformers," *The Tora u-Madda Journal* 11 (2002–2003), pp. 123–173. And yet, he freely admitted that during the forty years of his ministry he was erroneous twice. To be precise, not quite so; rather he acknowledged that twice he wrongly admitted that he had been in error. (Whether to be erroneous for having wrongly admitted that one had committed a blunder is to be regarded as 'error' is a matter too subtle to be examined by the writer of these lines). To appreciate the nuanced position of this illustrious rabbi it would be important to remember that in the *qedoshim* environment, rabbinic discussions and arguments are grasped in terms of a combat between knights; see Section V, n. 82. In the *hasagot*-mood, the contenders' main concern, as per heroic combat, is victory, rather than prosaic 'truth' or 'justice' (see Chapter 64). No greater humiliation could befall a hero than having to apologize or admit error. Therefore, it would be best to view queries and answers as clever stratagems, designed to trap the opponent and win victory. As the author of our *responsum* explained, the rabbis submitting questions to him were quite familiar with the usual views on the matter, and expected that

> ...perhaps he [i] could offer a fresh aspect (לחדש דבר), different than what the standard authorities [had exposed]. [ii] Or would differ from them (לחלוק עליהם), [iii] or to say that one should rely on the opinion of such an authority, etc.

In view of such a situation, the highest concern of a rabbi issuing a reply was to parry any possible attack, in case the party in question decided to investigate the subject and find a flaw in the rabbi's reasoning. In which case, he would be forced to admit error, since everyone could make a mistake.

> Therefore, I necessarily have to let him know the reason for having decided (the matter) differently than the opinion of the rabbi submitting the question. So that he should not scrutinize after me and find that I made a mistake, and (then) I would have to apologize and declare: 'What I have submitted to you was in error'—given that every human can err! That is why I have to make known [to those who submit a query before me] the grounds [for the decision I am making] and my rationale.

The query that our learned rabbi was examining was a criticism to a previous reply. Our rabbi realized that the rabbi submitting the question had investigated his reply and was raising some objections.

> Now, upon receiving his query again, censuring me, [inquiring] if I still maintained my original position, I see, however that his demonstrations are without merit. I have realized that he had scrutinized after me, but having not found [any contrary argument] except for a number of objections having no merits. Why should I have to reply to him and justify myself? Why I should bother with that?! Either way: if he would comply with my decision—that would be fine!—and if he would not comply—that would be even better—so that I would no longer be responsible! Since I fulfilled my responsibility and I have replied to him, and am no longer obliged to clarify the matter more!

Having dismissed the objections raised by the rabbi, he would no longer risk the possibility of admitting error and having to retract publicly. It is in this context that our rabbi disclosed that he had a spotless—or quasi spotless—record.

> However, if I am in error I would have to retract. Thank God, in the last forty years I have not [committed an error], except twice. Once, I was corrected by the erudite rabbi ... and I concurred with him. However, I have now studied ... and examined [the matter], and realized that I was mistaken for concurring with him ... The other time [that I acknowledged error] ... the erudite rabbi ... [corrected me] and I concurred with him. However, [another] erudite rabbi ... summarized my *responsum*, and concluded that I was mistaken in concurring [with the contender rabbi and to acknowledge error], but that the law was according to my original decision. Thank God, except for these [two cases] I don't know [of any error that I committed].

In a census taken in 1941 in Hungary, were counted 61548 Jews that had converted to Christianity; by 1944 the number was 100000. We should also note that 69400 Jews had passed over to the Russian Orthodox Church. In the year 1854, the number of Jews that passed over to the Russian Orthodox Church was 4439; see William O. McCagg, Jr., "Jewish Conversion in Hungary in Modern Times," in Todd M. Endelman, ed. *Jewish Apostasy in the Modern World* (New York: Holmes & Meier, 1987), pp. 142–164. It is true that the ministry of this celestial rabbi had taken place some 100 years earlier. What is truly baffling is that in spite of having been privileged with such a splendid stewardship, when the opportunity arose, a large number of Jews chose to convert to Christianity. Facing this mystery, even the most rationalistic mind would have to confess how recondite and inexplicable the ways of history are!

68. Settled Law

See *Studies in the Mishne Tora*, pp. 47–60. There is a concept in rabbinic legal discourse akin to 'settled law' in American legal tradition. It refers to a law assumed to have been settled by the courts in one way, but within the power of the court to change. In this sense, for example, it was used by John G. Kester in an oral argument before the Supreme Court, on October 4, 2006, p. 14: "This case came as a shock in 2004. And in fact, are the judges below in this series of cases all said we thought it was settled law the other way."

A similar idiom is "קבעו ... הלכה לדורות," *Tosefta Berakhot* 5:2, p. 25; *Berakhot* 11a; *Pesaḥim*100a; *Ketubot* 50b; *Teshubot ha-Rambam*, #310, vol. 2, p. 577 (in contradistinction with "הוראת שעה," which is a legal decision that *cannot be cited as precedent*, cf. *MT Sanhedrin* 24:4). The same applies to "הלכה רווחת," *Yebamot* 14b; *Ḥolin* 57b; *Yerushalmi Yebamot* I, 6, 3a; *The Mishnah of Rabbi Eliezer* (Heb.), IX, p. 169; *Teshubot Rab Neṭruna'e Gaon*, 2 vols. (Jerusalem: Ofeq Institute, 5754/1994), #223–224, vol. 2, p. 350; #329, vol. 2, p. 490; *Teshubot Ge'one Mizraḥ wu-Ma'arab*, #72, 18a; *Teshubot ha-Ge'onim ha-Ḥadashot*, #153, p. 210; #179, p. 253; R. Isaac Alfasi, *Halakhot, Ketubot* 44a. The same is with "קבע הלכה," *Tosefta Berakhot* 1:4, p. 2; 5:2, p. 26; cf. *Demai* 5:24, p. 93 and *Ḥolin* 57b; *Ta'aniyot* 2:5, p. 331; *Ḥagiga* 2:11, p. 385. An analogous expression is "הלכה קבועה," see *Teshubot Rab Neṭruna'e Gaon*, #223, vol. 1, p. 219; #321, vol. 2, p. 476 (= *Sh'are Ṣedeq* IV, 4, #56, p. 149). In R. Abraham ibn 'Ezra, Introduction, *Commentary to the Pentateuch*, s.v. *Ha-Derekh Ha-Rbi'it*, we find: "ויש שהוא כהלכה שאינה קבועה." A good example of 'settled law' is the note of R. Ḥanan'el on *Shabbat* 92b, cf. Shraga Abramson, *Perush Rabbenu Ḥanan'el la-Talmud*, p. 110.

To say that the anti-Maimonideans were not acquainted with any of the above is nothing less than a gross euphemism.

69. Relying on Legal Sources and Authorities

No reliable *halakhic* expert (סביר וגמיר בכל התורה כלה) would deem a quotation from a 'source'—any source—to constitute in and of itself a legal decision (פסק, הוראה). The trajectory from a source or sources to a legal decision (הלכה למעשה) is what Maimonides refers to as "the *path* of the law" (דרך המשפט); see Appendix 48 and Section V, n. 303. In this connection, it would be highly instructive to examine a few key-passages in a *responsum*, *Teshubot R. Abraham b. ha-Rambam*, #98, pp. 143–149. The case concerned a decision issued by a local judge. The issue was complex, and the case was submitted to Maimonides' son for review. What makes this case particularly significant is the fact that the sitting judge rendered the verdict on the basis of the *Mishne Tora*. The first point of concern was that fluency in and familiarity with legal texts were not sufficient to render a judgment without a proper conceptualization of the law and proficiency in "the path of the law" (דרך המשפט). Here is the passage in question:

> In particular, cases requiring judicial analysis and study (Ar. נט'ר ותפקה) require the exercise of sharp judicial investigation and impeccable procedure (Ar. חד'ק אלפקיה וחסן תצרפה =Heb. דרך המשפט) in (the interpretation) of the written text (of the law). It is because of cases like this, that (the Tora) stipulated that judges must be "wise and intelligent" (*Dt* 1:13)—since in

> the adjudication of the law, one (qualification) without the other is of no use. 'Wisdom' stands for knowledge of what was previously said (on the matter), and 'intelligence' is excellence in (legal) conceptualization and procedure (Ar. חסן אלתצור ואלתצרף, p. 144).

Turning to the quotation from the *Mishne Tora* (p. 147), R. Abraham Maimonides remarked: "The judge that based his view on the text of the work (*Mishne Tora*) has, doubtlessly read only the first half (of the paragraph)… and skipped the end." In law, a quotation is meaningless unless it is accompanied by solid judicial analysis. To accomplish this, the judge had to show the "conceptual gist" (טעם) of the edict that had been argued; see Appendix 19. In the case brought before R. Abraham Maimonides, the sitting judge failed to show how it was applicable to the case at hand (p. 146). Again, a quotation "from the work" (*Mishne Tora*) is no substitute for judicial analysis. The pivotal point to be asked is: "Did (the judgment) rendered, conform to the best judicial analysis and judicial process (Ar. חסן אלפקה ולאתצרף) of the *halakhot* (involved in the case before us)?"

It follows that a case cannot be resolved on the basis of legal citations without taking into consideration the specific circumstances present in the case at hand. Objectors to this view may want to make reference to the rabbinic principle that a "statement should not be quantified differently" (נתת דבריך לשיעורים, *Shabbat* 35b, etc.); i.e., it should be interpreted uniformly. Anticipating this argument, R. Abraham Maimonides explained the enormous difference between formulating a law or legal principle in the abstract [as when explaining a law in class; cf. Mishna *Berakhot* 2:5–7], where precision and consistency are of the essence, and a judge "sitting in judgment or rendering a judicial instruction on a specific case (Ar. בחסב וקאעה ג'רת)." Concerning the latter, he offered the following outline:

> In general, let me say, that a judge that bases his decisions only on the literal reading of the text, is weak and pathetic. This attitude, in fact, runs contrary to (what the rabbis instructed): "A judge must follow what his eyes showed him!" (p. 147)

In simple terms, this means that quoting the law will not suffice when rendering a legal decision! Rather, the text of the law should serve as the *basis* upon which a legal theory is construed.

> The manifest tenor of a legal text (Ar. אלאמור אלמסטורה) should function as the judicial doctrine (Ar. אצל of the case at hand). However, it is incumbent upon the judge, either adjudicating or giving judicial instruction, to analyze (the doctrine or doctrines) in light of each of the circumstances pertaining to the case before him. The judge must relate the judgment that he is rendering

> to a (legal) concept, which he construes on the basis of derivations (Ar. פרוע) stemming from those judicial doctrines. The numerous stories mentioned in the Talmud about legal decisions, were not brought for naught, neither were they cited in order to rely [uncritically] on them, but to educate the judge so that he should learn from them about the power of judicial analysis and the best judicial procedure (Ar. קוה פקה וחסן תצרף; pp. 147–148).

On the imperative for the judge to consider the specificities of the case at hand, rather than rely on generalities, see R. Joseph b. Susan quoted by R. Samuel de Oceda, *Midrash Shemu'el* (Amsterdam, 5627/1867), on *Abot* 1:18, 19b.

In essence, judicial reliance on the view of legal authorities, without proper analysis, is a form of advocacy which no competent judge would cite as as a source of textual meaning. I would like to call attention to a halakhic method developed in recent years. Rather than to examine the legal issue according to the traditional sources and judicial procedure, always taking into account the distinctiveness of the case at hand, as it was practiced in both the Sephardic and Ashkenazic rabbinate (I am thinking of the late R. 'Uzziel and R. Herzog, respectively, the first Chief Sephardic and Chief Ashkenazic rabbis of the State of Israel), it has become acceptable for unlearned rabbis to render halakhic decisions by rumbling 'sources,' without proper analysis of either the law or the case. (In the footsteps of scholastic 'proof' consisting of 'quoting' an authority; see above Chapter 53). According to the new methodology, a 'judical decision' is rendered simply by tallying the views expressed by different authorities in the course of time, and then 'relying' (לסמוך) on the 'majority view' (דעת הרוב), i.e., 18 *vs*. 17. If the number is the same on both sides, then if the prohibition were Biblical, it is forbidden and if rabbinical it is permitted. To my mind, this is like someone who is not a certified physician, prescribing a medical procedure by tallying medical opinions on the matter—without checking the patient! The method is fundamentally flawed. First, it is practically impossible to tally the total number of opinions on any given issue, particularly if one were to take into account mss and rare editions, as well as views issued on the matter that for a number of reasons never reached major libraries and publications. Moreover, to augment the 'total' number of authorities 'consulted,' these rabbis includes writers citing or making reference to one another. Furthermore, in the process of listing and classifying the various views, they are portrayed monochromatically, without examining either the nuance of the ruling or its specific context. Its principal shortcoming, however, is the failure to offer a critical appraisal of the views in question. Given that conclusions are reached on the basis of 'majority view' (דעת הרוב), the analysis is superficial and trite, as the rabbi attempts 'to explain' his decision through the use of lame analogies. Key issues are overlooked. Contrary opinions are often sidestepped in a dismissive vein (אין כאן מקום להאריך, etc). To assume a posture of self-assurance and mask lack of knowledge, the tone varies from condescension to irreverence and unabashed disrespect, interrupted here and there with irrelevant digressions. Because these rabbinic authorities are halakhically incompetent and intellectually insecure, often when they decide in favor of a more lenient position, they go on to counsel adoption of the stringent view (והמחמיר תבוא עליו ברכה). Concerning this type of semi-literate halakhists, see the penetrating remarks of R. Ḥayyim D. Sh. Zurafa, *Sha'ar Shelomo* (Leghorn, 5638/1878), 165c–166b. R. Israel Moses Ḥazzan called attention to the enormous damage that bogus-halakhists cause. In particular, how their halakhic decisions promote division and turn their supporters into fanatics and superstitious, rather than into men and women of faith; see my *R. Israel Moshe Ḥazzan* (Heb.) (Haifa: Academic Publishers, 1978), pp. 79–82.

There is nothing wrong if someone that does not know a *halakha* would 'rely' (סומך) on the opinion of an expert, just as we do when we file our Tax Returns; see above Appendix 10. Indeed, R. Joseph ibn Megas maintains that someone who is not a thoroughly competent Talmudist fully acquainted with the interpretations and ruling of the Geonim, and "relies on the Geonic responsa" (מי שמורה מתשובת הגאונים וסמך עליהם)" is preferable to someone "who thinks he knows Talmud and relies on himself" (שחושב שהוא יודע בתלמוד וסומך על עצמו), *She'elot wu-Tshubot* #195, 29d; cf. *Studies in the Mishne Tora*, pp. 39–40. Some of the great legal minds of Israel—among them the celebrated Maran Joseph Caro and the Rama—would 'rely' (לסמוך) on the 'majority view' or on the local authorities and traditions. However, they were, first and foremost, eminently legal scholars (גמיר וסביר בכל התורה כולה), and they knew how to bring into play the whole gamut of sources, as well as legal precedent and legal theory, to bear upon their own analyses and conclusions. Hence, the incisive, highly informed insights characterizing their writings. By way of contrast, contemporary rabbis tallying opinions are not consummate scholars (גמיר וסביר בכל התורה כולה). My dissatisfaction with their *halakhic* conclusions is not because they are *necessarily* wrong—indeed, many times they happened to be right! But because these rabbis act as if they were issuing a judicial decision (הוראה), when in fact they may only be *counseling* to rely (לסמוך) or not to rely (לסמוך) on this or that authority. In which case, their counsel may not be necessarily better (or worse) than a similar counsel advanced by any other such rabbi, and it would not warrant stirring up strife and contention among various Jewish communities and congregants. That is why, like the classical anti-Maimonideans, these rabbis make sure that their audience is made up of a halakhically illiterate or semi-literate (תלמיד שלא הגיע להוראה) public, unable to realize that what they promote as a judicial ruling (פסק, הוראה), is nothing more than an advocacy position, motivated in some cases by ideology and politics, rather than *halakha*.

For some sobering remarks on those who are not proficient in all legal sources (גמיר וסביר בכל התורה כולה), issuing decisions on the basis of ideology, rather than *halakha*, see *Birke Yosef*, *Ḥoshen Mishpaṭ*, XV, 3.

70. The Library of Lucena

Concerning the Library of Lucena, see R. Abraham Zacuto, *Yoḥasin ha-Shalem*, eds. Herschell Filipowski and A. H. Freimann (Jerusalem, 5723/1963), 214 a-b. On R. Abul'afia's ancient manuscripts of the Talmud, cf. R. Mordechai Sabato, *A Yemenite Manuscript of Tractate Sanhedrin* (Heb.) (Jerusalem: Yad Izhak Ben-Zvi, 1998), p. 217. On the collection of Talmud from the Geonim, and the private library of R. Samuel ha-Nagid and R. Joseph ibn Megas, see *Kitab Al-Rasa'yil*, pp. 79–80; cf. ibid, p. 68. From the substantial quotations of Geonic and early sources, it is evident that Ramban had some knowledge of these materials. However, it is not clear whether he had direct access to the library or only to some material circulating freely among the learned. The incunabula fragments of the Talmud printed in Spain, edited by H. Z. Dimitrovski, *S'ridei Talmud,* 2 vols. (New York: The Jewish Theological, 1977) are to be carefully examined. I only studied the fragments of *'Erubin*. Although they contain significant variants, many are consistent with later 'French' readings, rather than what is known as 'Andalusian.'

BIBLIOGRAPHY

BIBLICAL LITERATURE

Biblia Rabinica = *Miqra'ot Gedolot.* 4 vols. Venice, 5308/1548.

The Bible in Aramaic. 5 vols. Ed. Alexander Sperber. Leiden: E. J. Brill, 1962.

Targum Anqelos = *Targum Onqelos*. In *Miqra'ot Gedolot.*

Targum to Job from Qumran Cave XI. Ed. Michael Sokoloff Ramat-Gan: Bar-Ilan University, 1974.

Targum Neophyti 1. Ed. Alejandro Díez Macho. 6 vols. Madrid and Barcelona: Consejo de Investigaciones Científicas, 1968–1979.

Targum Pseudo-Jonathan. Ed. M. Ginsburger, *Pseudo-Jonathan*. Berlin: S. Calvary, 1903.

Sharaḥ. Arabic version. R. Se'adya Gaon. Ed. J. Derenbourg, *Version Arabe du Pentateuque*. Paris : Ernest Leroux, 1893.

JEWISH HELLENISTIC LITERATURE

Book of Maccabees. In *Apocrypha*. Ed. R. H. Charles. Oxford: Clarendon Press, 1978.

Eupolemus. In ed. J. Freudenthal. *Hellenistische Studien*. Vol. 2. Breslau, 1875.

Josephus. *Complete Works*. Loeb Classical Library.

Philo. *Complete Works*. 10 vols. and 2 Supplements. Loeb Classical Library.

RABBINIC LITERATURE

TANNAITIC and TALMUDIC

Mishna. In Maimonides' *Perush ha-Mishnayot.* Ed. and tr. R. Joseph Qafih. 7 vols. Jerusalem: Mossad Harav Kook, 1967.

Tractate Ma'aserot (Heb.). Ed. and com. Yehuda Felix. Ramat-Gan: Bar-Ilan University Press, 2005.

Mishna Shabbat. In Abraham Goldberg. *Commentary to the Mishna Shabbat* (Heb.). Jerusalem: Jewish Theological Seminary, 1976.

Tosefta. Ed. M. S. Zuckermandel. Jerusalem: Wahrman Books, 5035/1975.

Tosefta. Ed. Saul Lieberman. *Zera'im-Neziqin*. New York: Jewish Theological Seminary, 1955–2001.

Talmud Yerushalmi. Venice, 5283/1523.

Talmud Yerushalmi Fragments of the Genizah. Ed. Louis Ginzberg. New York: The Jewish Theological Seminary, 1909.

Yerushalmi Qiddushin. Constantinople, 5514/1754.

Talmud Babli. Standard Edition. 18 vols. Vilna: Re'em, 5668/1908.

Babylonian Talmud. Codex Florence. Jerusalem: Makor, 1972.

S'ridei Talmud. Ed. H. Z. Dimitrovski. 2 vols. New York: The Jewish Theological, 1977.

Treatise Ta'anit. Ed. Henry Malter. Philadelphia: The Jewish Publication Society, 1978.

A Yemenite Manuscript of Tractate Sanhedrin (Heb.). Ed. R. Mordechai Sabato. Jerusalem: Yad Izhak Ben-Zvi, 1998.

Tractate 'Abodah Zarah. Ed. Shraga Abramson. New York: The Jewish Theological Seminary of America, 1957.

Diqduqe Soferim. Raphael N. N. Rabbinovicz. 15 vols. Jerusalem, 5720/1960.

Abot de-R. Natan. Ed. Salomon Schechter. Vienna, 5647/1887.

Massekhet Soferim. Ed. R. Michael Higger. New York: Debe-Rabbanan, 1937.

Massekhet Kalla Rabbati. Ed. Michael Higger. Brooklyn: Moinester Publishing, 1936.

Masechet Derech Eretz and Perek Ha-Shalom (Heb.). Ed. Daniel Sperber. Jerusalem: Sur-Ot, 1994.

MIDRASHIM

Mekhilta de-R Yishma'el. Eds. H. S. Horovitz and I. A. Rabin. Jerusalem: Wahrmann Books, 1970.

Mekhilta de-R. Shim'on b. *Yoḥai.* Eds. J. N. Epstein and E. Z. Melamed. Jerusalem: Mekize Nirdamim, 1955.

Sifra. Codex Assemani LXVI. Ed. Louis Finkelstein. New York: The Jewish Theological Seminary, 5717–1956.

Sifra. Ed. Isaac Hirsch Weiss. Vienna, 5622/1862.

Sifre Bemidbar. Ed. H. Horovitz. Jerusalem: Wahrman Books, 1966.

Sifre Debarim. Ed. Louis Finkelstein. New York: The Jewish Theological Seminary of America, 1969.

Sifre Zuṭa. Ed. Menahem Kahana. Jerusalem: Magnes Press, 2002.

Bereshit Rabba. Ms. Vatican Ebr. 30. Facsimile. Jerusalem: Makor, 5731/1971.

Bereshit Rabba. Eds. J. Theodor and Ch Albeck. 3 vols. Jerusalem: Wahrman Books, 1965.

Midrash Rabba [*'al ha-Tora ve-Ḥamesh Megillot*]. 2 vols. Vilna. Reprinted: Jerusalem, 5735/1975.

Vayyiqra Rabba. Ed. Mordecai Margulies. 5 vols. Jerusalem: American Academy for Jewish Research, 1960.

Debarim Rabba. Ed. Saul Lieberman. Jerusalem: Wahrman Books, 1974.

Midrash Tanna'im, Debarim. Ed. David Z. Hoffman. Berlin, 5668/69–1909.

Ekha Rabbati. Ed. Salomon Buber. Vilna, 1899.

Aggadat Ester. Ed. Salomon Buber. Cracow, 5657/1897.

Shir ha-Shirim Rabba. In *Midrash Rabba* [*'al ha-Tora ve-Ḥamesh Megillot*].

Qohelet Rabba. In *Midrash Rabba* [*'al ha-Tora ve-Ḥamesh Megillot*].

Midrash Tanḥuma. 2 vols. Warsaw, 5611/1851.

Midrash Tanḥuma. Ed. S. Buber. 2 vols. Vilna, 5645/1885.

Midrash Tehillim. Ed. Salomon Buber. New York: Om Publishing, 1947.

Midrash Shemu'el. Ed. Salomon Buber. Cracow, 5653/1893.
Midrash Mishle. Ed. Salomon Buber. Vilna: 5653/1893.
Midrash Aggada. Ed. Salomon Buber. Vienna, 1894.
Midrash Zuṭa. Ed. Salomon Buber. Berlin, 1894.
Pesiqta de-Rab Kahana. Bernard Mandelbaum. 2 vols. New York: The Jewish Theological Seminary, 1962.
Midrash ha-Gadol. Bereshit. Ed. Mordecai Margulies. Jerusalem: Mossad Harav Kook, 5727/1967.
Midrash ha-Gadol. Deuteronomy. Ed. S. Fisch. Jerusalem: Mossad Harav Kook, 1972.
Yalquṭ Shim'oni. 2 vols. Jerusalem: Ch. Vegshel, n.d.
Tana de-Be Eliyahu. Lublin, 5657/1897.
Ozar Midrashim. 2 vols. Ed. J. D. Eisenstein. New York, 1915.
Great is Peace (Heb.). Ed. Daniel Sperber. Jerusalem: Massada Press, 1979.
Mishnat R. Eli'ezer. Ed. H. G. Enelow. New York, Jewish Theoloical Seminary, 1933.
Zohar. 3 vols. Leghorn, 5618/1858.
Tiqqune ha-Zohar. Leghorn, 5646/1886.

GEONIC LITERATURE

R. 'Amram Gaon. *Seder Rab 'Amram Gaon*. Ed. Daniel Goldshmidt. Jerusalem: Mossad Harav Kook, 1971.
Gaonica. Ed. S. Assaf. Jerusalem: Darom, 1933.
Genizah Studies. Ed. Louis Ginzberg. 2 vols. New York: Jewish Theological Seminary, 1928–1929.
Geonic Responsa (Heb.). Ed. Elazar Hurvitz. New York, 1995.
Geonica. Ed. Louis Ginzberg. 2 vols. New York: Jewish Theological Seminary, 1909.
Ḥadashim gam Yeshanim. Ed. Abraham E. Harkavy. Jerusalem: Karmiel, 5730/1970.
Halakhot Gedolot. Ed. Ezriel Hildesheimer. Vol. 1. Jerusalem: Mekize Nirdamim, 1971.
Halakhot Pesuqot. Ed. R. S. Sassoon. Jerusalem: Mekize Nirdamim, 1950. Hebrew version, *Hilkhot Re'u*. Versailles: Cerf et fils, 1886.
R. Ḥanan'el. *Perush*. In *Talmud Babli*. Vilna: Re'em, 5668/1908.
———*Pesaḥim*. Jerusalem. Makhon Leb Sameah, 5751/1991.
Harkavi, A. E. *Ḥadashim gam Yeshanim*. Jerusalem: Karmiel, 5730/1970.
Ḥazzan, R. Israel Moses. *'Iyye ha-Yam*. Ed. and annotated by Leghorn: 5629/1869.
Hilkhot Re'u. See *Halakhot Pesuqot*.
Mann, Jacob. *The Jews in Egypt and in Palestine*. 2 vols. Oxford: Oxford University Press, 1969.
———*Texts and Studies*. 2 vols. New York: Ktav Publishing, 1972.
Newly Discovered Geonic Responsa (Heb.). Eds. S. Emanuel and A. Shoshana. Jerusalem—Cleveland: Ofeq Institute, 1995.
R. Nissim Gaon. *Sefer ha-Mafteaḥ*. Ed. J. Goldenthal. Vienna, 1847.
———*R. Nissim Gaon*. Ed. Shrage Abramson. Jerusalem: Mekize Nirdamim, 1965.
Oṣar ha-Geonim. 13 vols. Ed. B. M. Lewin. Jerusalem, 1928–1943.

Oṣar ha-Geonim. Sanhedrin. Ed. R. Ch. Z. Tobias. Jerusalem: Mossad Harav Kook, 1966.

Perush ha-Geonim 'al Ṭahorot. Ed. J. N. Epstein. Berlin: Mekize Nirdamim, 1924.

Qehillat Shelomo. Ed. R. Solomon A. Wertheimer. Jerusalem, 5659/1899.

R. Se'adya Gaon. *Commentary on Exodus*. Ed. and tr. Y. Ratzaby (Jerusalem: Mosad Harav Kook, 1998.

———"Fragments." Ed. M. Zucker. *Sura* 2 (1955–1956).

———*Ha'egron*. Ed. N. Allony. Jerusalem: The Academy of the Hebrew Language, 1969.

———*Perush. Daniel*. Ed. and tr. R. Joseph Qafiḥ. Jeruslem: Deror, 5741/1991.

———*Perush. Mishle*. Ed. and tr. R. Joseph Qafiḥ. Jerusalem, 5736/1976.

———*Saadya's Commentary on Genesis* (Heb.). Ed. Moshe Zucker. New York: Jewish Theological Seminary, 1984. See Zucker, Moses. *Rav Saadya Ga'on's Translation of the Torah*.

———*Sefer ha-Galui*. Ed. Abraham E. Harkavi. In *Zikhron la-Rishonim*, vol. 5. St. Petersburg, 1892.

———*Tafsir Yesha'ya*. Ed. and tr. Y. Ratzaby. Kiriat Ono: Mkhon Moshe, 1993.

———*Teshubot. Traité de Successions*. In *Oeuvres Complète*, vol. 9. Ed. R. Joel Muller. Paris: Ernest Leroux, 1897.

Sha'are Ṣedeq. Jerusalem, 5726/1966.

"*Shelosh Teshubot le-R. Hayye Gaon*." *Ginze Kedem* 2 (1923).

R. Sherira Gaon. *Iggeret*. Ed. B. M. Lewin. Haifa,1921.

Teshubot Ge'onim Qadmonim. Ed. David Cassel. Berlin, 1848.

Teshubot ha-Ge'onim. Ed. R. Jacob Musafia. Lyck, 5624/1864.

Teshubot ha-Ge'onim. Ed. Abrahan E. Harkavi. Berlin, 1887.

Teshubot R. Neṭruna'e Ga'on. 2 vols. Ed. Robert Brody. Jerusalem—Cleveland: Ofeq Institute, 1994.

Teshubot R. Sar Shalom. Ed. R. Samuel ha-Cohen Weinberg. Jerusalem: Mossad Harav Kook, 1975.

Zikhron la-Rishonim. Ed. Abraham E. Harkavy. Petersburg, 1880.

JEWISH and RABBINIC WRITERS

R. Aaron ibn Ḥayyim. See Ibn Ḥayyim, R. Aaron.

Abarbanel, R. Isaac. *Mif'alot Elohim*. Lemberg, 1863.

———*Naḥalat Abot*. New York, 5713–1953.

Abendana, R. Isaac. *Discourses on the Ecclesiastical and Civil Polity of the Jews*. London, 1706.

Abi Zimra, R. David b. *Teshubot ha-Radbaz*. 2. vols. Warsaw, 5642/1882.

R. Abraham b. David (of Posquières). *Teshubot wu-Psaqim*. Jerusalem: Mossad Harav Kook, 5724/1964.

R. Abraham ibn 'Ezra. See Ibn 'Ezra, R. Abraham.

R. Abraham ibn Ṭawwa'ah. See Ibn Ṭawwa'ah, R. Abraham.

Abrahams, Israel. *Studies in Pharisaism and the Gospels*. Second Series. New York: Ktav Publishing House, 1967.

Abramson, Shraga. *Ba-Merkazim*. Jerusalem: Mossad Harav Kook, 5725/1965.

———*"Dibre Ḥazal be-Shirat ha-Nagid."* *World Congress for Jewish Studies*. I. Jerusalem: Hebrew University Press, 5712/1952.

———*Mi-Pi Ba'ale Leshonot*. Jerusalem: Mossad Harav Kook, 5748/1998.

———*"Mi-Torato shel R. Shemu'el ha-Nagid."* *Sinai* (Jubilee Volume) 100 (5748/1988).

———*Perush R. Ḥanan'el la-Talmud*. Jerusalem: Vagshal, 5755/1995.

———*Tractate 'Abodah Zarah*. Ed Shraga Abramson. New York: The Jewish Theological Seminary of America, 1957.

Abulafio, R. Hezekiah David. *Ben Zequnim*. Leghorn, 5553/1793.

Abul'afya, R. Isaac. *Pene Yiṣḥaq*. Vol. 6. Jerusalem, 5668/1908.

Abul'afya, R. Ḥayyim. *Miqra'e Qodesh*. Izmir, 5482/1722.

———*Yishrash Ya'aqob*. Izmir 5489/1729.

Abul'afya, R. Me'ir ha-Levi. *Kitab Al-Rasa'yil le-Rabbenu Me'ir ha-Levi*. Paris, 5631/1871.

———*Yad Rama* on *Baba Batra*. New York: Da'at, 5712/1952.

Adrete, R. Solomon. *Ḥiddushe ha-Rishba 'al Aggadot ha-Shas*. Ed. R. Sh. M. Weinberger. Jerusalem, 5726/1966.

———*Ḥiddushe ha-Rishba. Megilla*. Ed. Z. Dimitrovsky. Jerusalem: Mossad Harav Kook, 5741/1981.

———*Ḥiddushe ha-Rishba. Rosh ha-Shana*. Ed. Z. Dimitrovsky. Jerusalem: Mossad Harav Kook, 5741/1981.

———*Ḥiddushe ha-Rishba. Shabbat*. Ed. Y. Bruner. Jerusalem: Mossad Harav Kook, 5746/1986.

———*Teshubot ha-Rishba*. Vol. 1. Bne Brak, 5718/1958.

———*Teshubot ha-Rishba*. Ed. Ch. Z. Dimitrovsky. 2 vols. Jerusalem: Mossad Harav Kook, 1990.

Aghamati, R. Zekharya. *Sefer ha-Ner. Berakhot* (British Museum, ms. 11361).

———*The Tractates Baba Kamma*... London: British Museum, 1961.

Agus, R. Jacob. "Toynbee's Epistle to the Jews." *Commentary* 32 (1961).

Al'ami, R. Solomon. *Iggeret Musar*. Ed. A. A. Haberman. Jerusalem: Sifriyat Meqorot, 1946.

Al-Ashqar, R. Joseph. *Mirkebet ha-Mishne*. Ed. J. Shpigel 5753/1993.

Al-Ashqar, R. Moses. *She'elot*. Jerusalem, 5719/1959.

Albeck, Ch. *Mabo la-Talmudim*. Tel Aviv: Dvir, 1969.

Albelda, R. Moses. *Darash Moshe*. Venice, 5363/1603.

Albo, R. Joseph. *Sefer ha-'Ikkarim*. Ed. and tr. Isaac Husik. Philadelphia: The Jewish Publication Society, 1946.

Alexander, Edward. *The Jewish Wars: Reflections by One of the Belligerents*. Carbondale: Southern Illinois University Press, 1996.

Alexander, Philip S. "Mysticism." In Martin Goodman, ed. *Oxford Handbook of Jewish Studies*. Oxford: Oxford University Press, 2002.

Alfandari, R. Ḥayyim. *Esh Dat*. Constantinople, 5478/1718.

Algazi, R. Ḥayyim. *Ba'e Ḥayye*. Orta-Kivvae, 5479/1719.

Algazi, R. Israel Jacob. *Shalme Ṣibbur*. Saloniki, 5550/1790.

Algazi, R. Solomon. *Yabin Shemu'a*. Legohorn, 5552/1792.

Al-Ḥarizi, R. Judah. *Taḥkemoni.* Warsaw, 5659/1899.

Almadari, R. Judah. Ed. R. Y. ha-Levi Kuperberg. In *Sanhadre Gedola*. Vol. 2. Jerusalem: Makhon Harry Fischel, 5729/1969.

Almosnino, R. Moses. *Tefilla le-Moshe*. Israel: Hamakhon le-Ḥeqer Yahdut Saloniki, 5748/1988.

Amram, David Werner. *The Jewish Law of Divorce*. London: David Nutt, 1897.

'Arama, R. David. *Perush 'al ha-Rambam*. Saloniki, 5330/1570.

'Arama, R. Isaac. *Ḥazut Qasha*. Sabioneta, 5312/1552.

Ardiṭ, R. Joshua Sh. *Ḥinna ve-Ḥisda*. 3 vols. Izmir, 5633/1873.

Arragel, R. Moses. In *Biblia de la Casa de Alba.* Madrid:

Imprenta Artística, 1920.

'Arusi, R. Raṣon."*Birkat Hadlaqat ...*" *Sinai* 85 (5739/1979).

———"*Qeri'at Tirgum ha-Tora veha-Haftara be-Ṣibbur*." *Sinai* 89 (5742/1982).

Asher, R. *Hilkhot ha-Rosh*. Standard Edition.

———*Teshubot ha-Rosh*. Constantinople, 5277/1517.

———*Tosafot ha-Rosh. Berakhot*. In *Berakha Meshulleshet.* Warshaw, 5623/1853.

Assaf, S. "*Me-Ginze Bet-ha-Sefarim ...*" In *Minḥa le-David Yelin*. Jerusalem: Ruben Mass, 5695/1925.

———*Tequfat ha-Geonim*. Jerusalem: Mossad Harav Kook, 5715/1955.

R. 'Azriel. *Commentary of Talmudic Aggadoth* (Heb.). Ed. Isaiah Tishby. Jerusalem: Magnes Press, 1982.

Azulai, R. Ḥ.Y.D. *Birke Yosef.* Leghorn, 5534–36/1774–76.

———*Mar'it ha-'Ayyin*. Leghorn, 5564/1804.

———*Petaḥ 'Enayim*. Leghorn, 5550/1790.

———*Ya'ir Ozen*. Leghorn, 5552/1792.

Baḥur, R. Eliahu. *Meturgeman*. Izna, 1541.

R. Baḥye b. Asher. *Be'ur*. Ed. C. B. Chavel. 3 vols. Jerusalem: Mossad Harav Kook: 5737/1977.

Baer, Yitzhak. *A History of the Jews in Christian Spain*. 2 vols. Philadelphia: The Jewish Publication of America, 1961–5722.

———"The Kabalistic Doctrine in the Christological Teaching of Abner of Burgos" (Heb.). *Tarbiz* 27 (1958).

Baron, Salo W. *A Social and Religious History of the Jews*. Vols. 3, 4, 8. Philadelphia: Jewish Publication Society, 1957.

Belkin, Samuel. *In His Image*. New York: Abelard-Schuman, n.d.

Benamozegh, R. Elie. *Em la-Miqra*. 5 vols. Leghorn, 1862–1865.

———*Jewish and Christian Ethics.* San Francisco: Emanuel Blochman, 5633–1873.

———*Mabo le-Tora she-be-'al-Pe*. Ed. R. E. Zini. Jerusalem, 5762/2002.

R. Benjamin of Tudela. *The Itinerary of Benjamin of Tudela*. Ed. and tr. Marcus Nathan Adler. New York: Philipp Feldheim, n.d.

Benveniste, R. Joshua. *Sede Yehoshua'*. Constantinople, 5514/1754.

Berakha, R. Isaac. *Berakh Yiṣḥaq*. Venice, 5723/1763.

Berkovitz, R. Eliezer. *Essential Essays on Judaism*. Jerusalem: Shalem Press, 2002.

Besamim Rosh. Ed. R. Isaac de Molina. Berlin, 5553/1793.
Bickerman, Elias. *From Ezra to the Last of the Maccabees*. New York: Schocken Books, 1962.
———*The God of the Maccabees*. Leiden: E. J. Brill, 1979.
——— *The Jews in the Greek Age*. Cambridge, Mass.: Harvard University Press, 1988.
———"The Maccabean Uprising: An Interpretation." In ed. Judah Goldin. *The Jewish Expression*. New Haven: Yale University Press, 1976.
———*Studies in Jewish and Christian History*. 3 vols. Leiden: E. J. Brill, 1986.
Blau, Ludwig. "Methods of Teaching Talmud." *Jewish Quarterly Review* 15 (1903).
Blumenkranz, Bernhard. *Les auteurs chretiens latins du moyen age sur les juifs et le Judaism*. Paris: Mouton, 1963.
Bodoff, Lipman. "Abraham's Covenant, Chosenness, and the Binding of Isaac." *Midstream*. November/December 2006.
———*The Binding of Isaac, Religious Murders, & Kabbalah*. New York: Devorah Publishing, 2005.
———"The Message of the Prophet Elisha." *Midstream*. February/March 1999.
———"Religious Murders: Weeds in the Garden of Jewish Tradition?" *Midstream*. January 1988.
Boṭon, R. Abraham de. *Leḥem Mishne*. In *Mishne Tora*. Standard Edition.
Broyer, M. "The Ashkenazi Semikha" (Heb.) *Zion* 33 (1968).
Buber, Martin. "To Create New Words?" In Martin Buber, *A Believing Humanism*. New York: Simon and Schuster, 1967.
Cardoso, Yshac. *Las Excelencias de los Hebreos*. Amsterdam, 1679.
Caro, Maran Joseph. *Abqat Rokhel*. Saloniki, 5551/1791.
———*Bedeq ha-Bayit*. Standard Edition.
———*Bet Yosef*. Standard Edition.
———*Kesef Mishne*. In *Mishne Tora*. Standard Edition.
———*Shulḥan 'Arukh*. Standard Edition.
Castro, R. Jacob. *'Erekh Leḥem*. Constantinople, 5478/1718
Chazan, Robert. *European Jewry and the First Crusade*. Berkeley: University of California Press, 1987.
Chicatilla, R. Joseph. *Sha'are Ora*. Warsaw, 5643/1883.
Churgin, Pinkhos. *The Targum to Hagiographa*. New York: Horeb, 1945.
Cohen, R. Abraham. *Sabbath Sermons*. London: Soncino Press, 1960.
Cohen, Avinoam. *Ravina and Contemporary Sages* (Heb.). Ramat Gan: Bar Ilan University, 2001.
Crescas, R. Ḥasdai. *Or ha-Shem*. Tel-Aviv, 5723/1963.
Dan, Joseph. "*Ba'yat Qiddush ha-Shem*." In *Holy Was and Martyrlogy*. Jerusalem: The Historical Society of Israel, 1967.
———*On Sanctity* (Heb.). Jerusalem: Hebrew University Press, 1997.
———"The Vicissitudes of the Esoterism of German Hasidim." In *Studies in Mysticism and Religion*. Hebrew Section. Jerusalem: Magnes Press, 1967.
R. David ha-Kohen. *Teshubot ha-Radak*. Constantinople, 5297/1537.
De la-Ara, R. Ḥiyya ha-Cohen. *Mishmerot Kehunna*. Amsterdam, 5508/1748.

Dershowitz, Alan M. *The Genesis of Justice.* New York: Warner Books, 2000.
Dienstag, Israel. Ha-Im Hitnagged ha-Gra le-Mishnato ha-Pilosophit shel ha-Rambam? *Talpioth* 4 (1949).
Dubnow, Simon. *Geschichte des Chassidismus*. Vol. 1. Berlin: Judischer Verlag, 1931.
Duran, R. Isaac Profiaṭ. *Ma'ase Efod.* Vienna, 1865.
Duran, R. Simon b. Ṣemaḥ. *Tashbeṣ*. Amsterdam, 5498/1738.
———and R. Solomon Duran, *Yakhin w-Bo'az*. Leghorn, 5542/1782.
R. Eli'ezer Ashkenazi. *Dammeseq Eli'ezer*. Lublin, 5407/1647.
R. Eliyahu ha-Levi. *Zeqan Aharon.* Constantinople, 5494/1734.
Elitzur, Yehudah. *Israel and the Bible* (Heb.). Ramat-Gan: Bar-Ilan University Press, 1999.
Epstein, J. N. *Prolegomena* (Heb). Ed. E. Z. Melamed. 2 vols. Jerusalem: Magnes Press, 1957.
Fano, R. Menaḥem 'Azarya di. *Teshubot*. Venice, 5360/1600.
Farḥon, R. Solomon. *Maḥberet he-'Arukh*. Ed. S. Gottlieb Stern. Presburg 5604/1844.
Faur, José. "*'Aliyat Qaṭan li-Qro ba-Tora*." In *Studies in Memory of the Rishon le-Zion R. Y. Nissim*, vol. 1. Jerusalem: Yad ha-Rab Nissim, 5745/1985.
———"Basic Concepts in Rabbinic Hermeneutics." *Shofar* 16 (1997).
———"The Biblical Idea of Idolatry," *Jewish Quarterly Review* 69 (1978).
———"A Crisis of Categories: Kabalah and the rise of Apostasy in Spain." In eds. Moshe Lazar and Stephen Haliczer. *The Jews Of Spain and The Expulsion of 1492*. California: Labyrinthos, 1997.
———"Concerning the term *qore be-iggeret*" (Heb.). *Alei Sefer* 15 (1988–1989).
———"David Nassy: On Prejudice and Related Matters." In eds. Lea Dasberg and Jonathan N. Cohen. *Neveh Ya'akov: Jubilee Volume Presented to Dr. Jaap Meijer*. Assen, The Netherlands: Van Gorcum, 1982.
———"Delocutive Expressions in the Hebrew Liturgy," *Ancient Studies in Memory of Elias Bickerman* (*The Journal of the Ancient Near Eastern Society*) 16–17 (1984–1985).
———"Don Quixote: Talmudist and *mucho más*." *The Review of Rabbinic Judaism* 4 (2001).
———"El pensamiento Sefardí frente a la iluminación Europea." In *Pensamiento y Mística Hispanojudía y Sefardí*. Cuenca: Ediciones de la Universiad de Casilla-La Mancha, 2001.
———"Esoteric Knowledge and the Vulgar: Parallels between Newton and Maimonides." *Trumah* 12 (2002).
———"Francisco Sánchez's Theory of Cognition and Vico's *verum/factum*." *New Vico Studies* 5 (1987).
———"God as a Writer: Omnipresence and the Art of Dissimulation." *Religion & Intellectual Life* 6 (1989).
———*Golden Doves with Silver Dots: Semiotics and Textuality in Rabbinic Tradition.* Bloomington: Indiana University Press, 1986.
———"The Hebrew Personal Pronoun." In *Perspectives on Jews and Judaism*. New York: Rabbinical Assembly, 1979.

———"The Hebrew Species Concept and the Origin of Evolution: R. Benamozegh's Response to Darwin." *Rassegna Mensile di Israel* 63 (1997).

———"*Hora'at ha-Talmud ba-Masoret ha-Ḥinnukhit ha-Sfaradit,*" *Shebile Ḥinnukh,* 35 (1975).

———*Homo Mysticus*. Syracuse: Syracuse University Press, 1999

———"Idolatry." *Encyclopedia Judaica.*

———"Imagination and Religious Pluralism: Maimonides, ibn Verga, and Vico." *New Vico Studies* 10 (1992).

———*In the Shadow of History*. Albany, N.Y.: SUNY, 1992.

———"Jews, *Conversos*, and Native Americans: The Iberian Experience." *Annual of Rabbinic Judaism* 3 (2000).

———"The Jewish Mentality of Francisco Sánchez," *Mentalities* 7 (1992).

———"Law and Hermeneutics in Rabbinic Tradition." *Cardozo Law Review* 14 (1993).

———"The Legal Thinking of Tosafot." *Dine Israel* 6 (1975).

———"The Limits of Readerly Collusion in Rabbinic Tradition." *Soundings* 76 (1993).

———"Maimonides' Starting Precept" (Heb.). Forthcoming.

———"On Martyrdom in Jewish Law" (Heb.). *Annual of Bar-Ilan University*, 30–31 (2006).

———"Monolingualism and Judaism." *Cardozo Law Review* 14 (1993).

———"Newton, Maimonidean." *Review of Rabbinic Judaism* 6 (2003).

———"Of Cultural Intimidation and Other Miscellanea: Bar-Sheshakh *v*. Raba." *Review of Rabbinic Judaism* 5 (2002).

———"One-Dimensional Jew." *Review of Rabbinic Judaism* 2 (1999).

———"Performative and Descriptive Utterances in Jewish Law" (Heb.). In ed. Arye Edrei. *Studies in Jewish Law in Honor of Professor Aaron Kirschenbaum* (*Dine Israel* 20–21, 5760–5761).

———"Person and Subjectivity: A Linguistic Category." *Mentalities* 6 (1990).

———*Rabbi Yisrael Moshe Ḥazzan: The Man and his Works* (Heb.) Haifa: Academic Publishers, 1978.

———"Retórica y hemenéutica: Vico y la tradición rabínica." In ed. E. Hidalgo-Serna, *et al. Pensar Para el Nuevo Siglo.* Vol. 3. Napoli: La Cittá del Sole, 2001.

———"Sephardim in the Nineteenth Century: New Directions and Old Values." *Proceedings of the American Academy for Jewish Research* 44 (1977).

———"Sir Isaac Newton—'a Judaic Monotheist of the School of Maimonides.'" In eds. Gorge K. Hasselhoff and Otfied Fraisse. *Moses Maimonides (1138–1204).* Germany: Ergon Verlag, 2004.

———"The Splitting of the *Logos*: Some Remarks on Vico and Rabbinic Tradition." *New Vico Studies* 3 (1985).

———"The Status of Jewish Real Estate outside Israel's Territory" (Heb.). *In Honour of Prof. Avner H. Shaki*. Ed. Chief Justice Aharon Bark, *Law Review Netanya Academic College*, 4 (2005).

———*Studies in the Mishne Tora* (Heb.). Jerusalem: Mossad Harav Kook, 1978.

———"The Targumim and Halakha." *Jewish Quarterly Review* 66 (1976).

———"The Third Person in Semitic Grammatical Theory and General Linguistics." *Linguistica Biblica Bohn* 46 (1979).

———"Tosafot ha-Rosh le-Massekhet Berakhot." *Proceedings of the American Academy for Jewish Research* 33 (1965).

———"Two Models of Jewish Spirituality." *Shofar* 10 (1992).

———"*Ve-Niṣḥu Ḥakhme Ummot ha-'Olam et Ḥakhme Yisrael.*" In *Minḥa Le-Yiṣḥaq*. Eds. Chief Justice of Israel Supreme Court Aharon Barak and Professor Menashe Shawa. Jerusalem: Lishkat 'Orkhe-Din, 1999.

———"Vico, el Humanismo Religioso y la Tradición Sefardita." *Cuadernos sobre Vico* 7 (1997).

———"*Zekhut ha-Rofe ...*" *Dine Israel* 7 (1976).

Feldman, Leon A. "*Teshubat ha-Rishba ...*" *Sinai*. Jubilee Volume, 100 (1987).

Fijo, R. 'Azarya de. *Bina le-'Ittim*. 2 vols. Jerusalem: Vagshel, 5749/1989.

Finzi, R. Solomon. *Mafteaḥ ha-Gemara*. In *Temim De'im*. Venice, 1622.

Fleischer, Ezra. *Hebrew Liturgical Poetry in the Middle Ages* (Heb.). Jerusalem: Keter Publishing, 1975.

Friedman, M. A. "*Ve-Khatab lo ...*" *Sinai* 84 (5739/1979).

Frimer, Norman. See Schwarts, Dov.

Gaster, Theodor H. *Festivals of the Jewish Year*. New York: William Morrow and Company, 1952.

———*The Holy and the Profane*. New York: William Morrow, 1980.

R. Gereshom. *Perush R. Gereshom*. In *Talmud Babli*. Vilna: Re'em, 5668/1908.

Gershenzon, Shoshana G. *A Study of* Teshuvot la-Meḥaref *by Abner of Burgos*. Ph. D. Thesis. New York: The Jewish Theological Seminary of America, 1984.

Gilat, Y. D. "Kallah, Months of." In *Encyclopaedia Judaica*.

Ginzberg, Louis. *A Commentary to the Palestinian Talmud,* (Heb.). Vols. 3–4. New York: The Jewish Theological Seminary of America, 1941.

Glatzer, Nahum. "Peace in Classical Judaism." In his *Essays in Jewish Thought*. Alabama: Alabama University Press, 1978.

Glueck, Nelson. *Ḥesed in the Bible*. Cincinnati: Hebrew Union College, 1967.

Goiten, S. D. *Religion in a Religious Age*. Cambridge, Mass: Association for Jewish Studies, 1974.

Goldberg, Abraham. *Commentary to the Mishna Shabbat* (Heb.). Jerusalem: Jewish Theological Seminary, 1976.

Goodblat, David M. *Rabbinic Instruction in Sasanian Babylonia*. Leiden: E. J. Brill, 1975.

Gordis, Robert. "Democratic Origins in Ancient Israel—the Biblical *'Edah.*" In *Alexander Marx Jubilee Volume* (English Section). New York: The Jewish Theological Seminary of America, 1950.

Graetz, Heinrich. *History of the Jews*. Vol. 3. Philadelphia: Jewish Publication Society, 1894.

Gruber, Mayer I. "The Term *Midrash* in Tannaitic Literature." In ed. Rivka Ulmer, *Discussing Cultural Influences*. Lanham: University Press of Ametica, 2007.

———"God, Image of." In *Encyclopaedia of Judaism*, Supplement #1.

Ḥabib, R. Israel Jacob. '*En Ya'aqob.* Standard Edition.

Ḥabib, R. Levi b. *She'elot wu-Tshubot*. Venice, 5325/1565.

Ḥabib, R. Moses b. *'Azarat Nashim.* Leipzig, 5619/1859.

———*Kappot Temarim*. New York, 5713/1953.

———*She'elot wu-Tshubot*. Jerusalem: 5687/1927.

Ḥajez, R. Jacob. *'Eṣ Ḥayyim*. Verona, 5408/1648.

———*Halakhot Qeṭannot*. Venice, 5464/1704.

———*Teḥillat Ḥokhma*. Verona, 5407/1647.

Halkin, Abraham. "In Defense of Maimonides' Code" (Heb.). *Tarbiz* 25 (1956).

———"Why was Levi ben Hayyim Hounded"? *Proceedings of the American Academy for Jewish Research*, 34 (1966).

Harkabi, Yehoshafat. *The Bar Kokhba Syndrome*. Chappaqua, N.Y.: Russel Books, 1983.

R. Ḥatam Sofer. *Qobeṣ. Teshubot*. Jerusalem: 5733/1973.

R. Ḥayyim b. Isaac. *Or Zarua'.* Israel, 1958.

Ḥazzan, R. Joseph. *Ḥiqre Leb. Eben ha-'Ezer*. Saloniki, 5573/1813.

———*Ḥiqre Leb. Yore De'a*. Part I. Leghorn, 5554/1794.

Ḥazzan, R. Moses Israel. *Iyye ha-Yam*. Leghorn, 5629/1869.

———*Kerakh shel Romi*. Leghorn, 5636/1876.

———*Words of Peace and Truth*. Ed. Samuel Meldola. London, 5605/1845.

Hellenistic Views on Jews and Judaism. Jerusalem: Zalman Shazar Center, 1974.

Heinman, I. "*Midrash*." *Encyclopaedia Miqra'it*. Jerusalem: Bialik, 1988.

Helmreich, William B. *The World of the Yeshiva*. Hoboken, New Jersey: Ktav Publishing, 2000.

Hertz, Chief Rabbi J. H. *The Pentateuch and Haftorahs.* London: Soncino Press, 5758–1997.

———*Sermons Addresses and Studies*. 3 vols. London: Soncino Press, 1938.

Heschel, Abraham Joshua. *God in Search of Man*. Philadelphia: Jewish Publication Society, 1956.

———"Inspiration in the Middle Ages." In *Alexander Marx Jubilee Volume* (Heb. Section). New York: The Jewish Theological Seminary of America, 1950.

———*The Prophets*. New York: The Burning Bush Press, 1962.

———*The Sabbath*. New York: Harper & Row, 1952.

Ḥoq le-Ya'aqob. 2 vols. Jerusalem, 5755/1995.

Ibn 'Aqnin, R. Joseph ben Judah. *Hitgallut ha-Sodot ve-Hofa'ot ha-Me'orot*. Ed. and trans. A. S. Halkin. Jerusalem: Mekize Nirdamim, 1964.

———*Mebo ha-Talmud.* Jerusalem, 5727/1967.

Ibn 'Aṭṭar, R. Ḥayyim. *Or ha-Ḥayyim.* Warsaw, 5671/1911.

Ibn Bal'am, R. Judah. *Commentary to Isaiah*. Ed. M. Peretz. Ramat-Gan: Bar-Ilan University, 1992.

———*Commentary to Jeremiah*. Ed. M. Peretz. Ramat-Gan: Bar-Ilan University, 2002.

Ibn Daud, R. Abraham. *Sefer ha-Qabbalah*. Ed. tr. and annotated by Gerson D. Cohen. Philadelphia, The Jewish Publication Society, 1967.

Ibn 'Ezra, R. Abraham. *Commentary* to *Ecclesiastes*. In *Miqra'ot Gedolot.*

———*Commentary* to the Tora. In *Miqra'ot Gedolot.* Ms. Vat. Ebr. 38. Ed. Prof. Etan Levine. *Abraham ibn Ezra's Commentary to the Pentateuch*. Jerusalem: Makor, 1974.

———*Yesod Mora ve-Sod Tora.* Eds. Joseph Cohen and Uriel Simon. Ramat-Gan: Bar-Ilan University Press, 2002.

Ibn 'Ezra, R. Moses. *Kitab al-Muḥadara wal-Mudhakara*. Ed. and tr. A. S. Halkin. Jerusalem: Mekize Nirdamim, 1975.

Ibn Gaon, R. Shem Ṭob. *Migdal 'Oz*. In *Mishne Tora*. Standard Edition.

Ibn Ḥayyim, R. Aaron *Qorban Aharon*. Venice: 5369/1609.

Ibn Jannaḥ, R. Jonah. *Kitab al-Luma'*. Ed. Joseph Derenbourg. Paris: F. Vieweg, 1886. Hebrew translation, R. Judah ibn Tibbon, *Sefer ha-Riqma*. Ed. M. Wilensky. Berlin: Akademie-Verlag, 1930. Facsimile edition. 2 vols. Jerusalem: Academy for the Hebrew Language, 5724/1964.

———*Sefer ha-Shorashim*. Hebrew tr. R. Judah ibn Tibbon. Berlin: Mekize Nirdamim, 1896.

Ibn Leb, R. Joseph. *Teshubot*. Amsterdam, 5446/1686.

Ibn Megas, R. Joseph. *She'elot wu-Tshubot*. Saloniki, 5546/1786.

Ibn Faquda, R. Baḥye. Arabic original: *Kitab al-Hadaya illa fara'id al-Qulub*. Ed. A. S. Yahuda. Leiden: E.J. Brill, 1912. Hebrew tr. and Arabic originl, in *Ḥobot ha-Lebabot*. R. Joseph Qafiḥ. Jerusalem, 5733/1973.

Ibn Shu'eb, R. Joel. *Nora Tehillot.* Saloniki, 5329/1569.

Ibn Shu'eb, R. Joshua. *Derashot 'al ha-Tora.* Constantinople, 5283/1523.

Ibn Verga, R. Joseph. *She'erit Yosef.* Warsaw, 1909.

Ibn Verga, R. Solomon. *Shebeṭ Yehuda*. Eds. Azreil Shochet and Y. Baer. Jerusalem: Mossad Bialik, 5707/1947.

Ibn Ṭawwa'ah, R. Abraham. *Ḥuṭ ha-Mshullash.* In *Sefer ha-Tashbeṣ*. Amsterdam, 5498/1738.

Idel, Moshe. "Nahmanides, *Kabbalah, Halakha,* and Spiritual Leadership." In eds. Moshe Idel and Mortimer Ostow, *Jewish Mystical Leaders and Leadership in the 13th Century*. Northvale, New Jersey: Jason Aronson, 1998.

R. Immanuel of Rome. *The Book of Proverbs.* Naples, ca. 1487. Offset: Jerusalem, The Hebrew University Press, 1981.

R. Isaac b. Sheshet. *Teshubot ha-Ribash*. New York, 5714/1954.

Isserlich, R. Moshe. *Mappa*. In *Shulḥan 'Arukh*. Standard Edition.

———*She'elot wu-Tshubot*. Amsterdam, 5471/1711.

Jabès, Edmond. *Elya*. Berkely, Ca.: Tree, 1973.

R. Jacob Castro. See Castro, R. Jacob.

Jellinek, Adolph. *Ginze Ḥokhmat ha-Qabbala*. Leipzig, 1853.

Jessurun, Rehuel. *Dialogo dos Montes*. Ed. and tran. Philip Polack. London: Tamiesis Books, 1975.

R. Joel ibn Shu'eb. See Ibn Shu'eb, R. Joel.

R. Jonah ibn Jannaḥ. See Ibn Jannaḥ, R. Jonah.

R. Joseph ibn 'Aqnin. See Ibn 'Aqnin, R. Joseph.

R. Joseph ibn Leb. See Ibn Leb, R. Joseph.

R. Joseph ibn Megas. See Ibn Megas, R. Joseph.

R. Joseph ibn Verga. See Ibn Verga, R. Joseph.

R. Joseph b. Zabbara. *Sefer Sha'ashu'im*. Ed. Israel Davison. Berlin: Eshkol, 5685/1925.

R. Joseph Jabès. See Ya'beṣ, R. Joseph.

R. Joshua ha-Nagid. See Maimonides, R. Joshua.

R. Joshua ibn Shu'eb, R. See Ibn Shu'eb, R. Joshua.

R. Judah al-Barceloni. See R. Judah al-Bargeloni.

R. Judah al-Bargeloni. *Sefer ha-Sheṭarot*. Ed. S. J. Halberstam. Berlin: Mekize Nirdamim, 1898.

———*Perush Sefer Yeṣira*. Berlin: Mekize Nirdamim, 1885.

———*Sefer ha-'Ittim*. Cracow, 5660/1900.

R. Judah ha-Levi. *Kuzari*. Arabic original, *Kitab al-Radd wa-al Dalil fi-al Din Dhalil*. Ed. H. Baneth. Jerusalem: Magness Press, 1977. Hebrew version: *Kuzari*. Ed. and trans. Yehuda Even Shmuel. Tel-Aviv: Dvir Publishing, 1994.

———*The Liturgical Poetry of R. Yehuda ha-Levi* (Heb.). Ed. Dov Jarden, vol. 1. Jerusalem, 1978.

———*Selected Poems of Jehudah Halevi*. Philadelphia: Jewish Publication Society, 1928.

R. Judah b. ha-Rosh. *Zikhron Yehuda*. Eds. J. Rosenberg and D. Cassel. Berlin, 5606/1846.

R. Judah he-Ḥasid. *Sefer ha-Ḥasidim*. Ed. R. Reuben Margulies. Jerusalem: Mossad Harav Kook, 5724/1964.

R. Judah he-Ḥasid, Sir Leon. *Tosafot Berakhot*. In *Berakha Meshulleshet*. Warshaw, 5623/1853.

R. Judah ibn Bal'am. See Ibn Bal'am, R. Judah.

R. Judah Messer Leon. *Nofet Ṣufim*. Mantua ca. 1475. Offset: Jerusalem: The Jewish National and University Library Press, 1981.

Kasher, Rimon. "The Interpretation of Scripture in Rabbinic Literature." In ed. Martin Jan Mulder, *Mikra*. Philadelphia: Fortress Press, 1988.

Katsh, Abraham I. *Judaism in Islam* (Heb.). Jerusalem: Kiryat Sepher, 1957.

Katz, J. "Halakhah and Kabbala—First Contacts" (Heb.). In *Yitzhak F. Baer Memorial Volume*. Jerusalem: The Historical Society of Israel, 1980.

Kellner, Menachem. *Maimonides on the Decline of the Generations and the Nature of Rabbinic Authority*. Albany: SUNY Press, 1996.

———"Maimonides on the Decline of the Generations." In *Ḥazon Naḥum*. New York: Yeshiva University, 5758/1998.

———"A New and Unexpected Textual Witness." *Tarbiz* 75 (2006), pp. 565–566 (Hebrew).

Kimḥi (Qimḥi), R. David. *Hebrew Grammar* (*Mikhlol*). Trans. and annotated by William Chomsky. New York: Bloch Publishing, 1952–5713.

Kimḥi (Qimḥi). *The Commentaries on Proverbs of the Kimhi Family*. Ed. Frank Talmage. Jerusalem: Magness Press, 1990.

Klausner, Joseph. "Why was Jeremiah Ignored in the Book of Kings?" In *Alexander Marx Jubilee Volume*. Hebrew Section. New York: Jewish Theological Seminary, 1953.

Koppel, Moshe. *Seder Kinnim*. Israel: Aluma Publishing, 1998.

Konvitz, Milton R. *The Alien and the Asiatic in American Law.* Ithaca, N.Y.: Cornell University, 1946.

———"Conscience, Natural Law and Civil Disobedience in the Jewish Tradition." In *Of Law and Man*. Ed. Shlomo Shoham. Sabra Books: New York and Tel Aviv: 1971.

———"A Philosophy of Human Rights." In eds. Abraham I. Katsh and Leon Nemoy. *Essays on the Occasion of the Seventieth Anniversary of the Dropsie University.* Philadelphia: Dropsie University, 1979.

———*Religious Liberty and Conscience.* New York: Viking Press, 1968.

Kotler, R. Aharon. *Mishnat Aharon.* Vol. 1. Jerusalem: Makhon Yerushalayim, 5745/1985.

La Nazione Ebrea a Livorno e a Pisa (1591–1700). Edited and annotated by Professor Renzo Toaff. Florence: Leo S. Olschki, 1990.

Laniado, R. Samuel. *Keli Faz.* Venice, 5417/1657.

Leiman, Sid Z. *The Canonization of Hebrew Scripture.* New Haven: The Connecticut Academy of Art and Sciences, 1991.

Lerner, Meron B. "The Simple Meaning…" (Heb.). *Annual of Bar-Ilan University* 30–31 (2006).

Leon, R. Isaac de. *Megillat Ester.* Venice, 5352/1592.

R. Levi ben Gereshom. *Perush 'al ha-Tora.* Venice, 5307/1547.

R. Levi b. Ḥabib. *She'elot.* Venice, 5325/1565.

Levi, R. Judah ha-. See R. Judah ha-Levi.

Levi, R. Abraham ha-. *Ginnat Veradim.* Vol. 2. Constantinople, 5476/1716.

Levine, Étan. *Heaven and Earth, Law and Love: Studies in Biblical Thought.* Berlin: Walter de Gruyter, 2000.

Levy, Hans. "Cicero on the Jews in his Speech for the Defense of Flaccus" (Heb.). *Zion* 7 (1942).

———*Studies in Jewish Hellenism* (Heb.). Jerusalem: Bialik Institute, 1969.

———"Tacitus on the Origin and Manners of the Jews" (Heb.). *Zion* 8 (1943).

Lieb, R. Arie. *Sha'agat Arye.* Warsaw, 5629/1869.

Lieberman, Saul. *Greek in Jewish Palestine.* New York: Philipp Feldheim, 1965.

———*Hellenism in Jewish Palestine.* New York: The Jewish Theological Seminary of America, 1950.

———"How Much Greek in Jewish Palestine?" In *Biblical and Other Studies.* Cambridge, Mass.: Harvard University Press, 1963.

———"On Adjurations among the Jews" (Heb.). *Tarbiz* 27 (1958).

———*Shkiin.* Jerusalem: Bamberg & Wahrman, 1939.

———*Tosefta Ki-Fshuṭah.* 10 vols. New York: The Jewish Theological Seminary of America, 1955–2001.

——— *Yerushalmi Ki-Fshuṭo.* Jerusalem: Darom, 5695/1935.

Lonzano, R. Menaḥem de. *Shete Yadot.* Jerusalem, 5730/1970.

Luzzato, Samuel David. *Commentary to the Pentateuch* (Heb.). Tel Aviv: Dvir, 1965.

———*Philoxenus* (Heb.) Cracow, 1895.

———"*Viqquaḥ 'al ha-qabbala.*" In his *Meḥqare Yahdut.* Warsaw, 5673/1913.

Ma'arabi, Pereṣ. "*Ledarko ...*," *Sinai* (Jubilee Volume) 100 (5748/1988).

Mahler, Raphael. *A History of Modern Jewry*. New York: Schocken, 1971.

Maimonides, R. Abraham. *Milḥamot ha-Shem*. Ed. R. Ruben Margaliot. Jerusalem: Mossad Harav Kook, n.d.

———*High Ways of Perfection*. Ed. and tr. Samuel Rosenblatt. Vol. 2. Baltimore: John Hopkins Press, 1938.

———*Perush*. Ed. Sh. Weisenberg. Letchworth, 1959.

———*Teshubot*. Ed. A. H. Freimann. Jerusalem: Mekize Nirdamim, 1937.

Maimonides, R. David. *Al-Mirshad*. Ed. and tr. P. B. Fenton. Jerusalem: Mekize Nirdamim, 1987.

Maimonides, R. Joshua. *Teshubot R. Joshua ha-Nagid*. Ed. and tr. R. Y. Ratzabi. Jerusalem: Makhon le-Ḥeqer Mishnat ha-Rambam, 5749/1989.

Maimonides, R. Moses. *Epistle to Yemen* (= *Iggeret Teman*). Ed. Abraham S. Halkin. Tr. Boaz Cohen. New York: American Academy for Jewish Studies, 1952.

———*Guide for the Perplexed*. Arabic original, *Dalalat al-Ḥa'irin*. Ed. Issachar Joel and Solomon Munk. Jerusalem, 1931.

———*Iggeret Teman*. See *Epistle to Yemen*.

———*Iggerot*. Ed. and tr. R. Joseph Qafiḥ. Jerusalem: Mossad Harav Kook, 1972.

———*Iggerot ha-Rambam*. Ed. D. H. Baneth. Jerusalem: Mekize Nirdamim, 1947.

———*Letters and Essays of Maimonides* (Heb.). Ed. and tr. Isaac Shailat. 2 vols. Maaleh Adumim: Maaliyot Press, 5748/1988.

———*Mishne Tora*. Standard Edition.

———*Perush ha-Mishnayot*. Ed. and tr. R. Joseph Qafiḥ. 7 vols. Jerusalem: Mossad Harav Kook, 1967.

———*Qobeṣ Teshubot ha-Rambam*. Leipzig, 5619/1859.

———*Sefer ha-Madda'*. Eds. M. H. Katzenelenbogen and Saul Lieberman. Jerusalem: Mossad Harav Kook, 1964.

———*Sefer ha-Miṣvot*. Ed. and tr. R. Joseph Qafiḥ. Jerusalem: Mossad Harav Kook, 1971.

———*Teshubot ha-Rambam*. Ed and tr. J. Blau. 4 vols. Jerusalem: Mekize Nirdamim, 1975–1986.

———*Treatise on Logic*. Ed. and tr. Israel Efros. New York: American Academy for Jewish Research, 1938.

———*Treatise on Resurrection*. Ed. Joshua Finkel. New York: American Academy for Jewish Research, 1939.

Mal'akhi, R. Jacob. *Yad Mal'akhi*. New York: Keter, 5706/1946.

Malachi, Z. "*Abraham ibn 'Ezra neged Qalir*." *Peles*. Tel-Aviv: Tel-Aviv University, 1980.

Malter, Henry. *The Treatise Ta'anit*. Ed. Philadelphia: The Jewish Publication Society, 1978.

R. Manasseh ben Israel. *The Conciliator*. London: 5602–1842.

Mantel, Hugo. *Studies in the History of the Sanhedrin*. Cambridge, Mass. Harvard University Press, 1961.

Marcus, Ivan. *Piety and Society*. Leiden: E.J. Brill, 1981.

———"Robert Chazan, *European Jewry and the First Crusade*." *Speculum*, 64 (1989).

Margalioth, M. *Sefer ha-Razim*. Jerusalem: The American Academy for Jewish Research, 1966.

Masnut, R. Samuel. *Midrash Daniel wu-Midrash 'Ezra.* Eds. I. S. Lange and S. Schwartz. Jerusalem: Mekize Nirdamim, 1968.

Medina, R. Samuel de. *Teshubot Meharashdam. Ḥoshen Mishpaṭ*. Saloniki, 5358/1598.

Melammed, Ezra Z. *Essays in Talmudic Literature* (Heb.). Jerusalem: Hebrew University, 1986.

R. Menaḥem Me'iri. *Bet ha- Beḥira, Pesaḥim*. Jerusalem: Yad ha-R. Hezog, 5726/1966.

———*Bet ha- Beḥira, Sanhedrin*. Ed. A. Sofer. Jerusalem: Qedem, 5734/1974.

Mervaise [or Marvege], R. Jacob de. *She'elot wu-Tshubot min ha-Shamayim*. Ed. R. Reuben Margoliot. Jerusalem: Mossad Harav Kook, 1957.

Milḥemet ha-Dat. Ed. J. I. Kobakak. *Jeshurun* VIII (Bamberg, 1875).

Minḥat Qena'ot. Pressburg, 1838.

Mirsky, Aharon. *Ha'Piyut*. Jerusalem: Magness Press, 1990.

Miṭrani, R. Raḥmim Menaḥem. *Me'am Lo'ez*, on *Joshua*. Tr. to Heb. by Samuel Yerushalmi. Jerusalem: Ḥ. Vagshal, 5732/1972.

Morais, R. Sabato. *Italian Hebrew Literature*. New York: The Jewish Theological Seminary, 1926.

Morais, Vamberto. *A Short History of Anti-Semitism*. New York: W.W. Norton: 1972.

Mortera. R. Saul Levi. In Rehuel Jessurun. *Dialogo dos Montes.* Ed. and tran. Philip Polack. London: Tamiesis Books, 1975.

———*Gib'at Sha'ul*. Brooklyn, N.Y, 5751–1991.

———*Providencia de Dios con Yisrael*. Ms. Etz Hayyim 48C 20. Hebrew University Library.

Na'e, Sh. "*Ṭobim Dodekha Me-Yayyin.*" (Heb.). *Studies in Talmud and Midrashic Literature* in *Memory of Tirzah Lifshitz*. Jerusalem: Bialik Institute, 2005.

Naḥmanides, R. Moses. *Hasagot ha-Ramban*. Ed. C. B. Chavel. In *Sefer ha-Miṣvot le-ha-Rambam.* Jerusalem: Mossad Harav Kook, 1981.

———*Kitbe Ramban*. 2 vols. Ed. C. B. Chavel. Jerusalem: Mossad Harav Kook, 1963.

———*Perush ha-Tora*. 2 vols. Ed. C. B. Chavel. Jerusalem: Mossad Harav Kook, 1962.

———*Teshubot*. Ed. C. B. Chavel. Jerusalem: Mossad Harav Kook, 1975.

Nassy, David. *Lettre politico-theologico-morale sur les Juifs*. Paramaribo, ca. 1789.

R. Nathan b. Yeḥi'el. *'Arukh. Aruch Completum*. Ed. Alexander Kohut. 8 vols. Vienna and Berlin: Menora, 1926.

Neubauer, Ad. *Medieval Jewish Chronicles.* Oxford: Clarendon Press, 1887.

Neusner, Jacob. "The Constitutions of Judaism in Ancient Times: The Pentateuch and the Mishnah." *Journal of Reform Judaism* 36 (1989).

———*A Life of Rabban Yohanan ben Zakkai*. Leiden: E. J. Brill, 1962.

———*A History of the Jews in Babylonia*. Vols. 3–4. Leiden: E. J. Brill, 1968–1969.

———*Making the Classics in Judaism*. Atlanta, Georgia: Scholars Press, 1989.

———*The Philosophical Mishnah*. 3 vols. Atlanta, Georgia: Scholars Press, 1988–89.

———*The Social Study of Judaism*. 2 vols. Atlanta, Georgia: Scholars Press, 1988.

———*Understanding Seeking Faith*. Vol. 3. Atlanta, Georgia: Scholars Press, 1988.

Nieto, R. David. *Esh Dat*. London, 1715.

———*Maṭṭe Dan*. Spanish-Hebrew. London, 5474–1714

R. Nissim Gerondi. *Derashot ha-Ran*. Jerusalem: Mossad Harav Kook, 2003.

———*Teshubot*. New York: Publishing Corporation, n.d.

Oceda, R. Samuel de. *Midrash Shemu'el*. Amsterdam, 5627/1867.

Otzar Ḥilluf Minhagim. Ed. B. M. Lewin. Jerusalem: Makor, 1972.

Palache, J. L. *Semantic Notes on the Hebrew Lexicon*. Leiden: Brill, 1958.

Palaggi, R. Ḥayyim. *Ḥuqqot ha-Ḥayyim*. Izmir, 5632/1872.

———*Re'e Ḥayyim*. Vol. 2. Izmir, 5624/1864.

Pardo, R. David. *Sifre Debe-Rab*. Saloniki, 5559/1799.

———*Ḥasde David*. Vol. 2. Leghorn: 5650/1790.

Patai, Raphael. *The Jewish Mind*. New York: Charles Scribner's Sons, 1977.

Perrot, Charles. "The Reading of the Bible in the Ancient Synagogue." In ed. Martin Jan Mulder, *Mikra*. Philadelphia: Fortress Press, 1988.

Pines, Shlomo. "On the Concept of 'Spirits'" (Heb.) *Tarbiz* 57 (1988).

Qimḥi, R. David. *Commentary on Psalms*. (Heb.) Ed. Abraham Darom. Jerusalem: Mossad Harav Kook, 1971.

———*Sefer ha-Mikhlol*. See R. David Kimḥi (Qimḥi). *Hebrew Grammar* (*Mikhlol*).

———*Sefer ha-Shorashim*. Eds. J. H. R. Biesenthal and F. Lebrecht. Berlin, 1847.

Qimḥi, R. Joseph. *Sefer ha-Galui*. Berlin, 5247/ 1877.

Rabad (of Posquières). See R. Abraham b. David.

Rabbinowitz, L. *The Ḥerem Hayyshub*. London: Edward Goldstone, 1945.

Radaq. See Qimḥi, R. David; Kimḥi, R. David.

Rafel, Dov. "*Haqdamat Sefer 'Ma'ase Efod' le-Profiaṭ Duran*," *Sinai*. Jubilee Volume, 100 (1987).

Rama. See Isserlich, R. Moshe.

Reggio, R. Samuel Isaac. *Be'ur Yashar*. 5 vols. Vienna, 5581/1821.

———*Thora et Philosophia* (Heb.). Vienna, 1827.

Reif, Stefan C. *Judaism and Hebrew Prayer*. Cambridge: Cambridge University Press, 1993.

Reviv, Hanoch. *The Elders in Ancient Israel* (Heb.). Jerusalem: The Magness Press, 1983.

Riṭba. See R. Yom Ṭob as-Sibili.

Rosenthal, Abraham. "*Tora she-'al pe*." In eds. Moshe Bar-Asher and David Rosenthal, *Meḥqerei Talmud*. Vol. 2. Jerusalem: The Hebrew University, 1993.

Rozanes, R. Judah. *Mishne le-Melekh*. In *Mishne Tora*, standard edition.

Sabato, R. Mordechai. *A Yemenite Manuscript of Tractate Sanhedrin* (Heb.). Jerusalem: Yad Izhak Ben-Zvi, 1998.

Ṣabba', R. Abraham. *Ṣeror ha-Mor*. Cracow, 5365/1605.

Salvador, Joseph. *Paris, Rome et Jérusalem*. Vol. 1. Paris: Michel Lévy Frères, 1860.

R. Samuel Ashkenazi. *Yefe To'ar. Bereshit*. Venice: 5357/1597.

R. Samuel b. 'Eli. *Qobeṣ shel Iggerot*. Ed. R. Simḥa Assaf. Jerusalem: Makor, 5730/1970.

R. Samuel ha-Nagid. *Diwan Shemuel ha-Nagid. Ben Tehillim.* Ed. Dov Jarden. Jerusalem: Hebrew Union College Press, 1966.

———*Hilkhot Hannagid* (Heb.). Ed. Mordecai Margalioth. Jerusalem: The American Academy for Jewish Research, 1962.

R. Santob de Carrión. *Don Sem Tob Glosas de Sabiduría*. Ed. Agustín García Calvo. Madrid: Alianza Editorial, 1974. Ed. tr. and annotated by T. A. Perry. *The Moral Proverbs of Santob of Carrión*. Princeton: Princeton University Press, 1987.

Schechter, Salomon. *Aspects of Jewish Theology*. New York: Schocken, 1961.

———"*Ṣavva'a.*" *Bet-Talmud* 4 (5645/1885).

Scholom, Gershom. *Ha-Qabbala be-Probanṣ*. Jerusalem: Academon, 5746/1986.

———*Major Trends*. New York: Schocken Books, 1961.

———*On the Kabbalah*. New York: Schocken Books, 1969.

———*The Origin of the Kabbalah*. Princeton: Princeton University Press, 1987.

———*Reshit ha-Qabbala*. Jerusalem: Schocken, 5708/1948.

Schrieber, Aaron M. "The Ḥatam Sofer's Nuanced Attitude Towards Secular Learning, Maskilim, and Reformers." *The Tora u-Madda Journal* 11 (2002–2003).

———"*Hashqafato ...*" *BaDaD* 9 (5759/1999).

Schwarts, Dov. "*Ṣurot Shonot shel Magia ...*" *Proceedings of the American Academy for Jewish Studies*, 57 (1990–1991).

——— and Frimer, Norman E. *The Life and Thought of Shem Tov ibn Shaprut* (Heb.). Jerusalem: Ben-Zvi Institute, 1992.

Scott, Robert E. See Schwartz, Alan and.

Sefer Gezerot. Ed. A. M. Haberman. Jerusalem: Sifre Tarshish, 1945.

Sefer ha-Ḥinnukh. Ed. R. C. B. Chavel. Jerusalem: Mossad Harav Kook, 5729/1969.

Sepher ha-Razim (Heb.). Ed. Mordecai Margalioth. Jeruslem: The American Academy for Jewish research, 1966.

R. Sforno. *Be'ur 'al-ha-Tora*. Warsaw, 5617/1857.

Shalom, R. Abraham. *Neve Shalom*. Venice, 5335/1575.

Shatzmiller, Joseph. "The Forms of the Twelve Constellations: A 14th Century Controversy," (Heb.). In *Shlomo Pines Jubilee Volume*. *Jerusalem Studies in Jewish Thought* 9 (1990).

R. Shem Ṭob ben Isaac Arduṭiel. See R. Santob de Carrión.

Shepard, Sanford. *Shem Tov: His World and His Words*. Miami: Ediciones Universal, 1978.

Shiber, Y. "The status and confirmation of witnesses at wedding ceremonies in Jewish law." Ph. D. Thesis presented at Bar Ilan University, Fall, 2002.

R. Shimshon. *Perush ha-Mishnayot*. In *Talmud Babli.* Standard Edition. 18 vols. Vilna: Re'em, 5668/1908.

R. Shimshon of Chinon. *Sefer Keritut*. Warsaw, 5645/1885.

Shrem, R. Isaac. *Be'er Yiṣḥaq*. Leghorn, 5624/1864.

Silver, Daniel Jeremy. *Maimonidean Criticism and the Maimonidean Controversy*. Leiden: E. J. Brill, 1965.

R. Simḥa b. Samuel. *Maḥzor Viṭre*. Berlin, 5642–5657/1882–1897.

Sofer, R. Moses. *Ḥatam Sofer, Qobeṣ Teshubot*. Jerusalem: 5733/1973.

R. Solomon b. Melekh. *Mikhlal Yofi*. Amsterdam, 5445/1685.

Speiser, E. A. "The Biblical Idea of History in Its Common Near Eastern Setting." In ed. Judah Goldin. *The Jewish Expression*. New Haven: Yale University Press, 1976.

———"'People' and 'nation' of Israel." *Journal of Biblical Literature* 79 (1960).

Sperber, Daniel. *A Dictionary of Greek & Latin Legal Terms*. Ramat Gan: Bar-Ilan University, 1984.

Spiegel, Shalom. "Amos vs. Amaziah." In ed. Judah Goldin. *The Jewish Expression*. New Haven: Yale University Press, 1976.

———"The Legend of Isaac's Slaying and Resurrection." In *Alexander Marx Jubilee Volume*. Hebrew Section. New York: Jewish Theological Seminary, 1953.

———*The Last Trial*. New York: Schocken, 1969.

———"*Le-Farashat ha-Polmos ...*" In *Jubilee Volume in Honor of Professor Harry A. Wolfson*. Hebrew Section. Jerusalem: American Academy for Jewish Studies, 1965.

Stein, Leopold. *Untersuchungen uber die Proverbios Morales*. Berlin: Mayer & Muller, 1900.

Stern, Menahem. *Greek and Latin Authors on Jews and Judaism*, 3 vols. Jerusalem: The Israel Academy of Science and Humanities, 1974–1984.

Straus, Oscar S. *The Origin the Republican Form of Government in the United States*. New York: G. P. Putnam's Sons, 1885.

———*Roger Williams*. New York: D. Appleton-Century, 1936.

Sulzberger, Mayer. *The Polity of the Ancient Hebrews*. Philadelphia: Julius H. Greenstone, 1912.

Sussman, Y. "Tora she-be-'al Pe." *Meḥqerei Talmud*. Vol. 3, Part I (2005).

Ta-Shma, Israel M. *Early Franco-German Ritual and Custom* (Heb.). Jerusalem: Hebrew University, 1992.

———"*Ḥasidut Ashkenaz bi-Sfarad: Rabbenu Yona Gerondi, ha-'ish wu-fa'olo.*" In *Galut Aḥar Gola*. Jerusalem: Machon Ben Zvi, 1989.

———*Ha-Tfilla ha-Ashkenazit ha-Qduma*. Jerusalem: Hebrew University Press, 5763/2003.

———"Hilkhata Kebatrai" (Heb.). *Shenaton ha-Mishpat Ha-Ivri* 6–7 (1979–1980).

———"*Qeliṭatam shel sifre ha-Rif, ha-Raḥ, ve-Hilkhot Gedolot be-Ṣarfat wub-Ashkenaz beme'ot ha-Yod-Alef-Yod-Bet.*" *Qiryat Sefer* 55 (1980).

"Rabbi Yonah Girondi: Spirituality and Leadership." In eds. Moshe Idel and Mortimer Ostow. *Jewish Mystical Leaders and Leadership in the 13th Century*. Northvale, New Jersey: Jason Aronson, 1998.

———"*Shiqulim Pilosofim be-Hakhra'at ha-Halakha bi-Sefarad.*" *Sefunot* 18 (1985).

———"*Sifriyyatam shel Ḥakhme Ashkenaz bene ha-Me'a ha-Yod Alef-Yod Bet.*" *Qiryat Sefer* 60 (1985).

———"*Tosafot Gornish.*" *Sinai* 68 (1971).

Tcherikover, Victor. *Hellenistic Civilization and the Jews*. Philadelphia: Jewish Publication Society, 1961.

Templo, R. Solomon Rafael Judah Leon. *Massekhet Halakha le-Moshe mi-Sinai*. Amsterdam, 5494/1734.

Toaff, Professor Renzo. See *La Nazione Ebrea a Livorno e a Pisa*.

Tolan, John. *Petrus Alfonsi and his Medieval Readers*. Gainesville: University Press of Florida, 1993.

Torre, R. Lelio della. "Quelques mots sur la peine de mort et la séparation de pouvoirs chez les anciens juifs." In his *Scritti Sparsi*, vol. 2. Padova: P. Prosperini, 1908.

Tosafot. In *Talmud Babli*. Vilna: Re'em, 5485/1725.

———*Responsa of the Tosaphists* (Heb). Ed. Irving Agus.New York: Talpioth, Yeshiva University, 1954.

Ṭrani, R. Moses di. *Bet Elohim*. Venice, 5311/1551.

———*Qiryat Sefer*. New York, 1953.

Twersky, I. *Rabad of Posquières*. Cambridge: Harvard University Press, 1962.

Urbach, E. E. "The Participation of German and French Scholars in the Controversy about Maimonides and his Works" (Heb.). *Zion* 12 (1947).

Vital, R. Samuel. *Be'er Mayyim Ḥayyim*. Jerusalem, 5726/1966.

Weiss Halivni, David. *Peshat and Derash*. New York: Oxford University Press, 1991.

———"The Role of the Mara D'atra in Jewish Law." *Proceedings of the Rabbinical Assembly* (1976).

Whitfield, Stephen J. "Where They Burn Books ... " *Modern Judaism* 22 (2002).

Wolfson, Eliot. "The Mystical Significance of Torah Study in German Pietism." *Jewish Quarterly Review* 84 (1993).

Wolfson, Harry A. *Philo*. 2 vols. Cambridge, Mass.: Harvard University Press, 1948.

Ya'beṣ, R. Joseph. *Or ha-Ḥayyim*. Ferrara, 5314/1554.

Yafe Ashkenazi, R. Samuel. *Yefe Mar'e*. Berlin, 5485/1725.

Yahuda, A. S. "A Contribution to Qur'an and Ḥadith Interpretation." In *Ignace Goldziher Memorial Volume*. Part I. Budapest, 1948.

——— *'Eber ve-'Arab*. New York: Ha-Histadrut ha-'Ibrit be-Ameriqa, 1946.

———*The Language of the Pentateuch*. Oxford: Oxford University Press, 1933.

Yefet b. 'Eli. *Commentary to Proverbs*. Ed. Israel Gunzig. Krakow, 1898.

Yerushalmi, Yosef H. *Zakhor*. Seattle: Washington University Press, 1982.

R. Yom Ṭob as-Sibili. *Ḥiddushe ha-Riṭba*. Jerusalem: Mossad Harv Kook, 1985–1996.

Yosef, R. Ovadiah. *Yabbia' Omer*. Vol. 7. Jerusalem, 5753/1993.

Yuter, R. Josh. "Ramban." Unpublished.

Zabbara. See R. Joseph b. Zabbara.

Zacuto, R. Abraham. *Sefer Yoḥasin ha-Shalem*. Eds. Herschell Filipowski and A. H. Freimann. Jerusalem, 5723/1963.

Zacuto R. Moses. *Qol ha-Remez*. Ansterdam, 5479/1719.

Zahalon, R. Jacob. *A Guide for Preachers*. Ed. and tr. R. Henry Adler Sosland. New York: The Jewish Theological Seminary of America, 1987.

Zimmels, H. J. "Scholars and Scholarship in Byzantium and Italy." In ed. Cecil Roth, *The Dark Ages*. New Brunswick: Rutgers University Press, 1966.

Zucker, Moses. "'*Iyyunim*." *Porcedings American Aacademy for Jewish Rresarch* 49 (1982).

———*Rav Saadya Ga'on's Translation of the Torah.* (Heb.). New York: Philipp Feldheim, 1959,

Zurafa, R. Ḥayyim D. Sh. *Sha'ar Shelomo*. Leghorn, 5638/1878.

WESTERN SOURCES and WRITERS

Albright, W. F. "The Reform of Jehoshaphat." In *Alexander Marx's Jubilee Volume*. New York: The Jewish Theological Seminary, 1950.

Alonso, Ana María. "The Effects of Truth: Re-Presentations of the Past and the Imagining of Community." *Journal of Historical Sociology* 1 (1988).

Amoroso, Leonardo. "Vico e l'antichissima sapienza degli Ebrei." In ed. Giovanni Matteucci. *Studi sul "De antiquissima Italorum sapientia di Vico."* Bologna: Quodlibet, 2002.

Arieti, Sylvano. *Creativity*. New York: Basic Books, 1976.

Assmann, Jan. *Moses the Egyptian*. Cambridge, Mass. Harvard University Press, 1997.

Augustin, St. *The City of God*. New York: Modern Library.

———*Confessions*. Oxford: Oxford University Press, 1991.

Bacon, Francis. *Proficiency and Advancement of Learning*. Oxford: Oxford University Press, 2000.

Barnes, Albert. *The Book of Job.* Vol. 1. New York: Leavitt, Trow, & Company, 1845.

Barthes, Roland. "To Write: An Intransitive Verb?" In eds. Richard Macksey and Eugenio Donato. *The Structuralist Controversy*. Baltimore: Johns Hopkins University Press, 1972.

Bauckham, Richard. *The Bible in Politics*. Louisville, Kentucky: John Knox Press, 1989.

Bauval, R. G. "The Seeding of the Star Gods: A Fertility Ritual inside the Cheops's Pyramid?" In *Discussions in Egyptology* 16 (1990).

Beckwith, Roger T. "Formation of the Hebrew Bible." In ed. Martin Jan Mulder, *Mikra*. Philadelphia: Fortress Press, 1988.

Benveniste, Émile. *Indo-European Language and Society.* Coral Gables, Florida: University of Miami Press, 1973.

———*Problems in General Linguistics*. Coral Gables, Florida: University of Miami, 1971.

Berlin, Isaiah. *Vico & Herder*. New York: The Viking Press. 1976.

Bertalanffy, Ludwig von. *General System Theory*. New York: George Braziller, 1968.

Bishop, Joseph W. Jr., *Justice Under Fire: A Study of Military Law*. New York: Charterhouse, 1974.

Blackstone, Sir William. *Commentaries on the Laws of England.* Facsimile 1765 edition, Chicago University Press, 1972.

Borges, Jorge Luis. *Obras Completas*. Madrid: Espasa-Calpe, 1982.

———"Borges on Life and Death." Interview with Amelia Barili. *New York Times Review*, July 13, 1986.

———*Borges, Oral.* Buenos Aires: Emecé Editores, 1979.
———"El arte narrativo y la magia." In his *Discusión*. Buenos Aires: Emecé, 1964.
———*Nueve Ensayos Dantescos*. Madrid: Ultramar, 1977.
Borkowski, A. *Textbook on Roman Law*. Oxford: Blackstone, 1997.
Boman, Thorleif. *Hebrew Thought Compared with Greek*. New York: W. W. Norton, 1970.
Burkert, Walter. *Creation of the Sacred.* Cambridge, Mass.: Harvard University Press, 1996.
Byer, Anthony and Herein, Judith. Eds. *Iconoclasm.* Birmingham: University of Birmingham, 1975.
Camus, Albert. *The Stranger*. Vintage Book, 1946.
Canetti, Elias. *Crowds and Power*. Middlesex, England: Penguin Books, 1973.
Cardozo, Benjamin. *The Nature of the Judicial Process*. New Haven: Yale University Press, 1949.
———*The Paradoxes of Legal Science*. New York: Columbia University, 1928.
Carlyle, Thomas. *On Heroes, Hero-Worship, and the Heroic in History.* New York: Chelsea House, 1983.
Cassin, René. "From the Ten Commandments to the Rights of Man." In ed. Sh. Shoham. *Of Law and Man: Essays in Honor of Haim H. Cohn*. New York: Sabra Books, 1971.
Cassirer, Ernst. *Language and Myth*. New York: Dover Publications, n.d.
———*The Philosophy of Symbolic Forms*. Vol. 3. New Haven: Yale University Press, 1957.
Castro, Américo. "Disputa entre un Cristiano y un Judío." In his *De la España que aun no conocía*, vol. 3. Mexico: Finestere, 1972.
———*La Realidad Histórica de España*. Mexico City: Editorial Porrua, 1975.
Chattarjee, Ranjiit. "Before and Beyond Linguistics: The Case of Professor Nietzsche, Philologist." In eds. Colin E. Nicholson and Ranjit Chattarjee. *Tropic Crucible: Self and Theory*. Singapore: University of Singapore, 1984.
———*Wittgenstein and Judaism*. New York: Peter Lang, 2005.
Cicero. Loeb Classical Library.
Clement of Alexandria. Loeb Classical Library.
Coenen, Dan T. "A Rhetoric for Ratification: the Argument of *The Federalist* and its Impact on Constitutional Interpretation." *Duke Law Journal* 56 (2006)
Cohen, Morris R. "Property and Sovereignty." *Cornell Law Quaterly* 13 (1927–1928).
Cohn, Haim H. "Religious Human Rights." *Dine Israel* 19 (1997–1998).
Conybeare, F. C. "Christian Demonology." *Jewish Quarterly Review* 9 (1897).
———"Demonology of the New Testament." *Jewish Quarterly Review* 8 (1896).
Costa, Gustavo. "Fantasía y Magia Diabólica en Vico." *Cuadernos sobre Vico*, 15–16 (2003).
Cowley, A. *Aramaic Papyri of the Fifth Century B.C.* Oxford: Clarendon Press, 1932.
Crone, Patricia and Cook, Michael. *Hagarism*. Cambridge: Cambridge University Press, 1977.
Cuffel, Victoria. "The Classical Greek Concept of Slavery." *Journal of the History of Ideas* 27 (1966).

Curtius, Ernst Robert. *European Literature and the Middle Ages*. Princeton: Princeton University Press, 1973.

Daly, Mary. *Beyond God the Father*. Boston: Beacon, 1973.

Derrida, Jacques. "The Supplement of the Copula: Philosophy *before* Linguistics," *The Georgia Review* 30 (1976). [Reprinted in ed. Josué V. Harari, *Textual Strategies* (Ithaca, New York: Cornell University Press, 1979)].

——— *Writing and Difference*. Chicago: Chicago University Press, 1978.

Detienne, Marcel. *The Masters of Truth in Archaic Greece*. New York: Zone Books, 1996.

Devereux, George. "Charismatic Leadership and Crisis." *Psychoanalysis and the Social Sciences* 4 (1955).

Driscoll, James F. "Theocracy." *The Catholic Encyclopedia*. New York: Robert Appelton, 1910.

Dukeminier, Jesse. *Property* (Gilbert Law Summaries).

——— and Krier, James E. *Property*. Boston: Little, Brown, and Company, 1988.

Eliade, Mircea. *A History of Religious Ideas*. 3 vols. Chicago: Chicago University Press, 1988.

——— *Images and Symbols*. Princeton: Princeton University Press, 1991.

——— *Myth and Reality*. New York: Harper Torchbooks, 1975.

——— *The Myth of Eternal Return*. Princeton: Princeton University Press, 1974.

——— *The Quest: History and Meaning in Religion*. Chicago: Chicago University Press, 1969.

——— *Rites and the Symbols of Initiation*. New York: Harper & Row, 1975.

——— *The Sacred and the Profane*. San Diego: Harcourt Brace & Company, 1987.

Eliot, T.S. "The Three Voices of Poetry." In his *On Poetry and Poets*. New York: Farrar, Strauss and Cudahy, 1957.

Eisenhut, Werner. *Einfuhrung in die Antike Rhetorik und ihre Geschichte*. Darmstadt: Wissenschaftliche Buchgesellschaft, 1974.

Finley, M. I. "Was Greek Civilization Based on Slave Labour?" In *Slavery in Classical Antiquity: Views and Controversies*. Cambridge: Cambridge University Press, 1960.

Frankfort, Henry. *Kingship and the Gods*. Chicago: Chicago University Press, 1948.

Freud, Sigmund. *Civilization and its Discontents*. New York: Doubleday, 1958.

——— *Moses and Monotheism*. New York: Vintage Books, 1955.

Fromm, Eric. *The Anatomy of Human Destructiveness*. New York: Holt, Rinehart, and Winston: 1973.

——— *Escape from Freedom*. New York: Avon Books, 1965.

——— *The Heart of Man*. New York: Harper & Row, 1964.

——— *Man For Himself*. New York: Henry Holt and Company, 1947.

——— *Psychoanalysis and Religion*. New Haven: Yale University Press, 1950.

Forsythe, David P. "The Politics of Efficacy: The United Nations and Human Rights." In ed. Lawrence S. Finkelstein. *Politics in the United Nations System*. Durham and London: Duke University Press, 1988.

Galeazzi, Umberto. "Vico e la conscenza storica: Sui Sapere ermeneutico della Scienza Nuova." In eds. Antonio Quarta e Paolo Pellegrino. *Humanitas: Studi in Memoria di Antonio Verri.* Vol. 1. Lecce: Mario Congedo Editore, 1999.

Gancho, C. "Heroísmo Religioso." *Enciclopedia Bíblica*. Barcelona: Ediciones Garriaga, 1964.

Gardiner Janik, Linda. "A Renaissance Quarrel: The Origin of Vico's Anti-Cartesianism." *New Vico Studies*, 1 (1983).

Gesenius, Wilhelm. *Hebrew and English Lexicon*. Oxford: Clarendon Press, 1907.

Gibbon, Edward. *The Decline and Fall of the Roman Empire*. 3 vols. New York. The Modern Library, n.d.

Goodenough, E. R. "The Bible as Product of the Ancient World." In *Five Essays on the Bible*. New York: American Council of Learned Societies, 1960.

———*The Politics of Philo Judaeus*. New Haven: Yale University Press, 1935.

Gómez de Lino, Ignacio. *Mundo, Magia, Memoria*. N.p.: Taurus, 1981.

Gordon, Cyrus H. *Adventures in the Near East*. London: Phoenix House, 1957.

———*The Ancient Near East*. New York: W. W. Norton, 1965.

———*Before Columbus*. New York: Crown Publishers, 1971.

———*Evidence for the Minoan Language*. Ventnor, N. J.: Ventnor Publishers, 1966.

———"Rabbinic Exegesis in the Vulgate of Proverbs," *Jornal of Bibilical Literature*, 49 (1930).

Grassi, Ernesto. *Vico and Humanism*. New York: Peter Lang, 1990.

Hames, Harvey J. *The Art of Conversion*. Leiden: Brill, 2000.

Hart, H. L. *The Concept of Law*. Oxford: Clarendon Press, 1994.

Harris, Sam. *Letter to a Christian Nation.* New York: Alfred A. Knopf, 2006.

Heelan, Patrick A. "Perception as a Hermeneutical Act." In eds. Hugh J. Silverman and Don Ihde, *Hermeneutics and Deconstruction*. Albany: State University of New York Press, 1985.

Heidegger, M. *Early Greek Thought*. San Francisco: Harper & Row, 1975

———"…Poetically Man Dwells…" In his *Poetry, Language, Thought*. New York: Harper & Row, 1975.

Hengel, Martin. *Jews, Greeks and Barbarians*. Philadelphia: Fortress Press, 1980.

———*Judaism and Hellenism*. Philadelphia: Fortress Press, 1974.

Hertford, R. Travers. *Christianity in Talmud and Midrash*. London: Williams & Norgate, 1903.

———*The Ethics of the Talmud: Sayings of the Fathers*. New York: Schocken, 1962.

Hobbes, Thomas. *Leviathan*. London. Penguin Classics. 1984.

Holmes, O. W. "The Path of the Law," *Harvard Law Review* 10 (1897).

Horace. *Odes and Epodes*. Tr. and ed. Niall Rudd. Loeb Classical Library.

Husserl, Edmund. "The Crisis of European Man." In his *Phenomenology and the Crisis of Philosophy*. New York: Harper Torch Books, 1965.

Iliad of Homer. Tr. by Richmond Lattimore. Chicago: Chicago University Pres, 1951.

Illich, Ivan and Sanders, Barry. *The Alphabetization of the Popular Mind.* San Francisco: North Point Press, 1988.

Jacob, François. *The Possible and the Actual*. New York: Pantheon Books, 1982.

Jacobovici, Simcha and Pellegrino, Charles. *Jesus Family Tomb*. San Francisco: Harper, 2007.

Jolowicz, H. F. *Lectures on Jurisprudence*. London: University of London, 1963.

———*Historical Introduction to the Study of Roman Law*. Cambridge: Cambridge University Press, 1967.

Joyce, James. *A Portrait of the Artist as a Young Man*. New York: Modern Library, 1928.

Jung, C. G. *The Undiscovered Self*. New York: A Mentor Book, 1957.

Kahle, Paul. *The Cairo Geniza*. Oxford: Blackwell, 1959.

Kantorowicz, Ernst H. *The King's Two Bodies*. Princeton: Princeton University Press, 1957.

Kaufmann, Walter. *Religions in Four Dimensions*. New York: Reader's Digest Press, 1976.

Kockelmans, Joseph J. "Language, Meaning, and Ek-sistence." In his *On Heidegger and Language*. Evanston: Northwestern University Press, 1972.

Korey, William. "Human Rights at the U.N.: Illusion and Reality." In ed. Sh. Shoham. *Of Law and Man: Essays in Honor of Haim H. Cohn*. New York: Sabra Books, 1971.

Kristeva, Julia. "Psychoanalysis and the Polis." In ed. W. J. T. Mitchell. *The Politics of Interpretation*. Chicago: The University of Chicago Press, 1983.

Le Deaut, R. "Milenarismo." *Enciclopedia de la Biblia*. Barcelona: Ediciones Garriga, 1969.

Lerner, Daniel. "The Coercive Ideologists in Perspective." In *World Revolutionary Elites*. Eds. Harold D. Lasswell and Daniel Lerner. Cambridge, Mass.: M.I.T. Press, 1966.

Levin, David Michael. "The Living Body of Tradition." *Religious Tradition* (University of Sidney), 5 (1983).

Locke, John. *Two Treatises of Government*. Cambridge: Cambridge University Press, 1988.

Lomonaco, Fabrizio. "Critica storica e pirronismo: il modello olondese nell'età di Vico." *Bollettino Filosofico*, 15 (1999).

Luzzatti, Luigi. *God in Freedom*. New York: Mac Macmillan Company, 1930.

MacMullen, Ramsay. *Christianizing the Roman Empire*. New Haven: Yale University Press, 1984.

Maine, Henry. *Ancient Law*. New York: Dutton, 1965.

———*Lectures on the Early History of Institutions*. Port Washington, N.Y.: Kennikat Press, 1966.

Maitland, F. W. *The Constitutional History of England*. Cambridge: Cambridge University Press, 1950.

Marcuse, Herbert. *An Essay on Liberation*. Pelican Books.

———*One-Dimensional Man*. Boston: Beacon Press, 1964.

———"Repressive Tolerance." In ed. R. P. Wolff *et al*. *A Critique of Pure Tolerance*. Boston: Beacon Press, 1969.

Martínez Bibal, Josep. "*El* De Mente Heroica." *Cuadernos sobre Vico* 15–16 (2003).

Matteo, Ignazio di. "Il 'Tahrif' ad alterazione della Biblia secondo I musulmani." *Bessarione* 38 (1922).

Mayhew, Rev. Jonathan. *Discourse, Concerning Unlimited Submission and Non-Resistance to the Higher Powers*. Reprinted in *Religion in America*. New York: Arno Press, 1969.

———*Seven Sermons*. Reprinted in *Religion in America*. New York: Arno Press, 1969.

McCagg, William O. Jr. "Jewish Conversion in Hungary in Modern Times." In ed. Todd M. Endelman. *Jewish Apostasy in the Modern World*. New York: Holmes & Meier, 1987.

McCloskey, Susan. "Rhetoric is Part of the Lawyer's Craft." 10 *Journal,* November/ December 2002. New York State Bar Association.

McCloy, Shelby Thomas. *Gibbon's Antagonism To Christianity.* London: William & Norgate, 1933.

Merryman, John Henry. *The Civil Law Tradition*. Stanford: Stanford University Press, 1985.

Miner, Robert C. "*Verum-factum* and Practical Wisdom in the Early Writings of Giambattista Vico." *Journal of the History of Ideas* 59 (1998).

Momnigliano, Arnaldo. *Alien Wisdom*. New York: Cambridge University Press, 1975.

———*Essays in Ancient and Modern Historiography*. Middletown, Conn.: Wesleyan University Press, 1982.

———*Studies in Historiography*. New York: Harper & Row, 1966.

Moore, George F. "The Am-ha-Arez (The People of the Land) and the Haberim (Associates)." In F. J. Foakes-Jackson and Kirsopp Lake eds., *The Acts of the Apostles* (*The Beginning of Christianity*). Vol. 1. London: Macmillan, 1920.

———*History of Religions*. 2 vols. Edinburgh: T. & T. Clark, 1920.

———*Judaism*. 3 vols. Cambridge: Harvard University Press, 1966.

Morgan, Prys. "From a Death to a View: The Hunt for the Welsh Past in the Romantic Period." In eds. Eric Hobsbawm and Terence Ranger. *The Invention of Tradition*. Cambridge: Cambridge University Press, 1992.

The Nag Hamadi Library. Ed. James M. Robinson. New York: Harper & Row, 1977.

Newcomb, Steven T. "The Evidence of Christian Nationalism in Federal Indian Law: The Doctrine of Discovery, *Johnson v. McIntosh,* and Plenary Power." *New York University Review of Law and Social Change* 20 (1992–1994).

Newton, Isaac. *Principia.* 2 vols. Berkeley and Los Angeles: University of California Press, 1962.

Nicholls, William. *Christian Antisemitism*. Northvale, N. J.: Jason Aronson, 1993.

Nigg, Walter. *The Heretics: Heresy Through the Ages*. New York: Dorset Press, 1962.

Nietzsche, Friedrich. *Beyond Good and Evil*. Penguin Books.

———*Why I am so Wise*. Penguin Books.

Nirenberg, David. *Communities of Violence*. Princeton, N.J.: Princeton University Press, 1996.

Nunes Carvallho, David. *Forty Centuries of Ink*. New York: Banks Law Publishing, 1904.

Ortega y Gasset, José. *The Revolt of the Masses*. New York: W. W. Norton & Company, 1957.

Pagan Monotheism in Late Antiquity. Eds. Athanassiadi, Polymnia and Frede, Michael. Oxford: Oxford University Press, 1999.

Paz, Octavio. *Claude Lévi-Srauss: An Introduction*. New York: Dell Publishing, 1978.

Pearson, C. "Demons and Spirits." *Encyclopedia of Rreligion and Ethics*. Vol. 4. Edinburg: T&T Clarck, 1926.

Pellegrino, Charles. See Jacobovici, Simcha.

Perleman, Ch. *Justice, Law, and Argument*. Dodrech-Holland. D. Reidel, 1980.

Plato. *Collected Works.* Tr. by B. Jowett. New York: Greystone Press, n.d.

Pope John Paul II. "On the Mystery and Worship of the Eucharist." In ed. Austin Flannery, O. P. *Vatican Council II*. Collegeville, MN: The Liturgical Press, 1982.

Ribi, Alfred. *Demons of the Inner World.* Boston: Shambala, 1990.

Ricoeur, Paul. *Interpretation Theory*. Forth Worth, Texas: Texas Christian University Press, 1976.

Robinson, Theodore H. *Prophecy and the Prophets in Ancient Israel*. London: Duckworth, 1923.

Romilly, Jacqueline de. *Magic and Rhetoric in Ancient Greece*. Cambridge, Mass.: Harvard University Press, 1975.

Rousseau, Jean-Jacques. *Social Contract*. In ed. Charles M. Andrews, *Famous Utopias*. New York: Tudor Publishing, n. d.

Rudnick Luft, Sandra. *Vico's Uncanny Humanism*. Ithaca, N.Y.: Cornell University Press, 2003.

Russell, Bertrand. "How to Read and Understand History." In his *Understanding History*. New York: Philosophical Library, 1957.

———*Let the People Think*. London: Watts & Co., 1941.

———*The Scientific Outlook*. New York: W.W. Norton, 1962.

———*Why I am not a Christian*. New York: Simon & Schuster, 1957.

Russell, Jeffrey Burton. *A History of Medieval Christianity*. New York, 1968.

S. C. D. W. "Christian Faith and Demonology." In ed. Austin Flannery. *Vatican Collection Volume II*. Collegeville, MN: The Liturgical Press, 1982.

Sánchez, Francisco. *Quod nihil scitur.* In *Opera Omnia.* Ed. Joaquim de Carvalho. Coimbra: Universidade de Coimbra, 1955.

Schneider, N. "Die Unkundenbehalter von Ur III und die archivalische Systematik." *Orientalia* N.S. 9 (1940).

Schwartz, Alan and Scott, Robert E. "The Law and Economics of Preliminary Agreements," *Harvard Law Review* (2007).

Schwob, Marcel. *The King in the Golden Mask*. Manchester: Carcanet, 1982.

Seeskin, Kenneth. *Dialogue and Discovery: A Study in Socratic Method*. Albany, N.Y.: SUNY, 1987.

Selbie, W. B. "The Influence of the Old Testament on Puritanism." In eds. I. Abrahams *et al. The Legacy of Israel*. Oxford: Clarendon Press, 1928.

Shell, Marc. *The Economy of Literature*. Baltimore: Hopkins University Press, 1978.

Simon, Richard. *A Critical History of the text of the New Testament*. London, 1689.

Singer, Joseph William. *Entitlement.* New Haven: Yale University Press, 2000.

Slater, Philip. *The Pursuit of Loneliness*. Boston: Beacon Press, 1976.

Smith, Morton. *Jesus the Magician*. San Francisco: Harper & Row, 1978.

———*Palestinian Parties and Politics that Shaped the Old Testament.* New York: Columbia University Press, 1971.

———*The Secret Gospel*. New York: Harper & Row, 1978.

———*Studies in the Cult of Y.* 2 vols. Ed. Shaye J. D. Cohen. Leiden: E. J. Brill, 1996.

Steiner, George. *Martin Heidegger*. New York: Viking Press, 1978.

Tacitus. *The Complete Works of Tacitus*. Ed. Moses Hadas. New York: Modern Library, 1942.

Tarn Steiner, Deborah. *The Tyrant's Writ*. Princeton: Princeton University Press, 1994.

Tillich, Paul. "The Decline and the Validity of the Idea of Progress." In ed. Jerald C. Brauer, *The Future of Religions*. New York: Harper & Row, 1966.

———*Dynamics of Faith*. New York: Harper & Row, 1958.

Thomas, D. M. *The White Hotel*. New York: Viking Press, 1981.

Thomas Acquinas. *Summa Theologicae*. English version, by Timothy Mc Dermot. London: Eyre and Spottiswoode, 1989.

Torrey, Charles Cutler. *The Jewish Foundation of Islam*. New York: Jewish Institute of Religion Press, 1933.

Treaties and other International Acts of the United States of America. Volume 2, Documents 1–40; 1776–1818. Ed. Hunter Miller. United States Government Printing Office, Washington: 1931.

Trevor-Roper, H. R. *The European Witch-Craze*. New York: Harper Torch books, 1967.

Ullmann, Walter. *The Individual and Society in the Middle Ages*. Baltimore: John Hopkins Press, 1966.

———*Law and Politics in the Middle Ages*. Ithaca, N. Y.: Cornell University Press, 1975.

Unamuno, Miguel de. "Cómo se hace una novela?" In *Obras Completas*. Ed. M. Garcia Blanco. Madrid: Afrodisio Aguado, 1958.

———"The Word and the Letter." In his *The Agony of Christianity*. Princeton: Princeton University Press, 1974.

Van Buren, Douglas. "The *Ṣalme* in Mesopotamia in Art and Religion," *Orientalia*, n.s., 10 (1941).

Vaux, Roland de. *Ancient Israel*. Vol. 1. New York: McGraw-Hill, 1965.

Vico, Giambattista. *The Art of Rhetoric*. Atlanta: Rodopi, 1996.

———*The First New Science*. In *Vico Selected Writings*. Ed. and tr. by Leon Pompa. Cambridge: Cambridge University Press, 1982.

———*Il 'De mente heroica*.' In *Varia*. Naples: A. Guida, 1996.

———*The New Science of Giambattista Vico*. Tr. by Thomas Goddard Bergin and Max Harold Fisch. Ithaca, N. Y.: Cornell University, 1968.

———*On the Study Methods of Our Time*. Ithaca, New York: Cornell University Press, 1990.

Vinning, Joseph. *From Newton's Sleep*. Princeton: Princeton University Press, 1995.

Víves, Juan Luis. *El arte retórica/De ratione dicendi*. Barcelona: Anthropos, 1998.

Walaskay, Paul W. *'...And so we came to Rome.'* Cambridge: Cambridge University Press, 2005.

Walker, D. F. *Spiritual and Demonic Magic*. Notre Dame: University of Notre Dame, 1975.

Weber, Max. *The Protestant Ethic and the Spirit of Capitalism*. New York: Charles Scribner's Sons, 1958.

Weiler, Gershon. *Jewish Theocracy*. Leiden: E. J. Brill, 1988.

Wengst, Klaus. *Pax Romana*. Philadelphia: Fortress Press, 1987.
Wilhelm, J. "Heroic Virtue." *Catholic Encyclopedia*. New York: Robert Appelton, 1910.
Williams, Joshua. *Principles of the Law of Real Property*. London: Hodges, Smith and Co., 1865.
Wittgenstein, Ludwig. *Culture and Value*. Chicago: Chicago University Press, 1984.
——— "Lecture on Ethics." *Philosophical Review* 74 (1965).
———*Tractatus Logico-Philosophicus.* Tr. D. F. Pears and B. F. MxGuinnes. London: Routledge and Kegan Paul, 1961.
———*Worterbuch fur Volkess Schulen*. Vienna: Holder-Picher-Tempsky, 1977.
White, James Boyd. *Heracles' Bow*. Madison: Wisconsin University Press, 1985.
Wolin, Richard. *The Seduction of Unreason*. Princeton, N. J.: Princeton University Press, 2004.
Wood, Forrest G. *The Arrogance of Faith.* New York: Alfred A. Knopf, 1990.
Yoshino, Kenji. "The City and the Poet." *Yale Law Journal* 114 (2005).
Zerner, M. Ed. *Inventer l'hérésie*? Nice: Centre de etudes médiévales, 1998.

INDICES

Index of References

HEBREW SCRIPTURE

JEWISH HELLENISTIC LITERATURE

TARGUM

RABBINIC LITERATURE

TANNAITIC and TALMUDIC

MIDRASHIM

GEONIC WORKS

MAIMONIDES' WORKS

MISHNE TORA

MARAN JOSEPH CARO

Bet Yosef *Oraḥ Ḥayyim* XLVI, i 348; CCLXXII, i 387; CCLXXXV, ii 149; DCXXXI, i 398. *Yore De'a* CLXXXI, i 400; CCCXL, ii 152; CCLXXIV, ii 4. *Eben ha-'Ezer* XLII, ii 152

Shulḥan 'Arukh *Oraḥ Ḥayyim* XXIV, 2; CX, 12, CXC, 4, ii 13. *Yore De'a* CCXLV, 5, ii 128; CCLXXX, 2, ii 150. *Ḥoshen Mishpaṭ* CCCLIII, 32, ii 35. *Abqat Rokhel* 34c, i 273

WORKS BY JOSÉ FAUR

Studies in the Studies in the Mishne Tora, page(s): 1–2, i 379; 13–19, i 259; 14, i 53; 16, ii 94; 19–25, i 76; 21, i 87, 279; 21–24, i 73; 21–25, i 75; 25–32, i 76; 31–32, ii 116; 33–36, i 318; 34, i 331; 36, i 316; 38, i 73, 74; 39, ii 98, 105; 41, ii 104; 41–45, i 296; 43, ii 156; 43–44, i 296; 47, i 76; 47–60, ii 162; 49, ii 116; 52–54, i 312; 57, i 408; 136–137, i 309; 132, i 76; 147, i 81; 148–151, i 53; 181–182, i 411; 183–186, i 75; 184, i 309; 184–186, i 372; 189, i 309; 192, i 372; 219–230, ii 33; 230–238, ii 32; 230–237, i 160

Golden Doves, page(s): xiii–xiv, i 79; xvii, ii 58; xviii–xix, i 287; xix, 71, i 23; xvii, 121, i 268; xviii, i 78; xx, i 71; xxi, i 82; xxii–xxiii, i 11; xxiv–xxv, 83, ii 21; xxiv–xxv, ii 5; xxi–xxii; 25–26; 167, i 9; xxv, 109, 123–124, i 65; xxvi, i 61; xxv–xxvi, 13–14, i 63; xxv–xxvi, ii 81; 1–2, i 4, 33; 2, i 65; 4–7, ii 7; 7–8, i 15, 225, 245; 8, i 17; 10, i 46, 55, 152; 10–12, i 4; 12, i 60; 13, i 65; 13–14, 119, i 58; 14–15, i 250, 270, ii 55; 15, ii 59; 15–16, i 76; 16–17, i 271; 18–21, i 133; 22, 138, i 10; 23–24, i 10; 23–26, i 8; 24–25, i 10; 28, i 37; 29–30, ii 9; 30–35, ii 5; 32, i 15; 32–33, i 278; 32–33, i 29; 32–37, i 220; 41–47, i 28; 41–49, 80, i 22; 51–52, i 204, ii 124; 52–54, i 61; 53–54, ii 6; 54, ii 145; 56, i 40; 58, i 252; 59, i 9; 66–69, i 153; 66–69, ii 9; 6–7, i 4; 68, i 154; 74–76, 78, i 283; 77–78, ii 21; 83, ii 4; 84–85, i 28; 87, ii 65; 88, i 57, 65; 88–89, i 252; 89–96, i 373; 90–94, ii 70; 92–94, i 263, 267; 95–96, i 252 and Appendix 37; 95–96¸ i 270; 96, and n. 83, pp. 185–186, ii 108; 96, ii 80, 83, 84; 97, i 252, ii 62; 97–98, i 252; 98–99, i 251; 98–99, i 253; 98–99, i 264; 99–100, i 261, 276; 100–110, i 65; 101–102, ii 88; 102, i 255, ii 89; 102–103, ii 86; 103, i 65; 103–108, i 66; 104, i 67; 105–106, i 64; 107, i 6, 65, 107; 107, i 66; 108, ii 8; 108–109, i 69; 108–110, i 64; 108–111, ii 76; 109, ii 75; 109–110, i 317; 111–112, i 57; 111–113, i 266; 115, ii 121; 116, ii 5; 118–123, i 79, ii 5; 119–120, i 65; 121, i 4; 123–124, i 74, 82, 355; 124, i 397; 125, i 266; 119–123, i 19; 120, i 152; 132–133, i 54; 133, i 65; 143, i 66; 189, i 65; 136, i 389; 136–137, ii 5; 123–124, i 74, 82, 355; 124, i 397; 125, i 266; 136- 137, ii 58; 138–142, ii 80; 140–142, i 107, i 110; 140–142, i 264, 265; 142–145, ii 80; 144–145, i 246; 153 n. 81, ii 52; 167, i 10; 171 n. 29, i 4, 7, 22

In the Shadow of History, page(s): 2, i 356; 4–7, i 245; 4–8, i 187, ii 52; 6–7, i 188; 9–12, ii 132; 11–12, i 356; 14–15, i 392; 15, i 390, 391; 16–17, i 415; 18, i 420; 20, i 429; 22–23., i 424; 28–29, i 178; 29, i 175; 32–34, i 103, 176, 178; 33, i 422; 37, i 176; 39, i 179; 62, ii 133; 69–70, ii 133; 91–106, i 26; 180–181, i 283; 184–185, i 208; 185, i 146; 188, i 20; 189–190, i 229; 193–198, i 223; 199, i 244; 199–200,

Index of Subjects

D

I

T

U

V

W

Index of Names

Index of Terms

CPSIA information can be obtained
at www.ICGtesting.com
Printed in the USA
BVHW041312170420
577823BV00004B/17/J

9 781934 843185